THE DIRTIEST
RACE IN
HISTORY

BY THE SAME AUTHOR

In Search of Robert Millar: Unravelling the Mystery Surrounding Britain's Most Successful Tour de France Cyclist (HarperSport), 2007

Heroes, Villains and Velodromes: Chris Hoy and the British Track Cycling Revolution (HarperSport), 2008

Slaying the Badger: LeMond, Hinault and the Greatest Ever Tour de France (Yellow Jersey), 2011

Sky's the Limit: British Cycling's Quest to Conquer the Tour de France (HarperSport), 2011

THE DIRTIEST RACE IN HISTORY

BEN JOHNSON, CARL LEWIS AND THE 1988 OLYMPIC 100M FINAL

RICHARD MOORE

BLOOMSBURY

LONDON · NEW DELHI · NEW YORK · SYDNEY

To Virginie

First published in Great Britain 2012

Copyright © 2012 by Richard Moore

The moral right of the author has been asserted.

Every reasonable effort has been made to trace copyright holders of material reproduced in this book, but if any have been inadvertently overlooked the publishers would be glad to hear from them. Image on pp. viii–ix courtesy of Getty Images. Image on pp. 300–301 used with permission of *Philadelphia Inquirer* copyright © 2012. All rights reserved.

Bloomsbury Publishing Plc
50 Bedford Square
London WC1B 3DP

www.bloomsbury.com

Bloomsbury Publishing, London, New Delhi, New York and Sydney

A CIP catalogue record for this book is available from the British Library

ISBN 9781408135952

10 9 8 7 6 5 4

Typeset by seagulls.net
Printed and bound by CPI Group (UK) Ltd., Croydon CR0 4YY

CONTENTS

THE QUEST

This is a story mainly about four extraordinary men: Ben Johnson, Carl Lewis, Charlie Francis and Joe Douglas. Johnson and Douglas were both willing interviewees and could not have been more helpful. Francis, Johnson's coach, died in 2010. And Lewis, well, he proved so elusive that the title almost became *In Search of Carl Lewis*.

I tried to contact him through his agent, who, in the course of my efforts, became his ex-agent. I tried his sister-in-law, who acts as his manager; she didn't return emails or phone calls. I tried friends. But finally I met him: in a shop on Oxford Street in London. It was a strange, though somehow fitting, encounter.

A word about the title, too – the dirtiest race in history? I mean this in the broadest sense, referring not only to drugs, but also to varying degrees of skulduggery and corruption, and the enduring legacy of the Olympic 100m final in Seoul. There are those who take a more ambiguous, even ambivalent, view. It was the greatest race of all time, they say. And perhaps it was.

It was the best of times, it was the worst of times, it was the age of wisdom, it was the age of foolishness, it was the epoch of belief, it was the epoch of incredulity.

A TALE OF TWO CITIES, CHARLES DICKENS

PROLOGUE

THE GREATEST RACE
OF ALL TIME?

SEOUL, SATURDAY 24 SEPTEMBER 1988, 1.20 P.M.

Ben Johnson, hands on hips, stares at the lane ahead of him, his pose
giving him a studied casualness, which is in contrast to the lowered
head, squinting eyes and dilated pupils. His expression suggests he
is staring not at a hundred-metre stretch of rubberised track, but at
someone who has just challenged him to a fight.

Johnson relaxes as he paces a few strides down the track. He slowly
rolls his enormous shoulders and shakes out his limbs, then turns
and returns to his blocks. As he reaches them, a figure approaches
from behind.

The figure is Carl Lewis. In the warm-up area and now out on the
track, Lewis has been making his way around all the other Olympic
100m finalists, shaking each opponent's hand, looking him in the eye.
Whatever happens out there, guys, the gesture seems designed to say,
we're still friends.

But as far as Johnson is concerned, they're not friends. Lewis,
proffering his hand, appears to catch him unawares. Johnson half-
turns and returns the gesture, but he doesn't meet Lewis's gaze, and
he instantly regrets the handshake. As he would later explain, 'I don't

shake nobody's hand. We're not friends. I'm coming here to win. Carl is just trying to soften them up.'

Lewis returns to his lane: lane three. He peels off his all-white tracksuit. Johnson, in lane six, removes a pale yellow T-shirt. Underneath, both wear red shorts and vests: Johnson's kit is all red, like a British post box, Lewis has a white trim. Johnson's thick gold necklace doesn't hang around his neck; rather, it is laid out on his muscular chest. The race is between Lewis of the United States and Johnson of Canada; the other six are extras, with walk-on, non-speaking parts.

It's the contrast between the pair that makes the race so intriguing and their rivalry so beguiling. That and their mutual dislike. Johnson is rough; Lewis is smooth. Johnson exudes menace: he is a boxer, or a bull. Lewis is a butterfly: sleek, graceful, soft-featured. In the weeks leading up to the Olympics he had appeared on television in the guise of a pop star, dressed in a bright red and gold lamé outfit, dancing – but awkwardly, without the beautiful fluidity of his running – and singing,

'He had a special gift that came from above
He's a star! He's a star!'

Meanwhile, Johnson had been lying on a beach on the Caribbean island of St Kitts, eating and drinking, putting on weight and arguing with his coach as he recovered from an injury that had threatened his participation in the Olympics. 'The first time I ever enjoyed my life,' Johnson would wistfully recall more than two decades later. 'I had the best fun I ever had in my life on St Kitts before Seoul.'

Somehow, despite the competing distractions of making pop videos and lying on the beach, these two athletes have come together, in the best shape of their lives, as Lewis seeks to become the first man to successfully defend the Olympic 100m title, and Johnson bids to confirm himself as the fastest man in history. The American NBC commentary team of Charlie Jones and Frank Shorter agree that it is perhaps the first Olympic men's 100m final ever to feature two sprinters so evenly matched and at the top of their game. It is why it is the most anticipated race in history.

And yet the men's 100m final at the Seoul Olympics will surpass even that billing.

The psychological battle began in the warm-up area, before they even stepped on to the track. 'The warm-up area is the place where you learn everything about athletics,' says the British coach Frank Dick. Dick was helping the British sprinter, Linford Christie, but his attention was drawn to the American and Canadian camps. 'What happens out there on the track is nothing. What happens in here is the important thing. You could see these guys playing their games, and their totally different approaches. The surliness of Johnson and the flamboyance of Lewis. They were like two prizefighters. Gladiators. These were your heavyweight boxers. There was so much tension, it was… tingling.'

In the stadium, the noise is a thrum of nervous anticipation that manages to be low- and high-pitched at the same time. It's like a swarm of 90,000 bees, with regular bursts of clapping, and occasional yells of 'Ben!' or 'USA!' – never 'Carl!' The TV camera pans across the lanes. 'In lane six, number 159, the world champion and world record holder, Ben Johnson, Canada,' says the American-accented stadium announcer. Johnson gets the biggest cheer. 'Once again we request quiet to start, please,' adds the announcer when he has introduced the remaining two runners. The buzz drops an octave. The atmosphere is charged; as Dick says, it tingles.

The runners are called. They move forward in three waves: four step forward in the first group, led by the Canadian Desai Williams, all flared nostrils and pumped-up aggression, trailed by Calvin Smith, Dennis Mitchell and Christie; Robson da Silva, Raymond Stewart and Lewis appear a step behind; there's a longer pause, then a solitary figure ambles forward. Johnson. It's as though he is in a slightly different time zone.

Atten-hut! The Korean command, a call to attention. To your marks.

They settle in the blocks, Lewis digging his feet into the pedals like a climber ensuring he has a solid hold; Johnson still in his own time zone, the last man into the blocks, his shoulders appearing to force his arms out, so that his hands occupy the extreme corners of his lane. He twists rather than digs his feet into the blocks. 'Who's going to be last to settle?' asks David Coleman, the BBC commentator. 'Johnson's not going to fall for this; the others know that Lewis tries to psych them out a bit.'

Lewis sits up on one knee, extending his long frame, gazing into the distance, his left arm resting on his thigh. He scratches his nose, then bows his head and looks down at the track. Johnson, more compact, closer to the track, settles. But, setting himself apart again, while all seven opponents' heads are bowed as if in prayer, Johnson's is tilted up, his dead eyes focused on the full length of the track.

Atten-hut! Set... hold...

BANG!

Johnson lunges forward, throwing his arms behind him as though he is diving into water. While a wisp of smoke dissipates from the barrel of the starting pistol, he steals a foot on the rest of the field. Now it's the reverse image of the athletes' walk to the blocks: seven form an even line, with Johnson still on his own, but now a step ahead, approaching full speed while Lewis is still unfolding.

'And it's a fair start!' says Charlie Jones for NBC as they approach 10 metres, Ben Johnson six-hundredths of a second up on Carl Lewis.

TORONTO, FEBRUARY 2011

'I was fifty years ahead of my time,' says Ben Johnson, sounding both satisfied and bitter. 'Usain Bolt now is doing stuff I was capable of doing. What he's running on these fast tracks they're building now, I could have run.' He says it again, 'I was fifty years ahead of my time. *Fifty years!*' And he laughs, as he would at a sick joke.

He has suffered from bouts of depression over the past twenty-three years, especially over the past decade, but they have eased and he is doing better now. Sinking deep into an armchair in a room in a suburban Toronto home, Johnson glances across at Bryan Farnum, a large man whose hands are crossed across his ample stomach. Farnum is Johnson's spiritual adviser; he closes his eyes and nods slowly. 'Ben's doing well. His depression – the heaviness in his head – has completely gone.'

'I feel more content,' nods Johnson. 'Peace of mind.'

But when it comes to discussing his relationship with Carl Lewis, Johnson doesn't seem to have found peace of mind. In some respects he is still in the clutches of that old rivalry. Did he actually dislike Lewis? 'Well, he was my rival, so if I'm going to beat somebody, I don't want to be friends,' Johnson explains. 'He was the first and last major rival I had. The only one.

'But I haven't seen him in person for twenty years. I saw him once on TV, singing the national anthem.'

'I saw Lewis recently,' I tell Johnson.

'How does he look?'

'He looks quite well. He's got some white hair.'

'Some people say he looks very old.'

'He moves a little stiffly,' I say.

'He moves stiffly.' Johnson perks up. 'What do you mean?'

'A little bit jerkily.'

'Like he's in pain?' asks Farnum. Johnson leans forward, listening intently.

'I told you he was having problems, Ben,' Farnum says. 'I discerned it. So Richard's now confirmed that.'

Johnson sits back again. He looks satisfied.

'Unbelievable! ... NINE! ... SEVEN! ... NINE!'

Charlie Jones on NBC, his voice hoarse, screams as the clock stops. As Johnson crosses the line, he glances to his left towards Lewis, with the gesture that for ever encapsulates the race: right arm in the air, finger pointing to the sky. Lewis is a full two metres behind. Then Johnson turns towards the crowd, to accept their adulation.

The start had been extraordinary, but that isn't the most remarkable thing about the 100 metres Johnson has just run; it is that for the rest of the race his lead kept expanding. For the last 10 metres Johnson has been celebrating, and yet he has finished in 9.79, chopping four-hundredths of a second from the world record – from his *own* world record.

'And now – *now* – all the critics have been answered,' says David Coleman, 'there is no question about who is the fastest man in the world. Now he reigns supreme... '

'That probably is the best 100m ever run, technically,' says Frank Shorter. 'The race is over at 50 metres. He has another gear that we have not seen, even last year.'

Lewis's face crumples as he crosses the line and, as his jaw relaxes, he looks up and mouths something that seems less like a curse than a prayer. He resembles someone who has just witnessed a traumatic event: he looks on the verge of tears. In the second half of the race Lewis stole three separate glances at Johnson: at 65 metres, his head locked on to the human bullet and, as though in disbelief, he felt compelled to look again twice more in the closing 20 metres, when he would normally be closing the gap. Even while running the fastest 100m of *his* life, Lewis wore an anguished, horrified expression for much of it. Near the end he drifted to his right, towards his rival, as though Johnson exerted a magnetic pull. Later, the head-on angle would reveal that Lewis stepped clean outside his lane in the final 10 metres.

Beyond the line, Lewis jogs after Johnson, but the exchange between them – another half-turn, another handshake – is cursory.

Johnson doesn't smile when he looks at him; if anything, his expression darkens. Lewis stares at the big screen in bewilderment as Johnson takes off on a lap of honour with a Canadian flag, and then the beaten man gives an interview to NBC. 'I don't feel it was the best race I ran here,' says Lewis. 'The only thing I can say is, I talked to my mother last night, she had a dream two nights ago that my father just said, "I'm all right," and that's all I feel, I gave it my best shot.' His father, Bill, had died the previous year. Carl had buried him with the 100m gold medal he had won at the Los Angeles Olympics, as well as a promise that he would win himself a replacement in Seoul.

Had he not been aware of Johnson's explosive start? 'Well I didn't see him until about 60 or 70 metres,' replies Lewis, still visibly stunned, still anguished. 'He must have really caught a flyer... I just tried to run the best I could and I... I'm pleased with my race.'

'Well,' Charlie Jones comes back in, as Lewis, head lowered, disappears into the bowels of the stadium. 'The waiting is over, the questions have been answered.'

When he had finished his lap of honour, Johnson was asked which he treasured more – the world record or the gold medal. 'The gold medal,' he said, 'because they can't take that away from you.'

The news broke fifty-five hours later.

These were the days before the big TV channels would build an entire studio on-site, and present major events from whichever – invariably exotic – location they were staged. In Britain, the Olympic coverage was anchored in London, which lent a peculiar familiarity to events taking place in an unfamiliar setting, in a different time zone, and in such blazing heat that much of the footage had a hazy, other-worldly quality.

In contrast to events in Seoul, dapper Des Lynam, the BBC presenter famous for his smoothness and languid charm, sat in a brightly lit studio in Television Centre, presenting *The Olympics Day*. Few sights were as familiar and reassuring as that of Lynam, his calm, treacly voice, his grey hair and dark moustache. Today he wore a navy blue blazer and a stripy tie. A pale yellow silk handkerchief billowed from his pocket.

It was all so ordinary as we watched him being slipped a note by somebody off-screen, to his left. Lynam scanned the paper quickly. Then he looked back up. He didn't give much away, but his manner had changed in a subtle, barely discernible way. It was clear, in fact, that the impossible had happened: Lynam was ruffled. 'Now,' he said, looking directly into the camera. 'I've just been handed a piece of paper here that if it's right' – he swallowed and shook his head solemnly – 'it'll be the most dramatic story out of these Olympics, or perhaps any others.'

PART ONE
CARL AND BEN

'I want to be a millionaire,
and I don't ever want a real job.'
CARL LEWIS

1

THE SANTA MONICA TRACK CLUB

'It wasn't about money for Carl. Never.'
JOE DOUGLAS

SANTA MONICA, MAY 2011

Home to the most glamorous club the sport of athletics has ever known is an unpretentious three-storey apartment block on Ocean Park Boulevard as it heads away from the Pacific into the less celebrated part of Santa Monica.

There are two neatly typed stickers indicating suite 201. 'Joe Douglas' reads one. 'Santa Monica Track Club' reads the other. But there is just the one buzzer.

Up two flights of dark, dingy stairs, and the door opens with a light push to reveal Douglas, perched on a desk, his back to me. He is talking and gesticulating at a young, black athlete – a middle-distance runner, judging by his lean build – who sits impassively before him. 'You tell 'em you have to finish at three, OK? We're training at three.'

Then Douglas turns around and leaps from the desk as though scalded. 'I've seen you before!' he says and claps, once, then points at me. 'I know you!'

'I'm not sure... '

'Where have we met?' he asks.

'Er, Zurich?' I suggest. Zurich was on my mind. I wanted to know about Zurich in 1988.

'*Yes!*' replies Douglas, clapping his hands. 'I think that's right.'

Then he turns around and jumps back up on the desk, facing his athlete. 'Here, let me finish with Prince – this is Prince. Take a seat over there. Let me finish with Prince, I'll be' – he studies his watch – 'I'll be with you in a minute.'

At seventy-five, and no more than five foot four, Douglas remains a bundle of energy and enthusiasm. Since 1972 this has been his lair: an open-plan apartment in a residential block, taken over with desks and computers, the pale carpet heavily stained, the walls filled with images of the Santa Monica Track Club alumni, their chests bearing the famous logo of a yellow half-sun, its orange rays protruding like tentacles, set against a pale blue backdrop. They were the Harlem Globetrotters of track and field, the Real Madrid of athletics. Carl Lewis, to whom Joe Douglas was part-coach, part-manager, was Michael Jordan and David Beckham rolled into one – with a bit of Michael Jackson and Grace Jones thrown in for good measure.

It is the Lewis image that features in this gallery more than any other athlete, and the pictures trace his career, from fresh-faced prodigy to red stiletto-wearing, Pirelli-advertising superstar.

'Joe Douglas... Joe Douglas hated my guts. He was not a good person,' Russ Rogers, the American sprint team's coach at the 1988 Seoul Olympics, told me. And he wasn't joking: there was an audible shudder as Rogers spoke, as though the very mention of Douglas's name was enough to send a chill down his spine.

'Joe was involved in a lot of cloak and dagger stuff,' I was told by an American athletics writer. Another journalist, with two fingers intertwined to suggest closeness, said, 'Joe Douglas and Carl Lewis were like that.' The accompanying shake of the head suggested this might not always have been a good thing. 'If you want to understand Carl, you've got to understand Joe.'

Then again, there was the testimony of one of the US's most respected athletics writers, Dick Patrick: 'Joe Douglas and I had our disagreements, but the one thing I always liked about him is that at heart he is a hard-core track and field guy. And he still works with athletes, world-class athletes and older runners. He's still out there when they're running along little grass paths on Santa Monica Boulevard. He's incredibly authentic, in that sense. I mean it was kind of like he won the lottery when he stumbled into Carl and forged this relationship, and the two of them are really incredibly loyal to one another. Since Carl retired, Joe's not a major force, but he's still involved, he still loves track and field.'

'You gotta meet Joe: he'll have a million stories,' Patrick had urged me. 'I mean, I don't know if you can believe all of them… '

Douglas, having finished with Prince, appears in the adjoining room, which has a large table and must pass as the club's boardroom. He finds me studying the Pirelli poster. This shows Lewis, heavily muscled and veined, poised in the starting position, in a tight black one-piece suit, wearing those red stilettos beneath the legend 'La potenza è nulla senza controllo' (Power is nothing without control). Douglas stands gazing at the poster, admiring his prize athlete – the athlete who put him and the Santa Monica Track Club on the map – once more. 'That wasn't going to be shown in the US,' he says. 'We're too conservative.'

It's hard to reconcile this friendly and enthusiastic character with his reputation, or his reputed influence, which once stretched far beyond this apartment, and wasn't always benign, according to the gossip. He seems more grandfatherly than godfatherly. Does he have any kids? 'Thousands!' Douglas replies. He means his athletes, his club.

He sits down behind the table and starts telling me how, as a high school boy, he was third in the nation in the half-mile, before he went on to UCLA and became fascinated by coaching. He sets his elbows on the surface of the table as if to prop himself up. Though grey-haired and struggling with a persistent cough and breathlessness, his edge-of-the-seat posture adds to the overwhelming impression of boyishness. I can imagine his legs swinging beneath the table, like a hyperactive child's. Later, driving to lunch, Douglas tells me a little about his childhood in tiny Archer City, Texas, where, he says, they lived in 'basically a tent by the side of the railroad tracks'. 'It was my fault my parents split up,' he shrugs. 'My dad was an alcoholic. He was throwing me up and down. My mom started hitting my dad, and he left. Later we made up, my dad and me. But he was murdered. I don't know the circumstances.'

It is an extraordinary story, told as if it were very ordinary, but it could offer a clue as to where his steel comes from, and explain the drive and ambition that he channelled into athletics and his baby, the Santa Monica Track Club.

I'd love to know how the club got started, can he tell me?

'Yes sir, I can.'

And he outlines the beginnings of the club that would go on to become athletics' most dazzling brand, and how he found his calling as a coach: 'In college, with my physics teacher, we used to talk about training, different mechanics and so on. So for instance the concept of lifting the knee is incorrect.'

Douglas gets back up and stands in the middle of the room. He lunges forward, demonstrating. 'The concept is to lead with your knee, push your foot backwards and leave the ground at the right angle. Simple physics. But initially I was running on my toes! One of my first coaches told me to run on my toes. That was wrong. For a sprinter, yes. But I was a middle-distance runner.'

He gave up running because he kept getting injured. But before that, he trained at the Los Angeles Track Club under Mihály Iglói, a Hungarian middle-distance specialist who competed at the 1936 Olympics. Iglói was a decent athlete but a legendary coach (it wasn't him who told Douglas to run on his toes). His athletes set an astonishing forty-nine world records – Douglas's Santa Monica charges have set a mere thirty-eight. His methods were based on the then unusual technique of interval training. He was a disciplinarian, and an extremist: two sessions a day, with multiple repetitions of short, intense efforts, and only a brief rest in between. When he started coaching, Douglas copied some of Iglói's methods, but he wasn't so hard on his athletes. He also wrote detailed accounts of every session by every athlete.

In 1972, when Douglas was thirty-six, working as a maths teacher at Westchester High School in LA, and coaching in his spare time, he was given permission by the city council to use Santa Monica College as a training base. And Douglas, just like that, established the Santa Monica Track Club. It was a community club, open to anybody. 'Usually the best athletes could go elsewhere because they could be paid,' says Douglas. 'I didn't have money to pay them, they came to me because I could make them better runners. That's how it developed.'

The club grew, and the name started to gain recognition way beyond Santa Monica. The distinctive logo of sunrise, mountain and wave was the work of one of the runners, Ole Oleson, whose inspiration came from the club's training runs. They would jog along Ocean Boulevard in the mornings, watching the sun rise from behind the Los Angeles Hills. In the evenings they would see it set over the Pacific. And since it was a community club, the members included wealthy businessmen, lawyers and doctors. In 1978, the club president, Ed Stotsenberg, persuaded them to pay $500 each so Douglas's protégés could run in Europe.

'First, though,' he says 'I called Andy Norman.'

Norman, a London policeman and athletics promoter, would become one of the most powerful figures in the sport in the 1980s, as well as one of the most notorious. His influence was enormous. 'Norman was like an octopus, his tentacles were everywhere,' says Doug Gillon, the long-time athletics correspondent of the *Glasgow*

Herald. He was 'a bully and dictator', according to John Rodda of the *Guardian*, who, 'across three decades from the 1970s to the 1990s… influenced, manipulated and dictated events.'

In 1978 Norman was the man to call if, like Douglas, you wished to gain entry for your new and still-unknown club to the prestigious European meetings. So that's what Douglas did, telling him he had some decent milers who he thought could break four minutes. He had other middle-distance runners too but, at that time, no sprinters.

'How fast can they run?' Norman asked.

'They haven't run four minutes yet,' said Douglas. 'Jerald Jones has maybe done 4.01…'

'They're dogs!' replied Norman quickly. 'But I'm going to help you. I can put you in these meets – Oslo, Gateshead, Stockholm.'

Douglas has every single performance, in every meeting Santa Monica athletes have ever taken part in, recorded on his computer. He jumps up again, and leads me through, fiddling with his glasses, then scrolling through pages and pages of spreadsheets. 'One of my athletes lost all these records,' he says, 'but I had all my notes, so we went back and did them all again.'

They show that Douglas travelled to London with four athletes on 23 June 1978. They ended up running in eight meetings in nineteen days, including Stockholm – 'where Jerald went under four minutes, so I didn't lie to Andy,' he says with evident satisfaction. 'And I've gone to Europe every year since,' adds Douglas as he removes his glasses, stands up and hurries back through to the meeting room.

The financial arrangements were complicated in this amateur sport, but Andy Norman took care of them. 'Runners were always paid. When I was running, I was paid $50 a meet,' Douglas says. 'That was in the 1960s. When I went to Europe as a so-called amateur, I was paid under the table. I remember in Oslo, the organisers said, "OK, will all the officials leave, please?" Then we were given appearance money or prize money in brown envelopes. Let's be clear: the sport has never been an amateur sport. But Andy, he took care of all that; he also told the meet directors to accept me in the first place. He was a wonderful man.'

Two years after that first visit to Europe, Douglas came across Carl Lewis for the first time. They were at the US Olympic Trials in Eugene, Oregon. Douglas knew Tom Tellez, who was coaching Lewis at the University of Houston. 'Tom was very interested in science and mechanics – like me. We've always got on.'

Tellez asked Douglas: 'Will you take my sprinter?'

'No,' replied Douglas.

'Why not?'

'Because sprinters are flaky. I want to have athletes who are committed, dedicated, who, if I tell 'em to be in bed by eleven o'clock, they'll be in bed by eleven. I don't want 'em out chasing women. And when I tell them what to do, they do it. I don't want them to miss a workout. Because if an athlete misses a workout, I go mad, and the second time I kick them off the team. I don't allow that.'

'Joe, he's perfect,' said Tellez. 'He's the most dedicated person you could ever have.'

'No.'

But at the third time of asking, Douglas agreed to see the paragon. 'Carl came here and the first thing I told him was, "Carl, you do not run for money. You are running to be fast; you are not running for money. You understand?"'

By the time Douglas went to Europe for the first time with Lewis, he had already made a name for himself in the NCAAs, the US college championships. Not that the Europeans were impressed. 'They said, "We'll give you $400" for him. I said, "Fine." And he went out and ran well. I can tell you the results, I got em… ' – and Douglas gets up, and rushes again to the other room, to his computer, the glasses go on, he scrolls through the spreadsheets. 'Let's see. Here we go.

Milan, 3 July. Carl was second in 10.31. It's respectable. It's not top of the world... '

The phone on Douglas's desk, beside his computer, starts ringing, and Douglas stares at it. Then he answers. 'Athletics International... Hello Prince, yeah, you go for lunch. We'll join you. Eighty per cent I'll join you. Eighty per cent. OK, bye.'

As he replaces the receiver, he quietly adds: 'Fifty per cent.' Squinting once more at his spreadsheets, he continues, 'We went from Milan to Holland, the Hague, and Carl was second there again, $400 again. But he never complained, he didn't say a word. Then to Stockholm: first in the long jump, second in the 100. Helsinki...

'Eventually we go to Cologne, and Carl did not run as well as he wanted to. And in Zurich, he wasn't running well. Still getting $400 a meet. But Copenhagen was next, and they offered him $1,800 to run there. But Carl came up to me, and said, "Coach, I'm not running well, I think I should go home and train."

'That's when my mind told me: he's going to be a great runner. It wasn't about money for Carl. Never. I was surprised. Because if you go to track meets, most of the people running around, going to bars and chasing women, were sprinters. That was their reputation. Carl would go up to his room and he would stay there. He was very disciplined. He was focused. That's how I knew. It's how I knew he was going to be a great, great runner.'

2

PICKING DAISIES

'I was never a fighter when I was young.'
CARL LEWIS

Carl Lewis came from a background steeped in athletics. This in itself was unusual: track and field has never been a major sport in the US. But his family was unusual in other respects, too: both his parents went to college at a time when black kids generally did not.

His father Bill grew up in Chicago, where he encountered Jesse Owens, the quadruple Olympic gold medallist, who worked in a local dry cleaners. Then he went to a black college, Tuskegee Institute, in Birmingham, Alabama, the very heart of the segregated South.

At Tuskegee, Bill Lewis met Evelyn Lawler. He was a talented basketball player, sprinter and long jumper; she was a jumper and high hurdler who represented the USA in the inaugural Pan-American Games in Buenos Aires in 1951. Only a leg injury prevented her from competing in the 1952 Olympics.

Bill and Evelyn both became teachers: he taught social studies, she did physical education. They married, and they had three boys, Mack (born 1954), Cleveland (1955) and Frederick Carlton, known as Carl (1961), then a daughter, Carol (1963). In Alabama they were involved in the civil rights movement, marching with Martin Luther King – who baptised Mack and Cleveland, but not Carl. The issue of constant discrimination and occasional racial violence was a malignant reality. The family lived near the 16th Street Baptist Church, where four Ku Klux Klan members planted a bomb in 1963, killing four young black girls, one of them the daughter of a family friend.

But the Lewises, being teachers, were fortunate, and – again – unusual for a young, black family in Alabama. They were not trapped there; they were middle-class and mobile. After the bombing Evelyn spoke to her sisters, who lived in New Jersey. There, she was told, 'the civil rights movement was in the newspapers, not in the streets'.

So when Carl was two the family moved to Willingboro, a quiet, affluent, planned community in the suburbs of Philadelphia, but on the New Jersey side of the Delaware River. The Lewises had a four-bedroom house, 4 Thornhill Lane, with a large garden. Bill and Evelyn began teaching in different schools, she at Willingboro High, he at John F. Kennedy High.

Both became heavily involved in athletics, coaching girls' teams from their respective schools, and in 1969 set up the Willingboro Track Club. Carl and his sister would be dragged along to the meets, where they would play in the long jump pit. In his 1990 autobiography, *Inside Track*, Carl called the pit 'our babysitter'. But it was Carol who first made the transition from building sandcastles to competing. Carl was overshadowed, a point emphasised in the autobiography, 'I was small for my age, the runt of the family, the non-athlete, and my father wondered if that was the way it would always be... Every family seems to have someone who is not talented, and I thought I was the one.'

He suffered mainly by comparison: his siblings were all exceptional athletes. Mackie was a star high school sprinter and long jumper. Cleve was a soccer player, the first black American ever drafted by a professional soccer team, the Cosmos. Carol was a long jumper who, when she was seventeen, was described by one of her coaches as 'one of the most gifted athletes in history'.

Carl and his sister were inseparable. 'She was Carl's buddy, and nobody else's,' said their mother. 'When Carl took cello lessons and played in the school orchestra, Carol took violin and did the same.' So then he followed her into athletics, inevitably trying the long jump. And in 1973, aged twelve, he enjoyed his first significant success, winning the age-group long jump at the annual Jesse Owens meeting in Philadelphia. But Carl's size was an issue, as Owens himself highlighted when he addressed Lewis's fellow competitors, 'You should learn a lesson from this smaller guy. He was determined and tried really hard.' 'For once,' Carl said, 'I felt good about what I was doing.'

Lewis appears to have been something of a misfit at school, at least in his efforts to play traditional American boys' sports, football, baseball and basketball. All his attempts seemed to end in humiliation. According to a later – and highly contentious – profile by Gary Smith in *Sports Illustrated*, the eight-year-old Carl was fielding during a game of baseball when the ball was hit in his direction.

'His father's eyes followed the arc of the ball and then shifted to his son,' wrote Smith. 'His son was busy picking daisies. When the ball stopped rolling, Carl picked that, too. He didn't play baseball much longer.' With American football, he only got as far as watching. 'There were twenty-two boys on the field, each carrying out a role assigned to him by someone else. The ground was too hard and cold for daisies, and he saw a boy fall heavily on it. "Be tough!" he heard the coach holler when the boy lingered on the ground. "Get up! Be a man!" Carl didn't want to play a sport in which he couldn't be whoever he was, and he wandered away.'

A similar anecdote appeared in a Lewis profile in *Time* magazine on the eve of the 1984 Olympics, with an unnamed high school baseball coach saying, 'he was always picking daisies in centre field'. In contrast to such a hostile environment, the athletics track, reasoned the writer, 'became a comfort station, a self-sufficient arena where the contestants are allowed to be withdrawn'. Lewis himself was quoted as saying:

'I was never a fighter when I was young. I was shy, so I always found another way of getting around a tough situation.'*

Even the track did not always represent a 'comfort station' for Lewis. And his parents made few allowances. After he fell in one sprint relay, costing his school, Willingboro High, certain victory, he sat alone in a tent in the centre of the field. When Bill Lewis came in, Carl told him he had slipped because he was wearing a new pair of spikes, but: 'My father never liked excuses. He left the tent.'

After his father walked out, apparently without a word, Lewis said he was 'verbally attacked by my teammates. I sat alone, crying. That night I made two decisions. One, I was going to transfer to the other high school in town... Two, I was not going to be humiliated on the track again.'

By the time Lewis left school he had established a reputation as a promising sprinter and long jumper, helped by a growth spurt he experienced after transferring from Willingboro to John F. Kennedy High. He grew three inches in three months, from five-eleven to his adult height of six foot two. In his final year there he found himself targeted by universities eager to recruit him. What that actually meant, as he explained in his book, was 'hearing a lot of things you're not supposed to hear, like offers of money and gifts, all in violation of the rules that govern college sports. High school and college stars are supposed to be the purest of athletes. But they aren't.'

American universities' emphasis on sport can be a source of bemusement to non-Americans. College sports compete on almost equal terms

---

* Lewis's humiliations on the sports field would find an echo over three decades later, in 2003, when he was invited to pitch the ceremonial first pitch in a major league baseball game. His effort was pitiful; the ball dribbled out of his hand and bounced three times before it reached the plate. 'The case could easily be made that he's the greatest athlete of the twentieth century,' noted the commentator, 'but he sure as hell cannot throw a baseball.'

with professional sports for media coverage and popularity. In Britain, only the Oxford–Cambridge Boat Race even rates a mention in most newspapers. But in the US the major events are big box office, and vitally important to the income and status of the colleges involved. A lot of money swirls around, although it isn't supposed to end up in the pockets of the student-athletes.

Some of the incentives offered in Lewis's day were above-board, if not exactly in the spirit of the regulations, or fair on the other students. And not much has changed. According to the espn.com columnist Dan Shanoff, writing in 2005, the advantages conferred by sporting ability include, 'Not just a free room and board: the best dorm rooms on campus... not just free books and classes: first choice of any classes they want.' Shanoff calculated the total benefit at over $30,000 a year.

That was only the start of it, according to Lewis. He claimed in his book that Russ Rogers of Fairleigh Dickinson University in New Jersey 'talked more than any other coach about money, trips, shoes, and "taking care of me". He even said he'd be able to get me a car.' Rogers was 'the only black head coach I knew of... But the more I talked to him, the more I realised he was more like an agent than a coach. His whole recruiting pitch was money, money, money.'

Then again, Lewis was writing following several years of feuding with Rogers, which formed part of a larger, running battle between the Douglas camp and the US track and field authorities. Rogers was the national sprint coach. He shrugged off Lewis's accusations, telling me, 'Whatever Carl does, he runs into controversy. With Carl and me it was simple. He wanted to be an individual; he wanted to be on his own. And I was a team man. That's why we never got on.'

Another coach who tried and failed to recruit Lewis was Wayne Williams, of the University of Alabama. Williams spoke more warmly to me about him. He felt he had a chance because of the Lewis family's Alabama connection. Under the rules at the time, an athlete could make six official visits to colleges trying to recruit him. Williams recalls, 'I made a trip to Willingboro, and sat down with the family and we talked. I liked Carl, I had a good feeling about him, and I persuaded him to come and see us in Alabama. So he committed his number six visit to Alabama; he had already taken his other five. Well, two or three weeks before the visit, I begin to lose contact with him.'

He recognised the signs, 'I would call the house, but he wasn't home. The family would say, "Well, he's not here right now, call back later." Finally I begin to realise that the visit was not going to take place.' However, there was no limit at that time – though there is now – on the number of phone calls a coach could make. 'If I was trying to recruit an athlete I could probably average a dozen phone calls a week,' Williams went on. 'At the same time I was trying to recruit Calvin Smith, and I would call him in the morning, before school, and phone again at night.

'It was the same with Carl, but, after he went quiet, I found out that Houston had come into the picture, and they'd flown him out there for a visit. I believe one of the Nike reps was a big Houston person, maybe there was a bit of that kinda stuff going on. But there were no hard feelings. I saw Carl a couple of years ago at a track convention. He was having dinner, and I wandered over. He said, "Hey, Coach Williams, how you doing? Good to see you." And we talked a while. I don't hold those things against a kid. I know they gotta do what they gotta do. Sometimes they get their heads turned around. That's fine.'

Then there was the University of Tennessee, which tried to tempt Lewis with the offer of unlimited Adidas gear, while Jumbo Elliott, a recruiter employed by Villanova in Pennsylvania, actually offered to set the Lewis family up in business, with a franchise of the sports goods store, Athletic Attic. That was the clincher as far as Carl's brothers were concerned. But Lewis was only getting more confused. 'The phone was ringing ten times a night,' he recalled, 'and I was getting tired of talking to coaches.'

It was the University of Houston coach, Tom Tellez, who stood out. Yet Tellez was pessimistic about his chances. 'I told my assistant coach, "We can't get that guy. There's no sense in me recruiting him, he's too good, he won't come down here." My assistant kept telling me, "Why don't you just give him a call?"' So Tellez made the call, and Lewis was interested. He had already used up all his visits, but there was nothing to prevent him paying his own way – he made a stopover on the way back from a trip to Puerto Rico.

'So he visited the university and talked about track and field and then he left. Then, lo and behold, he called me and said, "I'm coming." I could not believe it. I have no idea why he chose us except that we had developed a good relationship during his visit.'

Tellez was impressed most by Lewis's long jumping and was convinced he could break the world record;* he was less interested in his sprinting. What impressed Lewis about the man he would call Coach T was his technical knowledge. And, according to Lewis, and contrary to what the grapevine was telling Wayne Williams, 'Coach Tellez had not offered money or a car or a shoe contract.' Yet, Lewis, having opted for Houston, told Tellez on his first day, 'I want to be a millionaire, and I don't ever want a real job.'

'I belonged to the old school,' says Tellez, 'but Carl was progressive. He had ideas for the sport and for himself that others didn't have. He could see things that I couldn't see in terms of how track and field could be a business.'

Lewis's apparent preference for the long jump over the 100m would become a source of curiosity. His own explanation hinted at a deeper motivation, that supports Russ Rogers's description of him as an individualist and a loner: 'Nobody was into the long jump so I always had a lot of time to practise. I never had to wait my turn and I got to run and jump.'

---

* He was wrong: Lewis never did hold the record. Bob Beamon's famous leap of 8.90 metres at the 1968 Olympics lasted until Mike Powell achieved 8.95 metres in 1991, which still stands more than twenty years later.

In his first year at Houston, Tellez changed his jumping technique, from 'hang' to 'double hitch', which involves air-running after take-off. And at the NCAA championships, that was the only running he did. And yet, when he did sprint, he generally won. A week before the NCAAs, Lewis, aged eighteen, ran an invitational 100m and beat James Sanford, then the world's top-ranked sprinter. 'Comparisons with Jesse Owens are inevitable,' said the *New York Times*, an allusion – the first of many – not only to his speed, but also to his versatility.

The following year, at the 1980 Olympic Trials in Eugene, Lewis finished fourth in the 100m, making the sprint relay team, and earning selection for the long jump by finishing second to Larry Myricks. His sister, Carol, then aged just sixteen, also made the Olympic team by finishing third in the long jump. The US eventually boycotted the Moscow Games. But the most enduring effect of those trials for Carl was his introduction to Joe Douglas.

Lewis did compete in one major championship that year. In late August, at the inaugural Pan-American Junior Games in Canada, he won a sprint treble, claiming gold in the 100 and 200m, then adding the 4x100m relay, too. (Curiously, he did not compete in the long jump.) He won the 100 in 10.43 seconds, with US teammate Calvin Smith second. And a distant sixth was a skinny Canadian sprinter, Ben Johnson. In his first meeting with Lewis, Johnson started fast, leading at halfway, but faded dramatically to finish in 10.88.

Lewis was embarking on his career as a world-class athlete at a time of seismic shift in the sport. The tension between the sport's amateur ethos and the cold reality of full-time athletes, paid by sponsors and promoters in the West and the state in the Communist-controlled East, was reaching snapping-point. Change was coming, and Lewis ('I want to be a millionaire, and I don't ever want a real job') knew it. The question is whether he was merely a beneficiary of the transition to overt professionalism or a prime mover in its arrival.

Contrary to what Wayne Williams had heard, it wasn't Nike but the German-based company Adidas who would become Lewis's first official sponsor. Adidas paid his travel expenses. But at meetings, with Lewis now competing for the Santa Monica Track Club almost as frequently as for Houston, Joe Douglas collected his appearance fees in cash, 'so there was no way,' as he told me, 'the NCAA or anybody at Houston would know'.

After his freshman year at Houston, Adidas attempted to tie Lewis to a contract and made him a formal offer: $8,000 for four years, plus bonuses. It was against NCAA rules, but it was not uncommon for shoe manufacturers to employ talented athletes as 'consultants'.

It wasn't Lewis's only offer, however. The Japanese sportswear firm Tiger – or one of their Florida-based representatives – offered him $15,000 a year. Lewis returned to Adidas and asked them to match that. He was told to take the $8,000 or leave it. He left it. It was a costly mistake. The Tiger 'offer' proved to be illusory.

Desperate, Lewis called a former sprinter, Don Coleman, who had become a mentor-figure to him after they had roomed together at meets in Puerto Rico and Moscow. Coleman now worked for Nike and persuaded them to make an offer of $5,000 a year with a sliding scale of bonuses. All the financial arrangements were spelled out in an official Nike memo dated 20 January 1981, with a handwritten 'Confidential!' scrawled by Coleman in the top left-hand corner. Nine years later, Lewis reproduced the memo in his book, *Inside Track*. 'I was a little surprised that Nike would put all this in writing – documenting rules violations,' wrote Lewis. But by then he had fallen out with Coleman and Nike.

These days, Coleman is a marketing director at Coca-Cola. He recalls that when he began working with Nike, in 1980, it was not the dominant brand it would become. Up till then their growth had been achieved largely, to quote their late 1970s advert, by 'word-of-foot'. Their first national TV commercial didn't appear until October

1982. Crucial to Nike's marketing had been their association with top sportsmen (they were all men): tennis star Ilie Nastase and distance runner Steve Prefontaine were the first. Distance running was their biggest market, which is why Nike's first TV ad was shown during the New York Marathon.

In the 1980s, apart from a blip when they underestimated the appeal of aerobics (that distinctly 1980s fad), Nike went from strength to strength. Arguably two sportsmen were fundamentally important to the rise of the brand and its signature 'swoosh': Michael Jordan, who was signed as an NBA rookie in 1985, and Carl Lewis.

Coleman was nine years older than Lewis, and had served in the air force in Vietnam. The difference between twenty-seven and eighteen meant their preferred topics of conversation were inevitably different but he liked Lewis. As he told me, 'I kinda knew this kid was for real.' In 1980, when Coleman began working for Nike as marketing manager for track and field, 'One of my duties was to look for talent. The first thing I did when I went to Nike was say: "Hey, look, we've got to sign this kid from New Jersey, because he's going to be the next great sprinter." Luckily for me it was the right call.'

Coleman is lost for words, though, when I ask whether it was easy to get around the NCAA regulations, or whether that was even a concern for him, or for Nike. There's a long pause, then he says, 'Uuuuuuhhh-hhh,' and laughs. 'This stuff happened a long time ago. I... I don't want to get anybody into any trouble, or raise something up from the dead. Look, Carl was a great athlete and we were trying to help him with his training. But Carl was really important to Nike, because he was the first sprinter they took on. We had problems later. It's in his book, though what Carl said in his book isn't quite correct. But our relationship went south, and it was kinda tough. He's the one that got upset with me because he thought I didn't pick his side in the legal matters.'

Lewis's problems with Nike and Coleman came much later. Later in 1981 he renegotiated his $5,000-a-year contract. It would now be worth $200,000 over the following four years, with an Olympic gold medal guaranteeing a bonus of $40,000. Lewis admitted in his autobiography, though, that his contract 'brought new pressure'. As well as incentives for good performances, it included, for the first time, disincentives; his payments would be halved if he was not in the top five in the world, or if he missed the Los Angeles Olympics. 'Track was business now,' he said. 'I was learning to play by their rules, and those were the rules of business.'

As the 1984 Olympics drew closer, Lewis was breaking championship records, earning constant comparisons with Jesse Owens, and creating a sense that, in LA, history beckoned. But there were clear differences in the two narratives. Owens shone brightly but briefly in Berlin, supposedly lighting a torch for equality, even if, in reality, he returned to a life of discrimination and segregation in the United States. For Owens, the Berlin Olympics represented an absolute peak. Whereas, for Lewis, the Los Angeles Olympics would offer a platform, a springboard. He became determined to seize the opportunities that would follow.

First, though, Lewis would have to match Owens's track and field feats. And the first indications that he might do that came in 1981. At the NCAAs in Baton Rouge, Lewis became the first athlete since Owens in 1936 – the year of his four gold medals in Berlin – to win both a track and a field title in the same championship. Then he did the same double, as Owens had also done, at the US national championships in Sacramento. There, he long jumped 8.62m; second only to Bob Beamon's 1968 world record, set in the rarefied air of Mexico City. 'He considers himself a long jumper who also likes to run the 100m,' noted the *New York Times*, the tone of mild surprise as effective as a raised eyebrow.

Yet the 100m world record also appeared within Lewis's grasp. Twice, in 1981 and 1982, he ran the distance in 10.00 seconds, the third fastest time ever, just five-hundredths of a second slower than

Jim Hines's world record, also set in Mexico during the 1968 Olympics. He actually ran 9.99 on his way to winning the 1981 NCAA title, but the following wind was just over the legal limit. In 1982 he accomplished the same NCAA-national championships double.

It wasn't just the winning; it was the way in which Lewis won. He won admirers for his openness and amiability off the track, and for his grace and panache on it. 'Beautiful' is a word that was – is – regularly deployed in describing Lewis the athlete. David Miller wrote in *The Times* of 'the magnetism of this beautiful athlete'. There have not been many male sports stars to whom such an adjective, with its connotations of feminine grace and aesthetics, has been applied.

But when it came to Lewis, sportswriters – an overwhelmingly male group – seemed to have no qualms about this kind of writing. In 1984, *Time* would describe him as 'gentler than a superman, more delicate than the common perception of a strong man'. Another, earlier, *Time* report highlighted his everyman popularity: 'This kid is going to be a star, and it's hard to think of anyone who will wear it more gracefully... You'd like your son to be Carl Lewis... He's just about perfect', while, in 1981, *Sports Illustrated* enthused, 'Carl is a paragon all right, but a likeable one. His manner is open and friendly, neither self-effacing nor aggressive. He answers questions thoughtfully and patiently and keeps his appointments to the minute.' As for his on-track attributes, 'You can freeze a film of a Carl Lewis long jump on any frame and then just sit back and marvel at the sculptural perfection of the picture in front of you. As in the leaps of a wild animal, an impala, say, there is no awkwardness.'

Lewis seemed unusually blessed. 'There is an ease about him,' said his coach, Tom Tellez, 'a kind of relaxed control that runs through his whole life, on the track and off.'

A 1981 feature in the *New York Times* described an idyllic family set-up, with the four Lewis siblings all having gravitated to Houston, like satellites orbiting ever closer to Carl. Cleve worked as a financial analyst, Mackie studied for a degree in geology, Carol also attended the university on an athletic scholarship. The newspaper feature painted a picture of the Lewises' life in Houston: 'Carl and Cleve share a two-bedroom duplex apartment near Houston's plush Galleria shopping district, Carl and Carol work out together. Mack drops by at practice daily, often reading a newspaper and discussing world problems with Carl and others. There is time to talk because Carl trains lightly these days. Mack says Carl is so lazy that he drives to classes across the street. Carl laughs and agrees… Lewis leads a pleasant life. He drives an Audi. He loves to buy clothes and records with his two credit cards.'

But the idyll was shattered the following year when Houston declared Lewis ineligible. It had nothing to do with his contract with Nike – though representatives of the university did call Nike to ask if they were paying him. The company denied it. Rather, it was due to a missed exam. In his junior (third) year, Lewis decided to sit out an American history paper. He felt he hadn't studied enough, and would fail, and so gambled on being allowed a re-sit. That gamble backfired, and the missed history exam created quite a stir, not least because he initially told Tom Tellez and journalists that he had completed the exam, and that the university must have subsequently lost his paper.

Lewis was given an ultimatum by the university's athletic director, Cedric Dempsey. He was told he had to take his classes seriously – all of them, not just the communications and media studies courses, which he was doing with an eye to a career in broadcasting beyond his athletics career. That was Joe Douglas's doing. 'I thought he was going to be a great runner,' says Douglas, 'but I suggested he take speech and English classes to learn how to communicate. Carl was extremely quiet at the beginning. If you, me and Carl were sitting here, and two more people appeared, he'd disappear to his room. He was shy. "Communication!" I told him. "You need those skills!"

Carl articulates extremely well now. Now you can't shut him up! He became a different person.'

Back in 1982, Dempsey told Lewis that he could return to the university, but only if he took part in fewer invitational meetings and focused more on his studies. To Lewis, it came down to a straight choice: athletics or university. By competing less, he reasoned, 'my athletic progress would be stifled. I wanted to continue to grow. I needed to grow.'

There is also the sense that Lewis took exception to being told what to do. Much to Dempsey's surprise, Lewis opted to end his university career, though he remained in Houston and continued to train under Tellez. But from 1982, said Lewis, 'I will compete for Santa Monica and myself.'

3

BEN AND CHARLIE

'A sprinter like me was born.'
BEN JOHNSON

TORONTO, FEBRUARY 2011

Ben Johnson, wearing a thick black jacket, black slacks and polished black shoes with a black woolly hat pulled down to his ears, is driving me through the grey, sprawling Toronto suburbs.

'I grew up on this street,' says Johnson, pointing out the window of his Mercedes, which is also black, although, with its salt-spattered sides, it is hard to tell. It's winter in Toronto: seriously cold, the roads wet and slushy, great mountains of filthy snow in lay-bys. 'It was a six-storey block we lived in, not a high rise,' Johnson continues, fidgeting and restless. He is distracted by the car in front, which is religiously observing the speed limit and holding him up. 'Oh man, the Canadians are like the British,' says Johnson, exasperated. 'The same rules. They love to follow the rules.

'This country, this town, it's about money. They'll bleed you, any way they can. They'll get in your pocket.'

It is thirty-five years since Johnson moved with two of his sisters from Jamaica to join his mother in Toronto. Having finally accelerated past the slow car, he can start to daydream again: 'I'm gonna go back to the Caribbean. Raise some chickens. Build a house. Just need to get some things sorted first.'

Has he never considered Toronto home? 'Well, yes and no. I was treated really bad, you know? Back home, where I was born, the life-style is different. There's no traffic, no police harassing you. It's just peaceful, quiet; you can relax and chill. I like that type of environment, you know? Not busy-busy-busy, going round all the time. That's not healthy at all. Hopefully, one day I'll just relax at home.'

Outside the Metro indoor athletics centre at York University, where Johnson trained from the winter of 1979 onwards, and where he now coaches a small group of young athletes, he locks his car and pulls the hat further down his head, over his ears.

'Hey, Ben Johnson?' a young black student stops as he passes, swiv-elling on his feet.

'Yeah,' says Johnson, reluctantly.

'Woah! Picture?' says the student, brandishing his phone.

'I'm in a hurry, man,' says Johnson, looking at his wrist. 'OK, quick… '

Johnson and the young student, who towers over him, stand and pose; then they shake hands and the student skips away, tickled pink with his celebrity snap. What will he tell his friends when he shows them the picture? That he bumped into Ben Johnson, once the fastest man in the world; or that he had a run-in with the man who brought shame to Canada, whose name, after all these years, is still prefixed by the word 'disgraced'?

Like Carl Lewis, Ben Johnson was small as a child. He is not particu-larly tall as an adult, either: an average five-foot-ten. In normal clothes his physique looks quite average, too. He's almost unrecognisable as the muscle-bound sprinter in the red vest and gold chain. Now he looks slightly built. It could have something to do with his diet. 'I don't drink beer,' says Johnson. 'Three years now, no alcohol. Mostly

I eat chicken, vegetables and lots of red, green and yellow peppers. It's hard, 'coz bad food tastes good, right?' He chuckles. Johnson laughs a lot; he is easy company. 'But I don't really miss drinking beer. Back then I drunk enough to enjoy myself.'

Now, says Johnson, he tries to avoid chemicals. 'It's just to be healthy,' he shrugs. Occasionally he struggles with a stutter that he claims he developed suddenly at the age of eleven. It seems to afflict him more seriously when he's trying to say something of importance. 'I-I-I mean, I'm going to die one day, but at least I can slow that process down. Just... s-s-slow it down.'

Johnson was born on 30 December 1961 – six months after Lewis – in Falmouth, the Jamaican port town. He was the second youngest in a large family, with an older brother, three sisters and a half-sister – another brother died in infancy. Baby Ben contracted malaria when he was just three weeks old. He was nursed back to health by his mother, Gloria, and then, as a young child, spoiled by her, and fussed over by his sisters. From his father there was a tougher kind of love. Ben senior was a hard worker who installed and repaired phones for the Jamaica Telephone Company during the week, and drove a taxi at weekends. He also kept chickens, ducks and pigs – and bees, selling honey on the side. 'You have to do many things to make a living in Jamaica,' he would say.

Johnson says his father, as well as being a hard worker, was 'intimidating' and a disciplinarian, who often raised his voice. He hints that he was beaten by him, too. His father was six feet tall and proud, Johnson says, and hugely respected in the community. Jamaica, meanwhile, was 'a big playground': life was spent outside in the heat and the sun, swimming in the ocean – a practice banned by his mother so there had to be much scrubbing to remove all traces of salt – and running barefoot on dirt roads, taking on his friends in impromptu races. Johnson was always small, wiry and quick. Later, he suffered slurs and innuendo about his intelligence. But at school in Jamaica he was, according to one of his teachers, 'average'. She added, 'He was shy and withdrawn. We really didn't know much about Ben.'

Johnson's family weren't wealthy, but, by Jamaican standards, they were not poor. All things considered, life for Ben was idyllic. At least it was, until Johnson's mother left when he was eleven – the age, coincidentally or not, when he says he developed his stutter. Gloria Johnson had travelled to Toronto to stay with her sister, and returned convinced that the whole family should move to Canada. In the event, she went alone and it was two years before Ben saw her at all, and another two before he joined her.

That was April 1976, by which time she was working in an airport kitchen. Ben's brother Edward and two sisters, Jean and Marcia, came too. The rest of the family stayed behind. 'Dad didn't like the cold much,' says Ben. That was the first thing he noticed there too, though he says it didn't bother him. 'I had Jamaica heat in my body,' he explains. 'The first time I ever saw snow I played in it with my sister for hours wearing just a T-shirt.' The next thing he noticed was the number of white people, who seemed quiet and reserved compared to Jamaicans. The colour television in his mother's small apartment also made an early impression: three months after he arrived he would spend days glued to the screen transfixed by the Montreal Olympics.

The Montreal Games would prove important in the context of Johnson's career, in ways nobody, least of all Johnson, could have foreseen. A Jamaican hero, Don Quarrie, won gold in the 200m, and silver in the 100, a hundredth of a second behind another Caribbean runner, Hasely Crawford of Trinidad and Tobago. But it was the diabolical performance of Johnson's adopted country, Canada, that was more significant. It remains the only summer Olympics when the host nation failed to win a single gold medal.

This failure prompted the kind of soul-searching that Canada would indulge in again twelve years later – in very different circumstances, and for very different reasons. One answer to the 1976 humiliation was to redirect funding from sport for mass participation, enjoyment and fitness, to a few elite competitors. The Athlete Assistance Programme was given a vast infusion of new government funding, allowing selected athletes to live, train and prepare like professionals.

The shift in emphasis was not uncontroversial. Some in Canada were uncomfortable with the naked ambition associated with such a focus on winning. It did not fit well with how many Canadians – polite, reserved, law-abiding, speed-limit observing – like to see themselves. There is a joke that Canadians are the only people who, after withdrawing money from an ATM, thank the machine. There were many who wished to avoid adopting what seemed a win-at-all-costs mentality. That was how the neighbours, the Americans, behaved. And, perhaps more than anything else, Canadians liked to define themselves as not the United States. 'Sometimes it has seemed that "winning" is a dirty word in Canada,' the swimmer, Alex Baumann, a double Olympic gold medallist in 1984, told me. Arguably that had been the case pre-1976; but it changed after Montreal, at least for the next twelve years.

As a fourteen-year-old, Johnson did not settle easily in Toronto, despite the fact that the city, and the country, was supposed to be a bastion of tolerance. He was small, he had a stutter, and, at school, his strong Jamaican accent meant he was not easily understood. Not surprisingly, he was put in classes for slow learners. There were also cultural hurdles to overcome. He failed to realise, for example, it was not the done thing in Toronto to kill a pigeon with a catapult, then roast it on a fire. He was also bullied at his school, Pierre LaPorte – 'not exactly the slums,' says Johnson, 'but close.' He does not dwell on the race issue, but his very dark skin made him a target for prejudice not only in Canada, but also in Jamaica, where lighter complexions convey higher status.

Johnson's stutter almost overcame him as he told me about some of the bullying. 'If I sat down in class they pulled the chair away from me, so I fall down, and… they threw my books around, and my lunch.

So I didn't go to class for a while.' Johnson was bullied by one boy in particular – though he claims that he managed to put a stop to it by challenging his tormentor to a race. The entire school watched. Johnson won, and says it stopped the bullying. Brother Eddie was fast too and serious about it, training with a local club, the Scarborough Optimists, and their coach, Charlie Francis. In May 1977, thirteen months after arriving in Toronto, fifteen-year-old Ben was dragged along by Eddie to meet the coach who, in the absence of his own father, would come to assume that role.

Their first meeting left Francis underwhelmed. 'I can't say that Ben bowled me over,' wrote Francis in his book, *Speed Trap*. 'At fifteen, he was at the ideal age to begin training, but he looked more like twelve: a skinny, awkward kid of 93 pounds... He looked slow, and he ran even slower than he looked. After a half-circuit around the track, he flopped down in the stands. I came over and asked him what was wrong, "F-foot weak, mon – gotta rest."'

Yet Francis saw something in Johnson. His main attribute was persistence: he 'refused to be discouraged, and showed up every day'. When an older sprinter gave Johnson his old running shoes, he was transformed, although the other boys found this hard to believe. Francis said one kid quit, complaining, 'Now everyone's beating me, even Ben.'

Francis and Johnson would form a formidable team, their bond apparently forged by their complementary talents and traits: the coach's sharp brain, eye for detail and knowledge of sprinting, the runner's capacity for work and potential for improvement. Francis was intense; Johnson laid back to the point of appearing horizontal, even if, as Francis put it, 'those big eyes of his were fixed on goals beyond my vision at the time'.

But there can have been few coaches more single-mindedly ambitious than Francis. That could be gleaned from his steely gaze and pensive expression. There are few photographs, in the public domain at least, of Francis smiling. But there is a telling one of him and Johnson during a quiet moment in training. Other than his tight blue shorts and thick gold chain, Johnson is naked and statuesque, his sculpted torso and thickly muscled legs those of a bodybuilder or male model. With his arms crossed loosely behind his back, he looks relaxed, supremely comfortable in his own skin. Walking beside him, Francis could be the archetypal embarrassing parent, down to the hint of paunch and the functional, swept-back hair. He appears bereft of vanity. With his arms locked by his sides in an awkward pose, he also looks faintly ridiculous, with his T-shirt tucked into his pink shorts, which are pulled up way too high. Never can a man have looked so oblivious to the trivial concerns of looking cool. From the serious expression, furrowed brow and thousand-yard stare, it is clear that he has other priorities.

Francis had been a sprinter, setting a Canadian juvenile record for the 100 yards, and he was recruited by one of the most prestigious colleges in the US, Stanford University in California. He began at Stanford in 1967, his own eyes by now fixed on a goal five years away: the Munich Olympics. But he was disappointed by Stanford, finding that the much-lauded and well-funded US collegiate system elevated rigorous competition above training. This was fine for the most obviously brilliant athletes, but failed to nurture more hidden talent. It was at Stanford that Francis first tried drugs. Amphetamines were popular among students studying for exams, and Francis thought they might boost his athletic performance. They didn't. His verdict was, 'If you're not prepared by your training... nothing will help you.'

Back home in Toronto for the summer of 1970, and frustrated at his lack of progress, Francis called a Canadian coach, Percy Duncan, who had equalled the world record for the 100 yards in the 1940s. His coaching methods were a revelation. On their first day together he massaged Francis's legs. 'Go home,' Duncan told him. 'Your muscles aren't ready to train; they're all tight and knotted. Come back tomorrow.'

It was another five days before Duncan deemed the legs to be in good enough shape to train, and even then he applied the 'less is more' maxim. His sessions were brief but intense (not dissimilar, at least in principle, to Mihály Iglói's interval training sessions with Joe Douglas). Duncan worked with Francis not only on his fitness and speed, but also on the mechanics of his sprinting, focusing on such details as arm swing, and loosening the hips by running along a lane-divider line.

Charlie Francis died of cancer in 2010, aged sixty-one, having been ill for five years. This is why *Speed Trap* is now the primary source for his thoughts on running. Luckily, the book is a treasure trove, full of nuggets of coaching wisdom. Among them is his analysis of Duncan's most fundamental lesson: 'Percy taught me the difference between running and sprinting – that while you run on the ground, you sprint over it, with the briefest possible foot contact. It's like the spinning of a bicycle wheel – a sharp slap of the hand will impart more speed to the wheel than would a more prolonged stroke.' Watch a world-class sprinter and observe Duncan's lesson in action: the airborne, floating athlete, the fleeting, jabbing contact with the track, as though the surface is almost too hot to touch.

Duncan's training served Francis well when he returned to Stanford. In June 1971 he ran the fastest 100m of his career, 10.1 seconds, at the Canadian trials for the Pan-American Games. At the Games themselves, in Cali, the winner was a familiar name: Don Quarrie. Francis finished a slightly disappointed fifth. Now his sights were set on the Munich Olympics, but his 1971 season proved difficult to follow.

Duncan was too busy to help, and he was not fully fit. There was another issue. The failings that would lead to Canada's inability to compete in Montreal four years later were becoming evident: other countries were already more sophisticated in their approach – in one area in particular. Francis alleged that an American hurdler asked him if he was using steroids, and was surprised when he said no. The

American went on to explain that there were no tests for steroids and that they were now essential to compete at the top level. 'I felt foolish in my ignorance,' said Francis, 'but also intrigued.' With good reason: he crashed out at the Munich Games in the quarter-final, trailing in last. 'In retrospect, I realised that my chosen sport was one of ultimate frustration for almost everyone who played,' Francis continued. 'There can be only one Olympic champion. The rest of us must confront our limitations.'

The rest of us must confront our limitations. With that sentence, Francis seemed resigned to his fate. Yet lurking in this passage, and throughout his discussion of his own performance, is a sense of bitter disappointment and frustration, of the kind that could either prompt resignation or fuel defiance. As his athletics career fizzled out, it was this frustration, perhaps, that was converted into the drive – or the chip on the shoulder, the sense of being hard-done-by – that would propel Francis, in his new guise as a coach, to try to transcend those limitations.

Because Francis had no intention whatsoever of confronting his or his athletes' limitations.

Another theme of Francis's book is his irritation, often spilling into anger, with sports officialdom in Canada. He mentions a 1973 track coaching conference in which a Soviet official described his country's 'wheel system, where the most promising athletes are fed to the best coaches at the centre'. The East Germans, meanwhile, deployed 'a pyramid system, in which the best athletes are moved to the top'. 'Canada has the mushroom system,' offered the Canadian delegate, Lynn Davies.* 'Keep the athletes in the dark and dump crap all over them.'

Francis needed an income and began working as an insurance underwriter after the Munich Games. But his competitive fires still

---

* The Welshman who won the 1964 Olympic long jump gold. He became technical director of the Canadian Track and Field Association but, unsurprisingly, not for long.

flickered. He still trained; he still competed. And, with Munich fresh in his mind, he began taking steroids. His description of this course of action is concerned entirely with the 'how' rather than the 'why'. And it was remarkably straightforward. He asked his doctor for a prescription, and his doctor obliged, prescribing Dianabol, the drug *du jour* among athletes. 'I soon began feeling less fatigued in training, able to push myself further without strain. I saw clear gains in muscle mass, yet lost several pounds of fat.'

Even so, Francis, now having to squeeze in his training around a job, was still unable to beat his personal best of 10.1. His conclusion was that steroids could not offer a quick route to success. They provided the icing on the cake, but first you needed the cake. There were no shortcuts: ultimately training hard was not enough, good coaching was not enough, knowledge was not enough, athletic ability was not enough and drugs were not enough. Each ingredient was essential.

As his athletic career wound down, Francis began coaching at the Scarborough Optimists, a Toronto track and field club run by an enthusiast called Ross Earl, who funded it by running regular bingo sessions. Desai Williams was another West Indian, originally from St Kitts, who came to athletics as an 18-year-old, having played football throughout his youth. His style was lop-sided and unconventional, but Francis spotted his potential. Even so, Williams's progress astonished his coach. In his first seven weeks working with Francis, he improved from 10.8 seconds to 10.5 over 100m, won a succession of national events and became recognised as one of the world's top teenage sprinters after a few months. And Francis soon had several more rough diamonds, ready to be polished – Tony Sharpe, Mark McKoy, Angella Taylor (later Angella Issajenko) and Ben Johnson. All were destined to become stars.

Training facilities in Toronto were inadequate, especially in the winter, when the athletes trained indoors at the Canadian National Exhibition Centre, on the shores of Lake Ontario. It sounds plush; it wasn't. The indoor training facility was known as Swine Pavilion, but nicknamed 'Pig Palace' by Francis's group of sprinters. It doubled as a venue for livestock shows. 'It stank, it was disgusting,' says Johnson. But in 1979 that issue was addressed when the Metro centre opened at York University. For Francis it was another piece of the jigsaw, another ingredient in the cocktail.

Thirty-two years on, it's the same building that Ben Johnson enters to meet up with the group he now coaches. A plaque in reception reads, 'Opened 13 October 1979, dedicated to the development of amateur athletics.'

On a Thursday evening in February 2011, it is packed with veteran joggers ambling around the track, sprinters and hurdlers practising, and small groups huddled around coaches. Johnson strolls across the track without attracting even a sideways glance, woolly hat still pulled down over his ears. And, remarkably, two other former members of the Francis group, Desai Williams and Angella Issajenko, are in attendance, as they are most days, doing their own work, looking after their own protégés. They continue the work of Francis. Up to a point.

'Charlie was brilliant at what he did,' Johnson had explained earlier in the day. 'A very smart guy. The programme we followed with Charlie was the best programme, simple as that. Even today people are using the same programme, and any time a guy runs 9.8 or 9.7, I'm telling you, Charlie should get $100,000 in his account. He's the one who changed sprinting and took it to the next level. Once he told the world, everyone copied.'

Johnson still talks about Francis in the present tense. He was with him the day before he died, just 'hanging out' as he had always done. 'Charlie believes in certain ways and certain ideas. You can't change his mind, he's a very stubborn guy. But Charlie and I worked together as a team, a unit.'

Johnson goes on to say – without a trace of arrogance, more as a statement of fact – that the unit brought together 'the best mind in the business and the best natural talent'. Did Johnson sense frustration in Francis over his own ultimate lack of success on the track? 'I don't think that… But it could maybe be because he didn't fulfil his potential that he worked through me to fulfil his great desire.'

Was their partnership like a father–son relationship? 'Yeah, it was,' Johnson agrees. 'We were together a lot of years. A lot of years. We trained together, we travelled together, we spent a lot of time together.' This aspect of their relationship comes across vividly in *Speed Trap*. When Johnson, aged seventeen, ran the 50-yard dash at the Maple Leaf Indoor Games against a field that included Hasely Crawford, Johnson surprised Francis by reaching the final. 'As he lined up for the final, I felt a spasm of protectiveness,' Francis wrote. 'Though Ben had grown to 150 pounds, his body still looked unformed, adolescent.'

As the youngest in the group, Johnson was also the butt of most jokes, increasing Francis's sense of paternal protectiveness. Yet, though Johnson was 'a natural target for practical jokes', they didn't appear to faze him. Nothing appeared to faze him. Desai Williams would later recall Johnson asking him for toothpaste, but taking a tube of heat rub from his wash bag by mistake. As he brushed his teeth, suddenly his eyes widened and he said 'What is this?' but he was quite calm and just muttered, 'This is how a mon learn to be careful around his friends.'

'He was a Shakespearean figure,' the Canadian journalist Jim Ferstle has said of Francis. 'Triumph and tragedy, great ambiguity, comic relief, lessons learned, and great stories… '

Ferstle speaks fondly of Francis, which is odd, because he was researching and writing about drugs in sport when few acknowledged the scale of the problem, and even fewer cared. From his home in Minnesota, Ferstle has spent many lonely hours delving into what he feels is the greatest threat to the integrity of sport. He is an unusual sports journalist in another respect: he has only attended one Olympics, in

1976. 'Too much of a cattle call,' Ferstle tells me. 'Ten thousand reporters chasing twenty thousand stories, all variations of the same thing.'

It was only years later, after the hordes of reporters learned the darker secrets of Francis's coaching methods, that Ferstle got to know him, but he found him utterly compelling. 'He was so inquisitive and thorough. Not warm, though. I wouldn't describe him as warm. There were so many aspects to his personality. That innate intelligence attracted you to him, while the arrogance put people off. One of the best descriptions of him was from a mutual acquaintance of ours at Stanford. He told me that it didn't surprise him that Charlie did what he did. But it also didn't surprise him that he came clean about it in the end.'

Ferstle says that Francis was quick to make friends with the East German coaches on the international circuit. They shared information on workouts, drills, spotting talent and, ultimately, doping.

'I always enjoyed talking to Charlie,' says Dick Patrick, the athletics correspondent of USA Today from 1986 to 2004. 'Tom Tellez avoided the limelight. Tellez had no need to have his ego stroked by his coaching Carl or wanting to tell everyone how brilliant he was. Charlie, I think, was trying to get a bit more attention for Ben, and maybe for himself, and he was more accessible to the press in general than Tellez. I thought he was a tremendous coach, very knowledgeable.'

Watching TV interviews with Francis, one is struck that beneath a calm Canadian veneer, there is a very un-Canadian intensity. That was obviously channelled into his coaching which, according to Angella Issajenko, was peppered by fits of temper. 'Intense' is also the word used by one Toronto journalist, Randy Starkman of the Star, who adds, 'He could be weird to deal with. But you talk to Charlie's athletes, and they swear by the guy. They felt he was looking after their best interests. And I think he was.'

This could be seen in the financial support Francis offered his sprinters, none of whom came from well-off families. He regularly subsidised his group, running up $17,000 in credit card bills in three years and having to re-finance, and eventually sell, the Aston Martin he'd bought with his earnings as an insurance underwriter. He bought his athletes groceries, paid their rent. When they travelled to compete, he asked them to put their spending money in envelopes and hand them over for safekeeping. The envelopes were frequently empty, in which case Francis would subsidise their trip. Bob Alexander, who would later grill Francis in his role as lead counsel at the post-Seoul Dubin Inquiry, says, 'Whatever you thought of Charlie, one thing was not in doubt: he really loved his athletes.'

In the case of Johnson, Francis appeared particularly keen to help, since he understood how short of money his mother was. On one early trip to Montreal, involving both Ben and brother Eddie, he discovered that they had only $6 between them. Later, Gloria Johnson handed Francis a bundle of dollar bills on the eve of Ben's first trip to Europe. He recalled, 'She'd taken a second job at night so that Ben could train without the interference of having to work after school... she gave me $100 to hold for Ben's spending money, and I knew what that sum must have meant to her. "Take care of him," she told me.'

Francis had some assistance too and among his supporters was Joe Douglas, who he had met in his Stanford days. 'I knew Charlie very well,' says Douglas, 'and I helped him get his athletes in meets when he first came to Europe. I got on with him very well... until he started giving his athletes drugs.'

'By the fall of 1979, my time had come to deal with the sport's great X-factor: anabolic steroids,' said Francis in *Speed Trap*. 'None of my men was yet advanced enough to make steroid use an issue. Angella Issajenko, however, was another matter... As I saw it, a coach had two options: he could face reality and plan an appropriate response, or he could bury his head in the sand while his athletes fell behind.'

Issajenko was not a conscript. Her transition from clean to tainted appeared as simple and straightforward, and as devoid of moral dilemmas, as that of her coach. She describes, in vivid but strikingly mundane detail, in her own book, *Running Risks,* what happened on 24 September 1979, when 'on a golden, early autumn afternoon', she went with Francis to see her family doctor and told him she wanted to start a programme of anabolic steroids: 'Charlie went downstairs to the pharmacy to have the prescription filled and returned to the office with 100 little pink pills in a bottle... '

'That afternoon,' according to Issajenko, 'I was nervous but very determined. I kept thinking about how I wanted to be the fastest woman on the planet.' The doctor, she said, 'briefly discussed the side effects of Dianabol, but I wasn't really listening, and he didn't seem all that concerned.' It was as easy as getting a prescription for an antibiotic. And some of the effects were immediate. 'Four days later, on 28 September, I turned twenty-one. I worked out, as usual, and made a note that I weighed 129 pounds. By Christmas Day, I weighed 138.'

Two years later, in September 1981, Francis felt the time had come to have the discussion with Johnson about drugs. His older athletes were already more worldly-wise, having been to college in the US. Johnson had failed to meet even the low standard of academic attainment required. But he understood very quickly what he had to do. He was still nineteen, in Francis's account, when they met to discuss the schedule for 1982.

'Then our conversation turned to steroids. It was immediately apparent that Ben understood how widespread they were, that he saw who was improving and why. I told him what I knew. I estimated the steroids represented at least one per cent of performance – or one metre in the hundred – at the elite level. Though the decision to take the drugs was Ben's, he had little choice if he agreed with my conclusions. He could either set up his starting blocks on the same line as his international competition, or he could start a metre behind... A few days later Ben called me to say he had decided: he wanted to use steroids... Without fanfare or moralising, our drug programme was in place.'

Johnson gently disputes his old coach's version of events. He says that there was a three-week period between his initial conversation with Francis and his decision. Did he wrestle with the problem? 'I asked myself many times in that three-week span. And I said to myself, "I don't want to, I don't want to take drugs to run. I can do it on my own accord."

'And then, one week goes by, and a week and a half goes by, and Charlie says, "Did you think about it?" And I say, "I'm still think-ing!" Then I thought, "Why should I do it clean when everybody else is doing it dirty?" Where would that leave me? The next day, I said to Charlie, "OK, Charlie, let's try it out." And that was it.'

Did he feel pressure? 'I feel there was a little bit of pressure, yeah. Because that's the only way I could train harder and recover faster, so I could get to the next level. But they were for training and recov-ery, that's all. People think I used drugs to make me run fast. That's annoying. Because scientifically that's not possible. A sprinter like me was born.'

Yet it was not something Johnson felt able to discuss with his mother. 'Well, my mum would disapprove, and I didn't want to get her involved in my career... I just trained my mind to ignore things like this, problems or trouble. My mum paid the bills, cooked my food and took care of things. I just eat, train and sleep. That was my life. Mum never asked me about my training, what I was doing, or wh...'

Johnson's stutter overcomes him. Eventually he continues, 'Or what I was taking.'

Even before he began taking steroids Johnson had shown signs of considerable improvement. After his last place behind Carl Lewis in the previous year's Pan-Am Junior Games, in an unremarkable 10.88 seconds, he ran 10.25 in 1981. And the following year, as Issajenko won the Commonwealth Games 100m title in Brisbane, Johnson won his first major medal, in the men's equivalent. He led until just two metres from the line, but finished second, in a wind-assisted

10.05 seconds, to Allan Wells of Scotland, the reigning Olympic champion. Francis's athletes won thirteen medals in Brisbane.

By 1981, Lewis had run 10 seconds flat, and was ranked first in the *Track & Field News* world rankings, as he would be for five more years. It would still be a few years before he would emerge as Francis's – and Johnson's – nemesis, though Francis's cynicism and suspicion is not difficult to detect in his book. He had first seen Lewis in 1979 when he was already six-foot-two but adolescent-skinny. Just one year later, he saw him again and he 'looked like he'd put on 25 pounds of muscle'.

'Charlie hated Carl,' says Randy Starkman, 'he would just go on and on about how much he hated Carl.'

4

THE QUIET ONE

'Help me to stay me.'
CALVIN SMITH

It was a Saturday evening, 14 May 1983, and Carl Lewis had just won the 100m in a low-key meeting in Modesto, California. The following wind was legal for a record: 1.48 metres per second (two is the limit). In the stand, watching, was Jim Hines, whose winning time over the distance at the 1968 Olympics still stood as the world record: 9.95 seconds. Now someone told Hines that Lewis had matched it.

'He tied the record?' said Hines, pulling his hat down over his eyes, pretending to hide. But Lewis's time was not immediately confirmed, and eventually one of the officials, Ed Hicks, said, '9.96… It wasn't half an inch from being 9.95, but it was 9.96.'

'Look again!' Lewis urged Hicks. It was his first legal run inside 10 seconds. But it hadn't quite been fast enough for the world record.

Still, if not now, the moment was bound to come. And as is so often the case when somebody emerges at the head of any pack, he was pulling others in his slipstream. If the man being called the next Jesse Owens was threatening to set new standards, he was challenging his rivals to do likewise, perhaps even encouraging them to believe that they could too. As a rival coach, Terry Long, put it, 'Carl's sprinting and jumping have made it like the time when the four-minute mile was first broken and suddenly it seemed like everyone could do it. He's raised the level of what can be expected in his events.'

This echoed the words written in 1937 by the pioneering sportswriter Paul Gallico: 'One broken record usually precipitates a whole host of them because the smashed mark immediately changes the mental attitude of the athlete towards the task of wrecking it further. We borrow a term from boxing and call it "softening up". A crack sprinter will run the hundred yards in 9.6, the world's record time, and never improve on it. Along will come a new phenomenon and lower the world's record to 9.4. The 9.6 man will suddenly, to his own great surprise, do it in 9.4, too. Why? Because he knows it can be done, has been done.'

Sure enough, the world 100m record fell two months later. It was broken by an American sprinter, a 22-year-old of great promise, but it wasn't Lewis. Instead, it fell to a small, slightly built runner with an unconventional style. Each time he ran his head fell back over the course of the race, as if pulled by some invisible force, then tilted to the left; he crossed the line with head and arms flung back, chest and throat thrust forward. His name was Calvin Smith.

Before Smith's breakthrough, Lewis had made another piece of history. In Indianapolis at the US national championships, he won three titles: the 100, the 200 and the long jump. Even Owens hadn't managed to do that: no one had since 1886. 'He's out of his head trying this,' Lewis's coach, Tom Tellez, had said as the meeting got underway. It was not a criticism; he was just awestruck by his protégé's audacity. But there was an extra incentive: the nationals would decide places in the US team for the inaugural world athletics championships in Helsinki, which Lewis was predicting would be better than the Olympics because only the best athletes would be allowed – weaker countries would have no right to send their best runner for the sake of it.

In Indianapolis Lewis duly claimed all three titles. In doing so, he produced the second-longest long jump in history, 8.79 metres, just 11 centimetres behind Bob Beamon's 'unbeatable' world record, which, like Hines's 100m record, had been set in the thin air of Mexico City at the 1968 Olympics.

The thinner air at high altitude confers special advantages for athletes in explosive events, whether runners or jumpers. For one thing, their event is anaerobic, so the lower concentration of oxygen in the air does not affect them as it does the endurance, aerobic, athletes – at least, not until after the event, when the effects hit the sprinter's oxygen-deprived body. More importantly, there is less resistance, and so objects, and humans, travel faster, and further. This is why airport runways at altitude are longer; it takes longer for planes to stop.

All of which underlines the quality of Lewis's long jump at low level in Indianapolis. After going so close he – and those watching – felt that the world record was on. But when he jumped a second time he did not quite match his first jump. That was it, Lewis decided. As the air stilled, the temperature dipped, and thunder began to rumble in the distance, he stopped, forgoing his remaining four jumps in order to rest for the 200m semi-final, thirty minutes later. Lewis's refusal to continue jumping prompted a frantic exchange, reported in *Sports Illustrated*. 'You must, you must get him to jump again,' an Italian photographer urged Lewis's father, Bill. The photographer was, according to the magazine, 'trembling'.

'Why?' asked Bill Lewis.

'Because of the conditions. Do you know how much electrostatic power is in the air?'

'He's over twenty-one.'

'You get these conditions once in a lifetime. In Mexico City, after Beamon jumped, the sky opened,' said the photographer. 'I was there.'

'What can I tell him?'

'Tell him there is energy!'

'And he'll tell me to pound sand,' shrugged Bill Lewis.

The photographer retreated in a mood of consternation. But it was a portentous exchange. Arguably, and with the considerable benefit of hindsight, that night in Indianapolis may have represented the greatest chance of Lewis's career to snatch the world record he most coveted, frequently threatened, but never attained. Ninety minutes later, he won the 200m final, opening such a gap on the bend that he was able to look around, smile, then look around again, and, with 10 metres remaining, throw both arms in the air.

'That was my way of showing the joy of what I do,' he explained. But had he kept pushing to the line then this world record surely would have been his. Lewis crossed the line in 19.75, the second-fastest 200 in history, three-hundredths down on Pietro Mennea's world record, also set in Mexico City, in 1979. 'I regret putting up my hands,' Lewis said when he realised how close he had been. 'But regret isn't the right word. I'm 0.1 from the world record in the 100, I'm 0.03 from the world record in the 200. I'm four inches from the world record in the long jump, so there's terrific suspense. It's still fun to compete.'

The world, it seemed, was Lewis's oyster, even if world records were proving tantalisingly elusive. He seemed sure he would get them. In the meantime, he was a triple national champion, the first in almost a century. And yet the atmosphere around Lewis mirrored the conditions that followed his second long jump. The air had cooled. Dark clouds were rolling in.

While Lewis's refusal to continue jumping annoyed some in the crowd, it was his behaviour in the 200m that irked some of his colleagues. 'I've talked to a lot of people,' Edwin Moses, the 1976 Olympic 400m hurdles champion, told the *New York Times*, 'and the words they used were lack of sportsmanship. Everybody knows he's a big winner, and nobody envies him or anything like that. But for some people, it's a little too much.'

'I guess you might call it showboating,' said Louise Ritter, the high jumper. 'It may be embarrassing to his competitors when he looks back after 30 yards, but I'd like to be in the position to be that good, to know that I don't have to worry.'

Larry Myricks, Lewis's long jumping rival, was more scathing, 'There's going to be some serious celebrating when Carl gets beat.'

Then there was Calvin Smith, the unheralded Calvin Smith. That changed on 3 July, in Colorado Springs. Smith, who had been third behind Lewis and Emmit King at the nationals, lined up for the 100m at the National Sports Festival with low expectations. He had been feeling jaded and below par. He had failed to make the progress he had hoped for after a remarkable 1982 season in which he had not only run a legitimate 10.05 seconds but a 9.91 in East Germany, at a meet where the wind assistance was the merest fraction over the permitted level – better than Hines's run, many thought.

Smith almost didn't travel to Colorado. 'I'd finished my college season, and I was just tired,' he says. 'I had taken some time off from doing any hard training. All I was doing was jogging. I went to the meet in Colorado just to see what happened, I guess. And I just got in the blocks, and I had a pretty good start, and I just ran, and I felt very good, very relaxed. It was effortless. Just… boom… it was over.'

At 2.55 p.m., on the Air Force Academy track – new and harder than most, which suited the sprinters – Smith, in all-green vest and shorts, sprang out of the blocks with the other seven runners, rather than lagging behind, as he so often was. After 35 metres there was daylight between him and the others, at 60 he had a clear and expanding lead: he seemed to be accelerating. Yet he didn't glance to either side as the finish approached, nor did he begin celebrating, he maintained his effort to the end. And, as he flashed across the line, the clock stopped at 9.93. Smith had sliced two-hundredths of a second from Hines's fifteen-year-old mark. The margin of victory was enormous: his nearest rival, Bernard Jackson, finished in 10.19. When Smith saw his time, and clocked that the wind was legal, he performed a little jig of delight before being overcome by self-consciousness, then he stopped and bowed his head to say a brief prayer.

Smith was a student at the University of Alabama, coached by the affable Wayne Williams. The same Wayne Williams who had tried to recruit Carl Lewis. But Smith had been almost as big a catch. 'I had got some information coming out of Mississippi about Calvin,' Williams recalls. 'Mississippi is not huge in track, but you get little inklings about talent. Calvin was running real well, but his coach in high school was a maths teacher. You know, he did not have good running form at that time.'

But Williams saw beyond Smith's huge Afro hairstyle, his modest times, set on an old dirt track, and his unusual style. He went down and talked to Smith and his family, who seemed interested. 'But Calvin was very, very quiet,' says Williams. 'Like with Carl, I would make my dozen phone calls a week. I don't know how irritated Calvin may have been with this, but he was a very quiet, polite, shy young man. As many times as I would talk to him, I would very rarely have a good conversation with him. Trying to get information outta Calvin was like pulling teeth. I'd ask, "How you doin', Calvin? How's your training going? What's happening with school?" You'd get these really short, "OK, yeah" answers. There was never a follow-up.

'I had a kinda technique for recruiting,' he explains, sounding mischievous. He followed a script, a set of twenty questions, but would turn them into statements. 'Instead of, "What kind of track facilities are you looking for?" I'd say, "We have the track facilities you are looking for!" I knew UCLA were looking to recruit him, so I'd say, "You know it's gonna be very expensive flying back and forth to California and having your family come and watch you compete..."'

His technique worked, both as a recruiting sergeant and as a coach, persuading his prodigy to keep control of his flailing arms. Just four years after Smith arrived at Alabama, he had the world record, one that would ultimately stand for five years, after Johnson's times were expunged. Yet, for all that, Smith's run was not universally hailed as one of the truly great athletic achievements. At 7,250 feet, Colorado

Springs is just 100 feet lower than Mexico City, so his run had the same, invisible, asterisk against it as Hines's record or, indeed, Bob Beamon's. Furthermore, Smith had recently lost to Carl Lewis at the nationals. Lewis had been due to run in Colorado, but pulled out with a leg strain. The question asked afterwards was not 'Did you see what Calvin Smith did?' but 'What would Carl Lewis have done?'

To further underline the advantages of the altitude, the women's record fell at the same meeting, Evelyn Ashford running 10.77 seconds – the first time the men's and women's records had gone on the same day. In the aftermath of his record, Smith was asked by reporters what he would say to Lewis. 'I'm not going to tell him anything,' he replied. 'I don't feel I'm any better than any of the other top runners. It's just who's running best that day.' What, he was asked, had he said when he dropped his head in prayer?

'Help me, God. Help me to stay me.'

'If cats could speak,' it is sometimes said, 'they wouldn't.' To meet Calvin Smith is to be reminded of this. He is feline and graceful in his movements, and low-key and unassuming when he does speak. His quietness, it seems, is not shyness. He says what he has to say. He comes across as sincere, in possession of a quiet, calm self-confidence.

Today, Smith is as slightly built as when he was competing. Yet he looks almost unrecognisable, mainly because of his long, flowing dreadlocks. He is sitting in his two-storey, pistachio-coloured home in a middle-class suburb of Tampa. There are athletics trophies and awards on display in the living room – but they belong to his son, also called Calvin, rather than him.

In the drive sits a small black Toyota. It's 5.30 p.m. and Smith has just finished work. When he retired as an athlete, in 1996, he became a middle-school English teacher for four years. Then he became a social worker, initially running a housing programme for ex-offenders. Now he is mainly deskbound, managing grant-aided projects to help the disadvantaged. 'But I enjoy getting out the office, meeting different clients,' he says. 'I do like that aspect.' Do any of those clients recognise him as the ex-athlete, the man who for five years – arguably the most competitive period in the history of the event – was officially the fastest man in the world? He seems a little embarrassed. 'Maybe some, not many,' he shrugs.

Smith grew up on the edge of Bolton, Mississippi, a town with just five hundred people, many of them his relatives. He was the youngest boy of ten children: six girls, four boys. His father died in his sleep when Calvin was five. 'My mother worked for different families in their homes, cleaning and stuff like that. We were poor, yeah, very humble. But still, it was a very enjoyable childhood. My grandmother and her sister lived in the house next door. It was just our family in our little area.'

It's only later, as I'm about to leave, hovering in the doorway, that Smith, leaning against the wall, tells another story about his childhood, which explains how he honed his speed. 'The local kids would play in the community centre at the end of the dirt road. Our house was probably a quarter-mile from where everything was, so many times I'd be down there playing with the kids, knowing the sun is going down, and it's getting dark – and you had to cross this little bridge and go down this dark dirt road. Well, I had one friend who lived close to me, and we had to both go down the dirt road... We'd jog, and say, "If any bad thing jumps out the bushes, we gotta run!" If we heard anything, or thought we heard anything, we ran.'

Like Lewis and Johnson he was small and struggled at team games, though not, in his case, for the want of trying. 'We played American football, and my teammates would give me the ball while they blocked. My teacher saw my speed and asked me to come out to the track. It was pretty much a natural progression from there.' Smith's style never lost that hint of the dirt road, although Williams came to feel that the head tilt actually helped his weight distribution on turns – the US would always use him on the third leg of the relay. And except for slinking out of Williams's weight training sessions, he was always the perfect pupil.

'Calvin never did anything other than exactly what I laid out,' said Williams. 'Now, in contrast to that, Emmit King would maybe come out and do half the workout, and say, "Coach, look, I gotta run, I gotta go over and see so-and-so, or I gotta go pay my gas bill... " I wouldn't bite him on the back. I'd say, "OK, Emmit, you go, do what you gotta do." Every so often Calvin would get a little bit upset with me because some of the other folks would – as he saw it – get away with stuff like that. Fact is he could have got away with stuff like that too, if he'd been that way. But he wasn't that way. He was going to do whatever I told him.'

Williams was an intuitive coach as well as an empathetic one. He focused on technique, not times, which he thought were a distraction. Only as a meeting approached did he produce his stopwatch. As he describes his philosophies and principles, Williams sounds like a throwback – a coach from a different, pre-scientific, pre-pharmaceutical era.

'I was not naive about drugs,' says Williams. 'I knew they went on. But I knew two other things: one is that I was not going to be one to suggest it to my athletes or have a part of it, and I knew my kids were clean. And I think that, if there had been an absolutely clean Olympics, Calvin would have won.'

One of the remarkable things about Smith is that, after leaving university and Wayne Williams, he never worked with another coach. 'Coach Williams was a great teacher, and, basically,' says Smith, 'I coached myself for the rest of my career using his techniques and workouts.' His great contemporary in the 400m hurdles, Edwin Moses, also went without a coach, but very few others contemplated managing without someone to offer moral support, encouragement, nannying and the occasional kick up the backside. 'Some athletes, they need guardians for ever,' Smith says. 'But I was a student of the sport, I learned and I had my own ideas about things. I still do. I didn't need someone to get on at me, to make me do something that I wanted to do.'

Living in Florida for much of his career – he moved there in 1987 – Smith would occasionally train with other sprinting groups, including that of another top American, Harvey Glance, but he was often isolated. He trained alone, on a grass field. It must have taken incredible self-discipline. 'It does,' Smith agrees. 'And a lot of people don't have that. But the key thing is to know your body. I would plan my workouts, but adjust them as I went along. I think I knew my body pretty well.'

'He's busted down the door of people's perceived limits,' said Terry Long as Carl Lewis homed in on three world records, even as Smith snatched one of them from his clutches.

But had Lewis really done such a thing? Was he merely the best of his time, or was he a mould-breaker: someone who could transcend his sport as Pelé, Muhammad Ali and, later, Michael Jordan transcended theirs?

The sports writer Gary Smith once suggested that, before Lewis, the public interest in the 100m – and in whoever could claim to be the world's fastest human – was as fleeting as the race itself, partly because of the nature of the event and its demands. 'The great ones have exploded upon us for one Olympics, then either dropped to the ground with twisted faces – thoroughbreds faster than their tendons or ligaments could bear – or lost half a finger-snap of speed and vanished from sight.' They did not linger long enough to gain a solid grip on the public imagination.

And, scanning the list of Olympic gold medallists and world record holders, it's tempting to agree. To the uninitiated, perhaps only two names leap out: Harold Abrahams in 1924 and Jesse Owens in 1936. And in Abrahams' case, this is now almost entirely because he was the central figure of the hugely successful 1981 film, *Chariots of Fire*, which showed him overcoming, among other things, a hidden layer of British anti-Semitism.

With Owens, it can be difficult to separate myth from reality. Owens also had to overcome prejudice, but being snubbed by Hitler at the 1936 Berlin Olympics was the least of it. In the United States, even after his four gold medals, he was not permitted to travel with whites, or stay in the same hotels. He returned from Berlin not to a hero's welcome, but to a life of segregation and exclusion, banned from continuing his career as an 'amateur' athlete, and reduced to racing horses and menial work to earn money. It was only much later that the legend developed: a legend that saw Owens, representing the free world and the land of opportunity, bravely defying Hitler.

In the years before Lewis's emergence, few people outside the athletics community could even name the Olympic 100m champion or the world record holder. This was partly because the event suffered from the introduction of electronic timing. With hand timing, there was, inevitably, a delay between the gun and the clock starting. Electronic timing eliminated the delay, which meant the recorded times were fractionally slower – a difference barely noticed in longer races, but critical in the 100m. The perception, then, was that sprinters were running more slowly.

In the 1970s and early 1980s other athletic feats attracted more attention. In Britain, one of the sport's heartlands, where the international federation had its headquarters and where the sport's 'amateur' values and ethos were enshrined, it was middle-distance running that inspired most interest, especially as the rivalry between Sebastian Coe and Steve Ovett began to heat up. Indeed, following the 1980 Olympics, it seems likely that more people would have been able to name the 800m gold medallist (Ovett) or the 1500m champion (Coe) than the fastest man in the Games. And yet the 100m champion was British, too.

In a way, that man's current situation underlines the point. I meet him in a café on the campus of the University of Surrey where he works

61

as a technician. It is his break and, towards the end of our meeting, he eyes his watch anxiously, so as not to run over his allotted hour.

Allan Wells was Carl Lewis's predecessor. In more ways than one. Wells, who grew up, the son of a blacksmith, in Edinburgh, was another scrawny youngster: he reputedly took a Charles Atlas bodybuilding course. He also took up long jumping and converted to sprinting, in his case aged twenty-four. Watching television one Sunday, he saw a former training partner, Drew Hislop, win a prestigious indoor 60m race. It was his epiphany.

Wells joined the same training group as Hislop, which, he says, had 'controversial methods of training'. Controversial in what sense? 'Speedball,' says Wells, though it should be added that he is referring to the spring-loaded punchball, not the cocktail of lethal drugs. 'And there was a lot of gym work,' he adds. 'I threw myself at their mercy.'

Wells's first major success as a sprinter came at the 1978 Commonwealth Games, where he won two gold medals, in the 200m and 4x100 relay, plus silver in the 100m behind Don Quarrie. He went to the Moscow Olympics as a contender but without the star billing of some of his British teammates – such as Coe, with whom he roomed. He might not have gone at all, with the British government keen to follow the American boycott in protest at the Soviet Union's invasion of Afghanistan.

'I got letters from 10 Downing Street,' says Wells. 'I opened one up and it had a photo of a little girl, with a doll six inches from her hand. She was dead, killed by the Russians. It was blackmail. I thought it was gutless. My wife Margot had intercepted four of these letters already and put them all in the bucket so I didn't see them. But I can still see the picture of that little girl.' Unlike the Americans, Britain ignored the government's objections and sent a team.

Drawn in a tough semi-final, with four first-round winners, including the defending champion, Hasely Crawford, Wells ran a personal best 10.11 to win. Even so, in the final he was an underdog. He had never even used starting blocks before these Games, the first time they were compulsory.

Wells, in his vest and short, tight shorts, was last to walk out on to the track. He was in lane eight. The man he wanted to watch was the Cuban, Silvio Leonard, the second-fastest man in history after Jim Hines and, in the absence of the Americans, the obvious favourite. But Leonard was right over in lane one and Wells couldn't see him. He did have another Cuban, Osvaldo Lara, on his inside, and that offered him a possible clue.

'I'd watched him training with Leonard over 30 metres. Leonard was taking about a yard out of him in that distance. So I thought, right, I could gauge myself against Lara. I got a good start, but I didn't pass Lara at 30 metres, it was more like 40 or 50, and that worried me a bit, because that was me just getting past him, not taking a yard off him, as I'd wanted to do.

'But I pass him, and the gap just opens up, I could kind of tell I was neck and neck with Leonard, but I think I got the lead, then he came back, and I dipped – and... '

'... And Wells has got it!' yelled the BBC commentator David Coleman.

'I have to say,' says Wells, 'that my event is the purest event and I say that with all respect. There's no hiding place. People see your character for what you are and how you run and how you handle yourself on the track. How you respond to winning or losing, they see all that.' Wells talks as he used to run: fast, without pausing for breath. He still looks fit, still has a full head of hair, but grey rather than black. And he admits he is shaking just thinking about the race.

'As much as we can put it into words, we cannot portray the physical feelings, the atmosphere around you and the fearful vibrations of everyone around you, and of what is going to happen. It is fear. Fear of the unknown: you are trying to establish the unknown.'

Yet, as with the high-altitude records, there is a problem with

Wells's gold. The absence of the US meant his victory was greeted with a great deal of scepticism. Some of the sceptics were close to home. Training in an Edinburgh park after the Games, a man shouted at him, 'You only won because the Americans weren't there!' It was, said Wells, 'a kick in the bollocks. And a kick up the arse.'

At his next major international meeting, the IAAF World Cup finals in Rome in 1981, Wells silenced the doubters by running 10.20, and beating all the highly rated Americans: Mel Lattany, Stanley Floyd, and the young Carl Lewis. Lewis was last, trailing home in 10.96, nursing a strained hamstring. Earlier, Lewis had competed in the long jump, earning Wells's public disapproval. 'It's not good sense to try what Lewis did,' Wells, with the authority of an ex-long jumper, told reporters. 'The US coaches shouldn't have permitted him to compete in both events. That's asking for trouble.'

He had offered Lewis the same bit of advice. And as with most rebukes, Lewis didn't appreciate it. 'I could live with losing a race, especially given the circumstances,' Lewis would say later. 'But I did not appreciate what Allan Wells said to me afterwards, "See, Carl, I told you, you can't do the hundred and jump the same day. Takes too much out of you."

'People like Wells,' added Lewis, 'inspired me to keep doing what I was doing.'

'The world is waiting for Carl Lewis,' claimed *The Times* on 5 August 1983, on the eve of the first World Athletics Championships in Helsinki. 'The only doubt concerns the number of gold medals that Lewis will win: will it be three or four?'

Lewis had just turned twenty-two and arrived in Helsinki with a swagger. He was charismatic, confident and charming. According to the *New York Times*, he 'carried out a news conference with polish and poise, meeting with finesse such potentially controversial issues as his endorsements or how American rivals may be jealous of him'.

Lewis's first event was the 100m, but on the blocks in the final, he was bothered by a bee, which forced a delay. When they got underway, Lewis began sluggishly. Wells started powerfully on his inside, all jabbing fists, head down like a charging bull. Emmit King was ahead at halfway. But the long, lean figure of Lewis, once fully extended and into his rhythm, bore down on them. While his rivals reached a plateau, Lewis kept accelerating. He overhauled King for a convincing win, in 10.07, with the slowest starter in the field, Calvin Smith – 'he fell asleep at the start,' said the *New York Times* – emerging from lane eight to claim silver ahead of King. It was an American one-two-three, with Wells in fourth. 'I believed in three medals for the USA, because we are the best runners in the world,' said Lewis. 'I'm not pleased with my time, but it was the best I could do in this stadium.'

A notable absentee from the final was Ben Johnson, who had only just managed to qualify from the first round and came sixth in his semi-final. It had still been something of a breakthrough year for him, including a personal best, 10.19, in winning his first Grand Prix event, in Munich. But by the end of 1981 he was ranked only eighteenth in the world.

'Ben's starts were the talk of the circuit,' insisted Francis. 'No one could match him out of the blocks.' But in Helsinki he sensed Johnson was starting to get over-stressed about the start. It was Jamaica's former champion, Don Quarrie, who suggested that Johnson was worrying about the wrong thing: he needed to focus on his weakness, not his strength. His start would take care of itself.

Wells had beaten Johnson at the Commonwealth Games in Brisbane, where he won both sprint golds. In Helsinki, a year later, he noticed that Johnson had added a great deal of muscle. 'People said he was squatting incredible weights.' But he liked Johnson, finding him 'friendly, laid-back, straightforward'. He was less keen on Lewis.

'The thing is, when you compete with people, you're not physically fighting them, but you're not friends with them. It's a very lonely existence, sprinting. But Lewis's demeanour, his attitude… he was a selfish individual. He didn't do himself any favours. I think he thought he would come into the sport, run over everybody and take everything that was going, then just walk away. I think a lot of the sprinters felt that about him. And he treated his countrymen like muck. I didn't like Lewis; I didn't like his attitude.

'But I beat Johnson and Lewis,' adds Wells with satisfaction. 'Calvin Smith was the only one I never beat.'

In Helsinki, Lewis duly won the long jump having again elected to jump only twice, sitting out his remaining four attempts, and opted to miss the 200, which Smith won. Still to come was the 4x100m relay. King ran leg one for the USA, yelling 'Don't leave me!' as he approached man two, Willie Gault, who he feared was sprinting away too fast to get the baton. Then Gault passed to Smith who passed to Lewis, a metre ahead of the field. Lewis took the baton in his left hand, switched it to his right, focused on the straight ahead of him, and opened the throttle and the gap. He crossed the line four metres clear, then looked at the scoreboard: 'I thought it said 38.8. For a second I was disappointed. It didn't make sense.' But in fact it was 37.86. It was the first time any team had broken the 38-second barrier. 'We wanted the world record as much or more than just the gold,' said King. 'We were trying to put it out of reach so it won't get broken again.'

But even more striking was Lewis's speed on the final leg. With his flying start as man four, he was timed at 8.9 seconds. 'There is no evidence that any man has ever run faster,' claimed *Sports Illustrated*. 'It reaffirms American sprint dominance,' said Lewis.

Lewis was fêted throughout Europe, labelled 'Superman' by *L'Equipe*, the French sports daily. In London, *The Times* had this headline: 'Owens, Louis, Pele, Ali... Lewis'. But the unalloyed adulation did not last long. On 15 August a report in a Norwegian newspaper, *VG*, claimed that Lewis had tested positive. The story took up a full page, with a large picture of a smiling, casually dressed Lewis, beneath the headline, 'Lewis Dopet?'

According to the paper, 'sources from the International Athletics Federation' had revealed that 'several of the samples from Helsinki were positive. One of them belongs to Carl Lewis.' The reporters, Jan Hedenstad and Arvid Eriksen, added that this was a preliminary analysis and that the samples would have to be re-tested before being declared positive. The story did not say what had allegedly been found in Lewis's sample. I contacted Hedenstad, who said that 'very good sources' told him there 'was something strange with his test, but for some reason the test did not lead to anything'.

Hadenstad points out that, at the time, 'the doping test technology was far behind those people developing new drugs. But the doping hunters at that time were able to see that something was wrong, but not to know exactly what and therefore not able to catch the users.' Exactly what might have been strange about Lewis's urine sample remains unclear.

Lewis issued a denial as he went on to run in Berlin. The writer, he told reporters, was 'just a kid'. (Hedenstad was thirty-four.) He added, 'He had absolutely no basis for it, just his feeling that nobody could do what I've done without artificial aid. Basically it was a guess. A destructive guess.'

And he was backed up by Arne Ljungqvist, the IAAF's medical chairman, who still maintains there was nothing to support the claim. 'It is true we had some suspicious findings, which is not rare,' Ljungqvist tells me, 'and this was in the early days of steroid analysis. We did have some suspicions about a handful of cases, but we never acted upon them because we were not convinced they were positives. I was very upset by the rumour about Lewis, and I have no idea where it came from. I would have been the first to know.'

So there were no positive tests at the inaugural World Athletics Championships, just as there had been none at the Moscow Olympics in 1980. That fact had encouraged Prince Alexandre de Mérode, head of the IOC medical commission, to describe Moscow as the 'purest' Olympic Games in history. Not everyone shared his confidence.

5

THE ROOTS OF EVIL

'I just saw athletes' bodies changing.'
DAVID JENKINS

Some facts about Moscow and Helsinki only surfaced years later, but they would appear to make a mockery of de Mérode's claims of purity.

Indeed, there were those who, like Charlie Francis, believed that elite sport had been impure for years, if not decades. As early as the 1950s, anabolic steroids had certainly been used by athletes, initially those from Communist countries. But the drugs soon moved west. The man described as the 'godfather of steroids' in the United States is a Maryland doctor, John Ziegler, who, at the 1954 World Weight-lifting Championships in Vienna, had his curiosity aroused by the dominance of the Soviet Union.

Ziegler was there in his medical capacity but he also worked out with a group of lifters and bodybuilders in a gym in York, Pennsylvania. He was a big man himself. But in Vienna, Ziegler was astounded not only by the performances, but also by the bulky physiques of the Soviet lifters. And so he sought out their team doctor, inviting him to a local bar and plying him with drinks and questions. He got his answer: they were taking testosterone, the male sex hormone, which acts anabolically, i.e. building muscles and stimulating growth. It also develops the sex organs and other male characteristics. This explained not just the bulk but also the hairiness of the Soviet lifters.

When he returned home Ziegler began experimenting with testosterone on some of the weightlifters in the York gym. And he collaborated with a pharmaceutical company, CIBA, to develop an anabolic steroid, derived from testosterone, conferring the same benefits but without, it was hoped, the side effects. In 1958 the product was ready: it came in little pink pills and was called Dianabol. Ziegler believed it was his – and sport's – Eureka moment. Dianabol appeared to offer gain without pain. The effects on his guinea pigs in the York gym were almost immediate, as well as so obvious that it was not long before they, like the Soviet doctor in Vienna, were being pestered for the secret.

Ziegler, however, became alarmed at their enthusiasm. While he prescribed his new wonder drug in small doses – no more than 5mg a day – he quickly realised that his clients were ignoring him, using ever-larger amounts in the quest for greater benefits. He couldn't understand why his clients wouldn't follow instructions. 'What is it with these simple-minded shits?' he complained. 'I'm the doctor!'

He had reason to be alarmed because he was starting to grasp that an anabolic steroid was not a simple masculinity pill. Long-term users of Dianabol also suffered side effects, some of them the very reverse of what one might expect from the male sex hormone, including shrinkage of the testicles and possible impotence. Robert Voy, later chief medical officer of the US Olympic Committee, knew all about Ziegler's steroid epiphany, and his second epiphany, which came when he understood what he had unleashed. 'He created a monster,' said Voy, 'a fact he regretted for the rest of his life.'

By the 1970s the use of steroids by athletes was believed to be rife. When a urine test for anabolic steroids was developed by British scientists and introduced in time for the 1976 Olympics, it was considered a huge step forward. In fact, it might have precipitated a step back to the use of pure testosterone, which was thought to be undetectable because it occurred naturally.

But there turned out to be a way round that, too. As the 1980 Olympics reached their conclusion, Manfred Donike, a former Tour de France cyclist-turned-chemist who sat on the IOC's medical commission, gathered the leftover urine samples from the Moscow laboratory and took them back to his lab in Cologne. He wanted to run some private, unofficial tests.

Donike suspected, as did his colleague Arnold Beckett, that athletes could have used steroids in training, stopped in time to allow the drugs to clear their system, then just used testosterone. But in testing the Moscow samples, Donike made a crucial discovery.

Although he could not determine whether an athlete had taken testosterone, he could compare the relative levels of testosterone and its epimer (or mirror image) in the body, epitestosterone. The testosterone/epitestosterone ratio in most people, he discovered, was pretty much constant: 1:1, or at most 2:1. But many of the Moscow samples showed fluctuating ratios, many in the 4:1 to 6:1 range, or even higher. The only plausible explanation for these fluctuating ratios was the administration of artificial testosterone. Donike said a fifth of the samples he tested showed T/E ratios above 6:1, sixteen of them from gold medallists. This was *his* Eureka moment.

The IOC were concerned by his findings, and testosterone was added to the banned list in 1982. But that, in the eyes of Robert Voy, makes what happened in Helsinki so inexplicable. Though Donike's T/E test was supposedly being used at the World Athletics Championships, there were no positives – or none reported. 'Did the IAAF choose to cover up the results in Helsinki?' asked Voy in his book, *Drugs, Sport and Politics*. 'They must have.'

Dick Pound, who would become founding chairman of the World Anti-Doping Agency, was also convinced something was wrong. He later told the *Los Angeles Times*, 'There either were positives that were not acted upon by the IAAF or directions not to test for certain compounds or substances.'* The IAAF, he added, was in serious jeopardy of becoming a laughing stock. But Arne Ljungqvist, who had been in charge of dope testing at Helsinki, suggested this was deliberate. He told me, 'We used the IAAF competitions for the purposes of trying methods to be used in the Olympic Games.'

Just days after Helsinki, the Pan-Am Games got underway in Caracas. The latest tests would be used here, as they had been in Helsinki. On the eve of the Games, word spread among the athletes that this time the testers were serious. 'Paranoia was in the air,' admitted Charlie Francis. Donike, known as 'the hunter' for his hard line approach, had flown in to supervise the testing personally. 'I don't know if any one of yours is taking drugs,' Evie Dennis, the US *chef de mission*, told Joe Vigil, the team manager, 'but if anyone is or has, tell him for God's sake go home.'

Two days before the track and field programme began, the American athletes were given another warning, at a meeting with their own doctors and coaches. They were told that the equipment being used in Caracas would be more sensitive than ever and (falsely) that Donike and his team could detect illegal substances used up to a year earlier. At 9 a.m. the next day, twelve US athletes, mainly but not exclusively from field events, flew home. During the meeting itself, there was an unusually large number of withdrawals with sudden injuries. Donike professed to be baffled.

He insisted that the drug-testing equipment being used in Caracas was no different from that used in Helsinki, or, indeed, at the previous year's football World Cup in Spain. And yet this time there were positives – fifteen of them: eleven weightlifters, a cyclist, a fencer, a

---

* Donike told the Dubin Inquiry in 1989 that two athletes were positive for testosterone in Helsinki, but that they'd been cleared because it was decided their urine samples were too dilute. He didn't name the athletes.

sprinter and a shot-putter. Many of America's top athletes, including Carl Lewis and Calvin Smith, were missing from Caracas, because it came so soon after Helsinki, and because they could earn more money on the European circuit. But Charlie Francis's athletes, including Johnson, ran in Caracas, with no success and no positive tests. Desai Williams reached the 100m final, but withdrew. He had injured his quadriceps, explained Francis.

I was curious to know more about the 1970s – the decade in which the presence of performance-enhancing drugs went from in-the-know rumour to common knowledge, and when the arms race between athletes and testers began. And so I paid a visit to a large hilltop house in the suburbs of San Diego, the home of David Jenkins.

Jenkins, like Allan Wells, is an Edinburgh boy. They were born weeks apart, in 1952. Wells went through the state school system, Jenkins to the more privileged Edinburgh Academy. Jenkins emerged more quickly: European 400m champion at nineteen, he won a silver medal in the relay at the Munich Olympics a year later. Now, however, Jenkins's name is synonymous with drugs. He never tested positive, and yet his name has been largely airbrushed from athletics history. 'If you go to the British Athletics website, there's not much there about David Jenkins,' he says.

On the phone, he is cautious, probing, non-committal. He says he will think about whether he will see me: 'due diligence', he calls it. When I call back, he says yes. Jenkins is well over six foot tall and, as he approaches sixty, still lean and athletic. He has been in the US so long that his accent and expressions have become mid-Atlantic. He leads me through his sprawling home, past bronze figures of stags and eagles, and into the living room, where a Buddha sits in the corner. This opens on to a terrace that looks out to the Pacific. Then he tells me about his journey from naive young athlete to drugs cheat. It is quite a story, and one that links in with the Seoul Olympics in 1988 partly because, as they were about to get underway, Jenkins was awaiting sentencing for smuggling steroids into the United States. Until the previous year he had been running a drugs ring, reportedly making $100 million a year.

When he became European champion in 1971, says Jenkins, he had no idea how to run races, and he didn't have a clue about drugs or money. He learned quickly. In his first race after he won the European title, he returned to the changing room where an official took a wad of money out of his briefcase and said, 'Buy everybody drinks!'

'I thought, buy everybody drinks? I can buy everybody drinks for a year!' And now he was a champion, it kept happening. When he went back to run in Edinburgh, he was handed an expenses form. He put in a claim for £3. 'And the official says, "I think you made a mistake." He takes the form, adds a couple of zeroes, and says, "OK?"'

Thus was Jenkins initiated into big-time athletics. And nothing was ever said. At meetings around Europe he soon commanded appearance fees of £100 a time, and apparently limitless expenses. 'I earned £10,000,' he says. 'After a couple of months I could buy a car.' A year later at the Olympics, he had to sign a piece of paper that said he did not get paid for running. Did that trouble him? 'Yes, it troubled me,' he says. 'Because you're lying. And I hadn't been lying before. Nothing I'd done up to then involved lying. So… I started lying. I didn't have a moral compass. My compass was provided by my surroundings, my environment. It wasn't internal. So I drifted. And you pay the price for that eventually.'

Jenkins did not even have a conversation about drugs until after he had won his Olympic medal. But he knew what was going on. 'I just saw athletes' bodies changing,' he says. 'I just became aware of it. Guys were reasonably open about it as well.'

Even after steroids were officially banned in 1975? Jenkins suddenly sits up, animated, 'You could buy steroids over the counter in every

European country we went to! The guys would stock up! They'd buy pharmacies out!'

In 1974 Jenkins, who had been feeling tired and anaemic, started injections of Vitamin B-12. They had an extraordinary effect. Jenkins felt energised, and he had a voracious appetite ('I was so frickin' hungry. I ate a pound of bacon, twelve eggs'). Vitamins were entirely legal, of course. But taking them via injections was another small step, he reflects now, on the path to steroids.

In 1975, still clean, he ran a British record 44.93 to win the US championships. It was the following winter, after doing a promotional event in Wolverhampton, that he took the decision to move on to steroids. 'There were three of us doing this promotional thing, to help raise money for the team for the Olympics,' says Jenkins. 'And we were running sprints. It was full on. We did ten, walking back in between. Normally I'd blow the doors off everybody. I'd get stronger as they went on. But we're getting to sprint number eight, nine, and this guy – who I know well, who I should be hammering – is right with me. I have absolutely nothing left in the tank. I thought, maybe I'm on a bad day or something. But it was when we were coming out the shower, I saw him, and I thought: what the fuck has happened to you? His body had... ' he pauses, '... changed.'

And so he found a doctor in Manchester who was supplying steroids to the local gym-users and was given a prescription for Dianabol, the testosterone derivative developed by John Ziegler. The irony is that Jenkins was a poor advert for what became his business. The dose he was given was way too big, and though his muscles strengthened, his tendons did not, and he kept getting injured.

'I never ran as fast as I had before going on the drugs. I ran faster in practice, in training, but never in a race.' In the 1976 Olympics, he fell back to seventh in the 400m and his only other major medal came in the sprint relay at the 1978 Commonwealth Games. He suffered, he says, 'a biomechanical reaction, a psychological reaction. And a serious emotional reaction.' How did that manifest itself? 'Short temper. You're not stable mentally. You don't feel calm. You're all over the place. I was just a mess. It was the last thing I needed. I'm not exactly Mr Placid.'

Jenkins's relationship with athletics also suffered. He no longer enjoyed it. 'You're absolutely driven,' he says, 'but you've lost the pleasure.' And yet that marked only the beginning of his relationship with drugs.

The World Championships in Helsinki were a significant milestone for athletics, and not only for Carl Lewis. It was an anomaly that the most popular sport on the Olympic programme did not have its own global event. They were an instant success, and the man basking in the limelight was the IAAF's Italian president, a man described by some as dynamic, charismatic and a consummate politician, and by others as autocratic, bullying and Machiavellian.

Primo Nebiolo, who had taken over as president of the IAAF in 1981, inherited the plans for the World Championships from his predecessor, Adriaan Paulen. Yet it was the diminutive, deeply tanned Nebiolo who, inevitably, seemed to take the credit.

Primo is 'first' in Italian. Neb[b]iolo is the country's darkest grape. Both seem somehow appropriate. His election as president was suitably murky and mysterious. Having secured the support of one of the most influential men in world sport, the Adidas founder Horst Dassler, Nebiolo set about securing the job.

Paulen, a former Olympic middle-distance runner, and leading member of the wartime Dutch resistance, was ambitious for his sport, but also loyal to its amateur ethos. He might not have been as hard line as his predecessor, the Marquess of Exeter, who declared after the 1968 Olympics that 'at future international competitions only shoes without identifying marks on them will be allowed', but he was respected for his integrity.

That was not something often said of Nebiolo, a construction magnate who had gained a foothold in sports politics through the World Student Games. Paulen did not resist his challenge for the presidency, having been told by Dassler and Nebiolo that they had enough votes and that they did not want to humiliate him. It was true that Nebiolo had been promised lots of votes, but his methods had been unusual. According to John Holt, general secretary of the IAAF at the time, Nebiolo sent tickets to all the African countries who normally could not afford to send delegates to the congress. There was, of course, one small condition.

Once elected, Nebiolo came to symbolise – arguably as much as Carl Lewis, the sport's poster boy – a new era of athletics, an era far removed from its roots.

He was an extraordinary figure, only the fourth president since the IAAF was founded in 1912. John Holt had been appointed the organisation's general secretary by the Marquess, the second president, gold medallist in the 400m hurdles in 1928, and (as Lord Burghley) one of the characters depicted in *Chariots of Fire*. Holt was still there in the Nebiolo era, and now lives in retirement in a remote village on the west coast of Scotland.

'I remember going up to Grosvenor House for my interview for the job in 1968. Lord Exeter was sitting there at the table doing a little jigsaw puzzle, he had his braces on, and I remember the braces, they had Botticelli nudes down them.' The president ruled with a light touch, and Holt ran things from a small office in Putney, as he did under Paulen. The values of the sport remained sacrosanct. Yet, beyond their reach, they were eroding fast. And when Nebiolo arrived, he made sure the IAAF reflected that.

'He said it was impossible to run a federation from a small office, and that we must have a bigger place,' recalls Holt. 'We moved to an office in Knightsbridge, overlooking Harrods. Nebiolo had this big suite, the president's room, with a conference table and beautiful antique furniture. He might have come to the office once a year.

'He was a huge bully; his staff quaked when he came into the room. He used to say to me, "You have an open door, it's ridiculous. You let your staff come into your room and talk to you! You must inspire fear in them! You must make them afraid when they come into your room – that is what I do." And he had to be referred to as Mr President. Unless you were having dinner with him, when you could call him Primo.'

Nebiolo would only ever travel first-class yet, according to the Scottish journalist Doug Gillon, he would sometimes miss a flight deliberately so he could charter a jet and arrive even more stylishly.

'Another of Primo's things,' says Holt, 'was that he'd say, "Every morning I wake up and I say to myself, how can I make Nebiolo bigger and greater today? I usually start with the press. Before breakfast I phone six or seven journalists to give them information, and they think I am very important."' They were not the only ones, as Holt recalls, 'Nebiolo could take you by the arm and say, "Tomorrow we will go and see the Pope." And he took us to Castel Gandolfo and, lo and behold, we sat on some chairs and the Pope came out to meet us.'

'He got things done.' Holt adds, with a shrug and a hint of exasperation.

Mr President had a grand vision for his sport as well as for his office. When it came to the inaugural World Championships, Nebiolo ensured that they were big and bold and with – as he was keen to point out – 159 competing nations. This was more than any other event in sporting history: more, crucially, than the Olympics. The 1976, 1980 and 1984 Olympics all suffered major boycotts.

Nebiolo was keen to convey a message: that the World Athletics Championships amounted to a better attended, more credible and more competitive gathering than the Olympics Games. According to

Dick Pound, the IOC president, Juan Antonio Samaranch, was 'terrified' by this upstart event and very wary of Nebiolo.

Livio Berruti, Italy's 200m gold medallist at the 1960 Rome Olympics, said that Nebiolo 'trampled, corrupted, and polluted the sporting ideals in which I believed'. But the paradox is that he brought some honesty into his sport, winning a significant victory soon after his election when athletes' 'trust funds' were approved at the annual meeting of the IAAF in Athens in 1982, after Nebiolo called on Andy Norman, the British promotions manager who helped Joe Douglas bring his athletes to Europe, to propose the resolution. It was the first official acknowledgement that athletes could be paid to compete, though the money was – in theory – to be squirrelled away for their retirement in funds managed by their national federations.

As everyone knew, athletes were paid long before this. 'Anyone who says they didn't get money for competing, they did,' says Allan Wells. Even Sebastian Coe, seen as the epitome of rectitude, admitted at the time that the system 'made honest people dishonest'. But when Wells was at his peak, in the late 1970s and early 1980s, the rewards were often derisory. In his first race as Olympic champion, at Meadowbank Stadium in his native Edinburgh, the under-the-table incentive was a video recorder!

In notoriously pricey Helsinki, the Americans were on a relatively generous £7 subsistence a day, but the British athletes had to get by on £1. 'It's all we can afford,' explained Bill Evans of the British federation. 'If I save up,' said the 800m runner Garry Cook, 'maybe I'll be able to afford a beer at the end of the championships.' The pace of change in the years that followed owed much to Nebiolo's vision, and his success at selling the sport to broadcasters and sponsors. Under Nebiolo, wrote Doug Gillon in the *Glasgow Herald*, athletics was dragged 'from antiquated amateurism into the commercial arena at a pace which launched athletes to millionaires and left critics gasping'.

'You could write a book of a thousand pages about Nebiolo,' chuckles Andreas Brügger, who for years promoted arguably the most prestigious annual track meeting, the Weltklasse in Zurich. 'You knew where you stood with him. He made no secret if he didn't like something, and he took very strong positions. But he was somebody who could make things happen.'

'He drove a hard bargain and thought big,' says Holt. 'For example, for a meeting in Düsseldorf the broadcasters said, "We're thinking of $400,000 for TV rights." And he'd say, "Well, go in the other room and think about one and a half million and come back and see me in ten minutes."'

One country was peculiarly resistant to Nebiolo. The British were less biddable than the Pope. 'He hated Britain,' says Holt. 'He didn't like the sports journalists; they asked too many questions. The other thing was that, wherever he went, I had to try and arrange for Nebiolo to be presented with an honorary degree from the local university, with a ceremony and everything. But in Britain, well, we're not very good at playing that game. The worst was when the World Student Games were in Sheffield, and the university refused. They said that people have to work for degrees in this country.' Outside Britain, Nebiolo was rarely thwarted or even challenged. And he dealt with the British problem eventually, by moving the offices from Knightsbridge to Monaco. Meanwhile, the president began planning to ensure the second world championships in 1987 would be an even greater success.

The issue of financial dishonesty among athletes was being addressed, but the issue of drugs was more intractable. The Helsinki championships closed with an estimated profit of £4 million and a vast reception, where European meeting directors courted athletes, trying to sign them up. Nebiolo, according to David Miller in *The Times*, strolled round the party, 'his entourage of courtiers following at a discreet distance, like some patriarchal nineteenth-century squire coming to see the workers were enjoying themselves at Christmas time. He could afford to smile.'

But, warned Miller, 'With a so-called amateur body making such astronomical profits, the moral obligation upon them to initiate immediately worldwide random drug-testing, highly expensive, is more mandatory than ever… The love of money is assuredly the root of evil in sport.'

Nebiolo predicted that the second championships would gross £10 million, and further underline the importance of the event. Even better, they would be staged in Rome, his home territory, convenient for a papal blessing.

6

WANNA BE STARTIN' SOMETHIN'

'Carl Lewis will be as big as Michael Jackson.'
JOE DOUGLAS

Even now, Joe Douglas adopts a conspiratorial whisper as he outlines the rise in earnings of his prize athlete, Carl Lewis. From an initial $400 a meeting in 1980, the figure climbed steeply. 'Carl's next minimum pay, in 1982, I think, was $10,000,' says Douglas matter-of-factly. 'Then $50,000, then $100,000. For the rest of his life, the minimum was $100,000.

'But he didn't ask for a dime! I asked for it for him.'

Douglas, by now, was leading his Santa Monica runners through Europe, negotiating their money and arguing for better hotels – a particular bugbear of his. He resembled a bandleader, leading his troupe on a merry dance around the major meetings: Oslo, Stockholm, Zurich, Berlin, Brussels. His athletes, on the other hand, were like the Musketeers: 'all for one, one for all'. Douglas sold them to event organisers as a collective, thus enabling up-and-coming athletes to gain entry to prestigious meetings purely because they happened to be in the same club as Carl Lewis.

Douglas's portrayal of Lewis as a team player is at odds with his reputation as a loner. It makes him even more enigmatic, as much of a mystery as the man Douglas was so keen for him to emulate: Michael Jackson.

Today, the Lewis enigma remains intact. Naturally I wanted to contact him and interview him, though he proved elusive. Getting in touch with Ben Johnson was relatively straightforward. And Lewis's old manager was easy to reach. But although I did finally meet Lewis, he proved far more difficult to track down – at times, intriguingly so. An initial, lengthy email to his agent, Andrew Freedman, ended with the question, 'Should I request an interview through you?' It met with a one-word response: 'Yes.'

Freedman and I exchanged several more emails – mine getting shorter, his getting longer – before, finally, when the trail seemed to have gone cold, he responded, 'I have hesitated in writing you back because I thought I might be able to convince Carl to participate. Unfortunately, I have been unsuccessful. I apologise. In addition, please know that I am no longer representing him. I wish you all the best with what sounds like an interesting book.'

I try another avenue, calling Lewis's best friend from Willingboro, Thomas Mayfield. He is friendly, and professes surprise that I have found it difficult to contact him. 'Oh, I speak to Carl every day,' he says. He promises to call Lewis's sister-in-law, Diane, and later he phones me back with her number. I call, leave a message, and wait. I have tried several more times. But I am still waiting. A film-maker friend spoke to Douglas about arranging an interview with Lewis; Douglas suggested a donation to Lewis's foundation. The fee mentioned was $100,000.

What seems most odd is that those close to Lewis – Mayfield, Douglas and others – affect surprise, even bemusement upon learning that I have found him elusive. It could be artifice. Because there is certainly a shield around him, just as there was in his days in the spotlight, partly maintained by his friends and family. It only makes Douglas's casual references to his star athlete all the more tantalising. 'Carl has his own room in my house,' Douglas told me. 'When I bought the house, I let him pick it.' Again like Michael Jackson, there is an agelessness about Lewis – a Peter Pan quality. Douglas talks about him sometimes as if he were a child rather than a man approaching his fiftieth birthday.

They made an impressive team. Douglas may have 'won the lottery' with Lewis, but Lewis leaned heavily on his manager when it came to planning his career in and beyond athletics. As far back as 1981, Douglas drew up a four-year, six-point 'marketing plan', designed – with the Los Angeles Olympics firmly in mind – to catapult him into the mainstream. It dictated that Lewis would limit his appearances at track meetings; that he would accept every public appearance offer in New York and LA; that he would appear in magazines such as *Esquire, Newsweek, GQ, Ebony* and *Time*, as well as on major TV shows; that he would limit endorsements pre-Olympics, holding out for the big ones, or preferably the big 'one' ('We want Carl to be identified with a major company the way O. J. Simpson is with Hertz,' said Douglas); that he would enhance his marketability by studying communication and taking acting lessons; and, finally, that he would, in the words of Douglas, 'Emote openly to the public after major achievements... I never told him to show an emotion he didn't feel, but if he was going to gesture, do it large enough so everyone could see.'

Like Primo Nebiolo, Douglas's eyes were wide open to the changes that were happening in athletics, and he was positioning himself, and Lewis, to take full advantage. 'He is not dumb, Joe,' says the promoter Andreas Brügger. 'Joe is a wheeler and dealer, and he was the toughest of all the managers. He was tough at negotiating, but he had a tremendous group. If you had the Santa Monica club at your meet, you could really organise something special, and get other stars, too. We always paid a flat sum for his entire group. How Joe shared that with his athletes – well, you'd have to ask him.' Douglas was every bit as concerned with the lowliest runner's pay as he was with Lewis's $100,000.

At Zurich in 1983, when his pay packet had just rocketed, Lewis failed to justify it. He was outshone by the sprinter so often in his shadow, Calvin Smith, who became the first man ever to break 10 and 20 seconds for the two sprint events at the same meeting. Smith was at the very top of his game and posed a real threat, it seemed, to Lewis's ambition of four golds in Los Angeles. And to Douglas's ambitions. Smith offered a contrast to Lewis in every way; he certainly had no marketing plan.

That partly explains why it was all about Lewis in the build-up to LA. Another part of the explanation was yet another Olympic boycott. The only other candidate city for the 1984 Games had been Teheran, which withdrew when the Shah's Western-focused regime was overwhelmed by Islamic revolution. But as the Games approached, Juan Antonio Samaranch and the IOC might have wished that they had been preparing for a fortnight in Iran instead.

Inevitably, after the US boycott of Moscow four years earlier, there was a sense of tit-for-tat in the withdrawal of the Soviet Union, East Germany and another twelve Eastern Bloc countries, as well as Libya and the one-time would-be hosts Iran. The Kremlin cited 'security fears', 'chauvinistic sentiments' and an anti-Soviet hysteria being whipped up in the United States. It was yet another blow to the Olympic movement and, with Nebiolo and his new championships yapping at their heels, the whole concept seemed in danger.

'Will there be another Olympic Games after Los Angeles?' asked David Miller in *The Times* on 28 July, the day of the opening ceremony. 'There are those who believe that these XXIII Olympics, opening today in front of President Reagan, will prove to have been so bedevilled by political boycott, excessive finance, shameless nationalism, acknowledged professionalism, rampant and undetected drug-taking, security against terrorism, immovable traffic and insufferable smog that future Games will be in jeopardy.'

This may seem exaggerated now but Los Angeles really did need to be spectacular to breathe life into the Olympic brand. And for that, they required a saviour. Just as Jesse Owens had detoxified 'Hitler's

Games' in 1936, so, to a lesser extent, LA and the Olympic movement needed a hero to rise above the politics and controversy, preferably an All-American hero.

They needed Carl Lewis.

Thus, perhaps, the *New York Times* was only half-joking in suggesting that, 'if anyone had to withdraw from the 1984 Summer Games, the Los Angeles Olympic Organising Committee would rather it have been the Soviet Union, not Carl Lewis'. Just how much America – and the Olympics – needed this one man was evident in the build-up. Lewis marvelled at how regularly he was on the cover of the national magazines. 'A year and a half earlier, nobody knew me,' he told me. 'But I'm going to the grocery store for nine months and I'm sitting there on the covers of those magazines. I'm getting checked out by people all the time.'

The level of interest in him was indeed extraordinary, not least because he was a track athlete. Track and field was hardly box office in the USA, and yet there were maybe signs, as the Olympics approached, that this could alter – and that Lewis could be the catalyst for change. A record crowd of 20,552 turned up for the US trials at the Coliseum, the Olympic stadium. The media focus on Lewis was relentless, not just on Lewis the athlete and sporting phenomenon, but Lewis the person and Lewis the puzzle, who did not appear to fit the established mould of male sporting superheroes. In the *New York Times* magazine, a seven-page feature began:

> The dark glasses go on as soon as Carl Lewis leaves the track, and a look of wariness replaces the easy joy that lights his face when he is running or jumping. He stares straight ahead, as hordes of reporters push and shove, and autograph seekers tug at his clothing with a frenzy usually reserved for rock stars. Carl Lewis is, at this moment, America's most dazzling athlete... a magnet for publicity, curiosity and criticism.

There was a similarly lengthy cover feature in *Time*, which opened:

> What he does is so simple, and how he does it so complicated, that Carl Lewis is a basic mystery. How fast he runs, how far he jumps, may serve to establish the precise lengths to which men can go. Gentler than a superman, more delicate than the common perception of a strong man, Lewis is physically the most advanced human being in the world, and about to become the most famous global sports figure since Muhammad Ali.

The LA Games would be the Carl Lewis Games, predicted the *New York Times*. It hardly mattered that athletes from the Eastern Bloc would be missing because 'Lewis is really competing with history'. Such articles dwelt on his background and his family, in particular the closeness of the relationship between Carl and his sister, Carol. The Lewis parents, too, attracted curiosity, and admiration. They were different, most agreed. Black, but middle-class. And they seemed to have managed their kids' careers perfectly. 'Most parents push too hard or too little,' said Carl. 'Our parents pushed just hard enough and then backed off.' 'I am not a believer in taking over a kid's mind,' said their mother, Evelyn. 'We never had to bully them, because they were always doing something they wanted to do, and as long as they were interested, we helped them all we could.'

The paper that once wrote about his two-bedroom duplex now noted his 'elegantly-appointed Victorian house' in Houston complete with expensive collectables, acquired on trips to Europe and the Far East: Provençal furniture, Baccarat crystal, Christofle silver, Oriental rugs, Samurai swords. He had six telephones, whistle-operated lights, and an early home computer, with details of his finances and schedule, connected to Joe Douglas's computer in Santa Monica.

And in the drive sat a white BMW 735i, with – almost unheard of in 1984 – a telephone installed. The discrepancy between Lewis's apparent spending power and his amateur status – which entitled him to withdraw a maximum $7,200 a year in living expenses from his trust fund – was duly noted, though without much comment. *Time* mentioned that Lewis had a dog, Sasha, a Samoyed; his answer phone message ended, 'And Sasha thanks you.' It was also reported that Lewis had been taking acting lessons, with a view to life post-athletics.

'We want him to be known as Carl Lewis the athlete,' Douglas told *Time*, 'Carl Lewis the sportscaster, Carl Lewis the actor.' Having encouraged him to study communication in college, Douglas helped him enrol at the Warren Robertson Theatre Workshop in New York. Robertson was Douglas's cousin. 'Great actors have a kind of vibrant containment, and Carl has that,' Robertson said. 'There is a depth of vulnerability in Carl. A lot of athletes create a partition on their emotions. It's that masculine, fixed idea that men don't cry, don't show pain. It was not hard to get Carl to touch the more fragile interior.'

Lewis seemed happy to fuel this image of himself as the antithesis of the traditional male athlete. When he won, and he celebrated, it was joy, he explained, not showboating. It was simply down to 'emotion... It's me. I was that way when I was six years old. I don't mind that other people don't show emotion like I do, but I mind when they say I shouldn't. Men, athletes especially, have to be like King Kong. When we lose, we can't cry and we can't pout. We're not supposed to be touched. We have to be carved in a certain way just to be men.' He rapped his chest with his knuckles. 'Chests of steel, and all. I think it's disgusting.'

The tone of most of the articles that introduced Lewis to mainstream America at that time tended towards curious, admiring, in some cases bordering on hagiographic. But that was not the case on 18 July 1984 – ten days before the Olympics started – when *Sports Illustrated* published Gary Smith's mammoth, 8,830-word portrait. This piece began:

He stands at the top of the runway, his warm-up jacket collar flipped up over his neck in the style of someone who wants very much to be different, which he does, and his expression saying, Oh, it's up. Breeze must've caught it. Around his neck is an orange headband – quite happy to be the only orange headband in the arena being worn around a neck – advertising the TV station he works for in Houston. On his feet are a pair of long jump shoes moulded specially for him. That was his idea, too. On the back of his custom-tailored warm-up suit, in case you confused him with another jogger, is stitched his name. Oh, that's Carl Lewis.

Smith, a writer who joined *Sports Illustrated* in 1982, specialised then – as he still does now – in long, probing, almost psychoanalytic features. He tends to spend considerable time with his subject, as well as speaking to their nearest and dearest (and not-so-dearest). So exhaustive – and perhaps exhausting – is the process that he is required by his employers to write just four or five such articles a year.

Smith's portrait of Lewis must stand as one of the most contentious and controversial of his career. In it, he paints a picture of the athlete as supremely self-conscious, vain, shallow and self-absorbed. For instance, on a tourist trip to Kyoto, he seemed more concerned with his outfit than with the place itself. 'He's the only person I know who has been around the world five times and never taken a picture,' his friend, and Nike contact, Don Coleman, told Smith.

'Lewis is a child,' wrote Smith, 'who has climbed a tree and lost himself in the self-absorption of seeing how far out on a limb he can go... Now, in August 1984, at age twenty-three, Lewis will glance down and notice the whole world watching him. He will smile a distant smile. "They think if I don't win four gold medals, I'll be a bum," he says. "But failure doesn't loom in me."'

After athletics, Smith suggested, Lewis will move into acting and singing: 'Four gold medals, a gold record, a golden Oscar – none would be an end in itself for him. Each would merely give the child in the tree a surer grip, more control, to assure him he could move a few more feet out on the limb – out to the frail, lonely end, where the wind whips and only the true original clings.'

In the feature, Lewis comes across as someone trying desperately hard, too hard. 'My main goal is to control,' he said. 'It makes me feel comfortable.' But he exposed some vulnerability. Long before the word 'metrosexual' had entered the vocabulary, Smith was intrigued by the way Lewis bucked traditional ideas of masculinity. Lewis told him that he spent a lot of time as a child with his sister, which 'may explain why I didn't have to develop the macho side a lot of boys did, and why Carol gained more masculinity. My dad was a very strong personality, but if I was playing with a doll when I was young, he wasn't the type to take it away and say, "Be a man." Our parents let us be ourselves.' Smith summed up, 'He could press his hands together and say, "Isn't that cute?" without feeling self-conscious.'

The story is not uniformly negative: Smith acknowledges Lewis's mesmerising talent ('It's a joy to watch him run, a small happiness just to see him walk') and his ebullience ('His humour, sharp and sarcastic, zings constantly... He seems terribly sophisticated for his age, but there is an exuberance about him, a joyful knowledge of what he's capable of, that makes him good company').

Nevertheless, Smith's profile crushed its subject, who spent a great deal of time trying to rebut the article. 'The person he kept calling Carl Lewis was not me,' he complained in his autobiography. For Dick Patrick, 'I think it was a damaging blow from which Carl and his image never quite recovered.' Which would be an incredible achievement for a single story. But it also hints at Lewis's sensitivity. Did it hurt because he thought it was unfair? Or that it was all too close to the truth?

Yet the comments Gary Smith elicited were very similar to those one still hears, even from contemporaries like Calvin Smith. 'We were never close friends, or anything like that,' says Smith. 'I'd say "Hello," and that was it.'

Yet they were teammates at two Olympics; they must have spent time together?

'Carl Lewis was, I guess, in his own world, and had his own group of people, and other people, well, he didn't seem to bother with. That's just the way it was.' Ray Stewart, another 100m finalist in 1988, told me, 'Carl's personality was a little different. Apart from "hello" and "how are you doing?" we never exchanged more than ten or twelve words.'

Later, Ben Johnson would be critical of Lewis's perceived arrogance – and he still is. There was also criticism from Lewis's early long jumping rival, Larry Myricks. 'Trying to know Carl Lewis is like trying to know Michael Jackson,' said Myricks. 'You can't. He lives in a different world. He's brought all the rumours on himself.'

The aloofness appeared to extend to relationships, too. 'My peer group never affected me,' Lewis told Gary Smith. 'I affected them. I weeded out the ones that didn't want to be independent, and the ones that did came with me. I never got involved with drugs or drinking. I have no time for people that dawdle. My objective is not to adjust to others.'

This, suggested his family and friends, is why he was not in a relationship. 'Fall in love?' his brother, Cleve, asked. 'It won't happen to Carl. Nothing will happen to Carl that he doesn't want to happen. He doesn't even have someone he really unburdens all his feelings to. That would mean giving control to someone else.'

Inevitably, there was speculation about his sexuality. Lewis strongly denied that he was gay. He blamed jealous track rivals, saying three of them had started rumours to make 'the ultimate attack on a man'. But in many of the stories written about him at the time there is an undercurrent of suggestiveness, which Lewis actually courted. For instance, Smith observed Lewis, about to conduct a TV interview, searching in his bag for an eyebrow pencil. 'He finds it and applies it, peering into the car window at a face that feels a razor blade only once a week… He reaches into the bag, pulls out a stick of orange gloss and runs a lap around his lips. Then he grabs a powder pad and pats it on his cheeks. "I'm a notorious shiner on camera," he says.' After the broadcast, Lewis changes out of an outfit that resembled 'something an alien might wear on *Star Trek*', and digs around in his car for his training gear. All he could find were pink running tights. 'If I wanted to run out in front of people with pink tights, I would.'

Lewis tells Smith, 'They say I'm a coke freak, that I'm a homosexual. They say it because no one knows what I'm doing. I don't even stay in the same hotel as the other athletes any more, because if I stand in a lobby with them there'll be eleven kids and six reporters and four photographers there. I could be sleeping with a horse for all they know. It's the same reason they say Michael Jackson's homosexual, because he keeps to himself. I'm not homosexual. If I was weak-minded, God, I'd be paranoid that I was being called that. But as long as I know what I am, it doesn't matter what people say.'

Gary Smith, who has profiled so many of the major American sports stars of the last three decades, was amused when I asked him if he had ever met another one like Lewis. 'He's pretty distinctive, I must say. He's not one of those guys you say, "Oh yeah, I met two or three other guys who remind me of Carl." Carl was very Carl.

'But, you know, I still tell people that the two most beautiful things I've seen in sports are Mike Tyson hitting a heavy bag and Carl Lewis running.'

1 AUGUST 1984

Arguably, the first major event of the Los Angeles Olympics was not the opening ceremony, but the Carl Lewis media conference, held four days later, two days before the heats for the 100m, and before a crowd bigger than would attend many of the Games' minor sporting events.

'I would like to keep this on a positive note,' Joe Douglas began, as he sat down beside Lewis and his mother. He had a reason to say that: the opening days had been negative for Lewis. As the USA team marched into the Coliseum for the opening ceremony, he hung back to make a grand entrance with Michael Jordan, rather than the rank-and-file. Lewis was criticised, but not Jordan. Now Douglas outlined his dual ambitions to the international press: Lewis winning four golds, then becoming the sporting equivalent of Michael Jackson.

Afterwards, Douglas and Lewis reflected that the conference had gone well. It had not bothered *them* that Lewis had arrived an hour late, but the journalists were feeling vengeful. 'Carl Lewis Is Slow Getting There, Then He Quickly Puts Media Away,' read the headline in the *Los Angeles Times*. 'Carl Lewis, who hates wasting time unless it's somebody else's, kept about a thousand of the world's journalists waiting an hour, arriving at eleven o'clock for his scheduled 10 a.m. press conference,' continued the story.

'He arrived fashionably late,' said the *New York Times*. 'He was dressed in a red leather sleeveless shirt – zippered on the side – and jeans. It has become part of documenting Lewis's exploits to describe his trendy attire and reporters elbowed one another for descriptions of today's outfit. "His shoes," a reporter said. "Did anyone see his shoes?"'

The British papers appear to be have been more forgiving even though the time difference between Los Angeles and London meant the daily reporters were dangerously close to their deadline, and the delay would have been infuriating. 'He had kept us waiting, as busy men often do, for more than half an hour, but then he talked honestly,' said *The Times*. In 1984 Britain had reason to be susceptible to Lewis's appeal. Football was out of fashion due to hooliganism. Athletics was on the up: the country's stars, Seb Coe, Steve Ovett and Daley Thompson, were all big names and strong personalities. Lewis represented not a figure of curiosity and intrigue, but a bona fide star, a legend in the making.

'The American journalists disliked Lewis immensely,' says the *Glasgow Herald*'s athletics correspondent Doug Gillon. 'There were comments you routinely heard: the Flying Faggot was one. It was all disgustingly homophobic.' An American sportswriter I spoke to, who preferred not to be named, argued that it was more complicated than that. 'I think with Carl, there was the perception of a lack of sincerity or candour – for whatever reason – that Americans see through. I think it was about his personality more than the question of sexuality.' Gary Smith emerged with a similar view, 'It was not the sexual ambiguity that annoyed Americans. I feel it was more the calculation.'

During the press conference, Lewis appeared relaxed, in good spirits. He said he was aware of rumours that he was on steroids, but put that down to jealousy. He felt a responsibility to convey the message that success was possible without drugs; he said that his life, and his achievements, were about sacrifice, not drugs. The line that emerged from the conference, though, was the Michael Jackson comparison, and the idea that Lewis was as focused on status and wealth as he was on winning.

'It's my fault,' Joe Douglas says now. 'I take responsibility.' Douglas was the one who mentioned Jackson. He was also to blame for the lateness: Lewis was staying, under protection, in a distant corner of the metropolis and Douglas had to fetch him. It was also Douglas who had taken the decision that Lewis should stay away from the athletes' village, which did not bother the press but undoubtedly widened the rift between him and his fellow competitors.

Douglas accepts all the blame, though he is unapologetic. 'Here's my opinion,' he tells me. 'I want him to be where he can be focused on his running. I don't want people coming into his room. I don't want him having roommates who are going to stay up late and bother him.' In fact, Lewis, under pressure from the US team, did check into the village, but promptly left. In the brief time he was there, he would later claim, he was bombarded for autograph requests – from other athletes. Douglas was adamant this was the right thing to do. 'We went to his room in the village and I forget how many people were in the same room. I said, "No." People sharing a room? Sharing a bathroom? No. Before the Olympics, Carl and I had talked, and I said we should probably rent a house. We took the house, that's where Carl stayed. You're there to perform. It's not a social event. Sorry.'

Lewis's bolthole was a two-storey white stucco house with a small pool, six miles from the Coliseum. Mother Evelyn, father Bill and sister Carol, who was also competing and would come ninth in the long jump, were all there. Evelyn cooked for everyone. When free, Carl relaxed by the pool. In the first week, before the athletics started, he even managed to spend the odd evening with Douglas in his Santa Monica apartment, watching the swimming. And on another evening Lewis visited the broadcasting centre, sitting behind the legendary ABC producer, Roone Arledge, as he supervised his channel's Olympic coverage.

'Do you want to try it?' Arledge asked Lewis.

'No thanks, I don't want to be in the hot seat yet,' replied Lewis. Note the 'yet'.

But the very fact he was there at all said something remarkable about Carl Lewis. It suggested that, before he had won a single medal, he was already looking further ahead. And that set him even further apart from his fellow athletes, who spent their days lounging around the village, playing pool, queuing for food, or waiting for buses.

4 AUGUST 1984, 7 P.M.

Carl Lewis has breezed through the three heats of the 100m, to reach his first final of the Games. And this one is the event he is most worried about. If he could win this, he believes he will be '60 per cent' of the way to the four golds. But his task is eased by the absence of Calvin Smith, who had been struggling with injuries and only made the relay team.

Lewis had won his heat, as has the improving Canadian, Ben Johnson. The same thing has happened in the quarter-finals, Lewis running in the fastest time so far – 10.04. In the semi-final he and Johnson went head-to-head, Lewis winning easily in 10.14, Johnson second in 10.42. That puts both in the final. The line-up reads, from lane one to lane eight: Ron Brown (USA), Mike McFarlane (Great Britain), Tony Sharpe (Canada), Ben Johnson (Canada), Sam Graddy (USA), Donovan Reid (Great Britain), Carl Lewis (USA), Raymond Stewart (Jamaica).

In a blue tracksuit, Lewis paces up lane seven, shaking out his long limbs, scanning the crowd in the packed Coliseum. Then he strips off to his red vest and shorts. Then, leaning forward, head hanging, arms dangling, he bounces gently three times, stretching his hamstrings. Then he focuses on the lane stretching 100 metres in front of him. He has tunnel vision, and without a glance to either side, he settles in the blocks.

The gun goes. But it's a false start and they're called back. The culprit is the runner in lane four, the man already earning attention for possessing the fastest start in the world. Ben Johnson.

Now, as the gun goes a second time, the runners in the middle, along-side each other in lanes four and five, are quickest out the blocks. Both Graddy and Johnson are short, wiry and powerful; and now they are neck-and-neck as they approach 50 metres, with clear daylight back to the others. But Lewis is approaching, gazelle-like, and, though Johnson and Graddy believe they are still racing for gold at 70 metres, Lewis engulfs them in the final quarter of the race, his lead expanding outra-geously all the way to the line, as he wins in 9.99 seconds. Two-tenths of a second later, Graddy dips for silver, with Johnson claiming bronze.

'As we got to 80 metres and I was still ahead,' Graddy said later, 'I got excited, and thought, "Hey, I'm going to win a gold medal!" Then I saw him out of the corner of my eye… ' But even now no one can catch Lewis to congratulate him: he is elusive, bounding away, indulging in an elaborate celebratory jig, bouncing from foot to foot, then darting over to the stand, and reaching into the crowd to grab a flag from a supporter, a giant Stars and Stripes. A chant of 'U-S-A, U-S-A, U-S-A' fills the arena as he completes his flag-waving lap of honour.

The next morning, the cover of *Time* featured a picture of Lewis, an Olympic gold medal dangling from his neck. How was this possible? The medal ceremony had been too late, surely, to process a colour picture using 1980s technology. The clue was in tiny writing inside, on the contents page: 'Copyright Carl Lewis' it said of the cover picture. It had been taken in advance of the Games: another Joe Douglas ploy, to ensure maximum exposure not if, but when Lewis delivered.

'The Carl Lewis Show, a mini-series in four parts'. So began *The Times* report of the 100m final, acclaiming the first gold medal for an athlete 'who is demonstrably bound for Hollywood, 15 miles down the road from here'. Elsewhere it noted that 'Lewis is beautiful to behold in his sprinting or jumping because he seems to be moving without effort.'

American papers were less gushing. 'He stayed out there waving the flag too long,' said Dave Anderson, in the *New York Times*, 'so much so that his reaction seemed to be structured, not spontaneous… Carl Lewis appears to project an atmosphere of arrogance rather than humour.' There were suggestions that the stunt had been orchestrated, that the flag had been planted, that the 'stranger in the crowd' was a US coach.

Later, the *Los Angeles Times* cleared up the 'planted flag' story by finding the man who had handed it over – Paul Tucker, a fifty-year-old fan from New Orleans. Again, Joe Douglas is quick to take responsibility. 'I told him to take the flag! I told Carl to take a flag from the crowd, because he's running for America and he's honouring America. I don't care what some other people's opinions are. I'm sorry. I want him to recognise everyone in that stand and say, "I am running for America."'

And no amount of negative press – 'constant sniping', according to Doug Gillon, 'Carl-bashing', as Lewis called it – could prevent his march to glory. He won the long jump so easily that the crowd was diverted by the women's javelin and the men's 10,000m, even though there was no chance of an American victory. Lewis won with a jump of 8.54m, 30cm further than the silver medallist, Gary Honey of Australia. But still there was criticism and controversy.

After Lewis established his mark, which he did in the midst of trying to qualify for the final of the 200m, he returned to old habits, passed up the rest of his attempts and was duly booed. Again, the transatlantic perspective was different. 'His first jump was clearly not going to be beaten, so he stopped,' says Doug Gillon. 'The reaction reflected people who don't actually understand track and field or the Olympics.'

There was also a defence of Lewis from a less likely source – *Sports Illustrated*, whose reporter, Kenny Moore, pointed out that Bob Beamon, when he set his world record in Mexico, 'hadn't run the 100m. He hadn't run a pair of 200m heats that morning. He'd had a following wind of exactly the maximum allowable, 2.00 metres per second.' And Beamon had also jumped at altitude. 'I was shocked at first,' said Lewis of the booing. 'But after I thought about it, I realised they were booing because they wanted to see more of Carl Lewis. I guess that's flattering.'

Forty-eight hours later, Lewis duly won the 200m final in an Olympic record 19.80, leading an American one-two-three, with Kirk Baptiste, Lewis's Santa Monica teammate, and Thomas Jefferson taking silver and bronze. So Lewis had three golds, with the relay to come on the closing weekend. It was a replay of Helsinki, but with a slightly different line-up. Sam Graddy and Ron Brown had replaced Emmit King and Willie Gaul, joining Calvin Smith and, of course,

Lewis. The same quartet ran all three rounds, progressing with ease to the final, where the race was theirs to lose. 'What if you drop the baton?' Lewis was asked on the eve of the final. 'I pick it up and we win anyway,' he replied.

He might not have been exaggerating. The race was described by one American commentator, Al Michaels, as 'Carl Lewis's historic moment'. He also noted that, 'It would be a good race if the Americans weren't in it. If you look at the Jamaicans, the Canadians, the Italians, the British... They should have a nice battle for silver.'

Graddy ran a first leg of 10.29, establishing a small lead for Brown, who increased the advantage as he handed over to the best third-leg runner in history, Calvin Smith, who passed to Lewis, who completed his usual trick of passing the baton from left to right hand, then powered down the home straight, covering the final hundred metres in 8.94 seconds, to win by 15 metres. And the time, 37.83, beat the record they had set in Helsinki.

However, the celebrations this time were strangely low-key considering that, with gold number four, Lewis had just matched Owens. He jogged in the direction of his teammates, then embraced them as they completed a subdued lap of honour. In his post-race interview, Lewis admitted that the world record 'makes it really special... for us to come together like that with all the adversity we've had'. It was a reference to yet another controversy – Lewis's reluctance to train with the others.

On the podium, during the medal ceremony, there is a scene that, with hindsight, makes for fascinating viewing. Standing directly in front of Lewis, as 'The Star-Spangled Banner' began to play and the twelve athletes from the three medal-winning teams turned to watch the flags being raised, was Ben Johnson, who had run the first leg for the Canadians on the way to their bronze medal. While Lewis's eyes fill with tears as he mouths the words to the anthem, Johnson fidgets distractedly, not knowing what to do with the small bunch of flowers he's been handed.

That ceremony was not the one that was noticed at the time, however. The British decathlete Daley Thompson had seen off his German rival Jürgen Hingsen and won gold, as he had done in Moscow. On the podium, his T-shirt attracted some attention. On the front, 'Thanks America for a good Games and a great time.' And on the back, 'But what about the TV coverage?' The coverage had been 'a little biased,' Thompson explained. This, according to most non-Americans present, was an uncharacteristic understatement. But later, during his winner's press conference, he revealed another T-shirt, this one asking, 'Is the world's second greatest athlete gay?'

When he was asked about its significance, Thompson said, 'Oh, in England gay means happy.'

But who did he mean? 'I don't know,' said Thompson. 'It could be anybody. It could be Carl Lewis, it could be Jürgen Hingsen.' What is most remarkable, reading contemporary reports of Thompson's stunt, is that it was dismissed as a harmless jape. Thompson appeared to receive no criticism at all. When I asked his former coach, Frank Dick, about the prank, he shrugged, 'Daley wasn't very kind to Carl. I ended up catching it in the neck from one or two of the American coaches because of that. "You can't keep control of your boy?" That's right! I couldn't.'

The postscript came a quarter of a century later when a gay dating website organised an internet poll to choose Britain's top gay Olympic icon. The runaway winner was Daley Thompson.

While Lewis emulated Jesse Owens, and proved himself the star of the 1984 Olympics, 22-year-old Ben Johnson quietly registered his presence in Los Angeles. It had been a breakthrough Games for him. Two bronze medals encouraged him and his coach, Charlie Francis, to believe that at the next Games, in Seoul, he could be a contender for gold. By now they were perfecting the secret weaponry that could make that possible. The previous winter Francis had decided that his group needed to work with one medical professional, rather than relying on the athletes' individual doctors to supply drugs – an approach he described as 'a scattershot system'. He 'wanted more control and more reliable feedback.'

In October 1983 Francis and Angella Issajenko had paid a visit to a Toronto doctor. George Mario Sahely Chehin Astaphan – known as 'Jamie' since childhood – had left the Caribbean island of St Kitts after high school for university in Montreal, graduating in 1967 and going on to Toronto Medical School. After qualifying as a doctor in 1971 he practised throughout Canada, though he also spent two years back on St Kitts as the island's medical officer. Wherever he worked, he was popular with his patients. Astaphan came across as confident, charming and dashing, with his jet-black hair, dark eyes and mahogany tan. However, he did have a facial tic that seemed to afflict him at moments of stress.

At their first meeting, Francis found Astaphan 'refreshingly jovial and easy-going'. Another trait stood out: he was extremely talkative. He admitted he knew next to nothing about performance-enhancing drugs, but also said he was keen to learn – and to help. He seems to have been easily convinced by what Francis told him about the need for a steroid programme, later explaining, 'The axiom among track and field and other athletes was, "If you don't take it, you won't make it," so if I didn't monitor them and if I didn't give it to them, they were going to get it elsewhere... They came to me for advice and for supervision, and I thought it was my responsibility to do this.'

Issajenko already had gone elsewhere, to Robert Kerr, a Californian known to supply top athletes with steroids and the latest in-vogue product, human growth hormone (HGH). He had also written a book, *The Practical Use of Anabolic Steroids*. As Issajenko put it, 'Dr Kerr's philosophy was that athletes were going to take steroids anyway, so he might as well prescribe them and give the athletes proper counselling on their use. At last, a practical approach!'

Kerr had drawn up a recommended drugs protocol for Issajenko: a combination of anabolic steroids, growth hormone and (legal) amino acids. Astaphan was willing to defer to Kerr's expertise while continuing his own research, which led him to add testosterone to the mix. This was the protocol followed by Johnson, as well as some of Francis's other athletes, in the build-up to Los Angeles. Though Johnson's bronze medal in the 100m suggested the programme was working, trial and error characterised Francis and Astaphan's approach. They were still experimenting.

The strangest incident involving Johnson in LA involved another Lewis, not Carl but Lennox – then boxing for Canada before he moved to Britain and became world heavyweight champion. Johnson was often the butt of jokes in Francis's sprinting group, and Lewis perhaps cottoned on to this when, in the athletes' village, he encountered Johnson in the games room.

Johnson had the key to his room hanging around his neck, which was a problem when he went to play pool because it got in the way. So he put it on a chair. It vanished. Six hours later, according to Johnson, Lewis brought it back. The time may be an exaggeration – there are inconsistencies in the accounts. What is not in doubt is that when Lewis re-appeared, Johnson flipped. Lewis responded to the yelling by putting Johnson in a headlock. In theory it was a mismatch: Johnson's opponent was seven inches taller as well as being a champion fighter, but he managed to flip him over his shoulder and send him sprawling over the pool table. Unfortunately, he strained his neck in the process, which he said hampered him in the 100m.

But it was Carl not Lennox who obsessed Johnson after the Games ended. He spent much of the following winter studying videos. The tapes included a race that followed the LA Games, in Zurich, which saw Johnson take on Lewis, and lead him for 94 of the 100 metres. With six to go, Johnson broke a sacred rule of sprinting and looked round wondering where Lewis was. The answer was all-too-close. Johnson finished third. 'After LA I knew Carl was good, but I knew I could beat him,' says Johnson now. 'I knew it.'

7

THE PRINCE AND
THE MISSING PAPERWORK

'This is crazy. Why would an athlete, who's sorta the
cream of the crop, and in good physical shape, and
very healthy, what are they doing with a drug?'
DON CATLIN

It was a very hot night in LA, and at 3 a.m. Don Catlin was still outside the front of his house, talking to his wife Bernadette. The 1984 Olympics had ended about thirty hours earlier amid scenes of utter American triumphalism. The US had dominated the medals table in unprecedented fashion, winning a record eighty-three golds, more than their five nearest rivals combined. Of course, the figure was distorted by the absence of the Eastern Bloc, but no one in Los Angeles was worrying about them.

The pessimism that had preceded the opening ceremony had melted away. David Miller of *The Times*, so gloomy at the start, described the event as 'a triumph'. American can-doism had restored the confidence of the Olympics, and established a new precedent: a profit.

But Catlin did not share the mood. For him, the Los Angeles Games were not yet over and he had only just returned home after a very, very tough day at the office. He said to his wife, 'You know, something happened today. I don't know what it is, exactly, but some day it's gonna come out. And someone is lying.' He was the man in charge of the drug-testing laboratory. And to this day he seems a little perplexed about the 'something'.

Catlin has a wonderfully calm manner, and a languid, soothing voice. He also has a very clear sense of right and wrong. Now seventy-three, he remains at the forefront of the fight against drugs in sport – 'the father of drug-testing in sports' as he has been called by the *New York Times*. And today he is sitting opposite me in the offices of Anti-Doping Research, the Los Angeles-based organisation he runs with his son. Just down the road is Muscle Beach, a place world-famous for its exhibitionist bodybuilders. Catlin's office is very discreet. Only the mailbox gives it away: 'Anti-Doping Research' it reads in a font suggestive of the military or FBI. You wonder what kind of mail Catlin receives. Urine samples, presumably, and blood.

Over the years, Catlin tells me, he has received hate mail. Some time ago his car was firebombed. He cannot be certain it had anything to do with his work but, he says, matter-of-factly, 'You know, I think organised crime is involved in this issue.'

Catlin had first become involved in the drug question as a young army medic in 1968, based in Washington DC and trying to work out how to combat diarrhoea, which was bedevilling US troops in Vietnam. But diarrhoea was hardly the only health problem in that war: an estimated 10 to 15 per cent of the GIs there were using heroin. There was also a big heroin problem in Washington. 'It was driving the city crazy,' says Catlin.

He volunteered to work in a local centre that was using novel methods to treat addicts. The Pentagon became aware of his growing expertise and wanted him to go to Vietnam to test soldiers so users could be weeded out and locked up. Catlin pleaded for a different approach. 'Let's try the medical model,' he urged the generals. Instead, they stuck with what they knew, and kept locking them up.

When he left the military he continued his work on drugs at UCLA. And, as the 1984 Games approached, his reputation reached the ears of the IOC. The new Olympic president, Juan Antonio Samaranch, was not much interested in the drugs issue. But the members of his medical commission certainly were. They wanted a dedicated local laboratory in Los Angeles to test the competitors, and so – nearly three years before the Games – four of them flew out to meet Catlin: Manfred Donike, Prince Alexandre de Mérode, Arnold Beckett and Robert Dugal.

De Mérode, a Belgian aristocrat whose title dated back to the twelfth century, had chaired the IOC medical commission since its inception in 1968. He was a historian with no medical training. He was also a chain smoker with a gravelly voice, but he had committed himself to tackling drug use in the early years of the commission when the reactionary Avery Brundage was still president of the IOC. Brundage felt strongly that drug-testing should be the responsibility of the international sports federations, not the IOC.

Donike was the West German chemist who, after the Moscow Games, took away the leftover samples and worked out a test for testosterone. Beckett, from Britain, and Dugal, from Canada, were scientists who were among the world's foremost experts in anti-doping. Beckett had developed the first test for stimulants in 1965, and had overseen drug-testing at the 1966 football World Cup; Dugal had run the anti-doping lab in Montreal during the 1976 Games.

'When the Prince came with the other guys, they wanted a major medical centre, they had heard of me, and bingo – we started to talk,' says Catlin. He refers to de Mérode as 'the Prince' throughout. 'Arnold was at the vanguard, in terms of what he wanted. But Manfred was the one who could really tell me what was involved. He had competed in the 1972 Games, and he was a chemist. He knew exactly what was needed. But the Prince,' Catlin adds, 'he's all over the map. I love all those guys. They're great guys.' He speaks of the four men in the present tense, though all of them are dead.

Testing athletes was a new one on Catlin. He had no knowledge of drugs in sport, and struggled to comprehend the nature and scale of the problem, and even the reason for it. 'When I first looked at it,

I thought this is crazy. You know, why would an athlete, who's sorta the cream of the crop, and in good physical shape, and very healthy, what are they doing with a drug?'

Initially, Catlin said thanks, but no thanks. 'I thought it was too complex for me. I'm in internal medicine. I'm not a chemist. And it wasn't clear in the beginning what kind of funding there'd be for it. But it became clear after a while that they were talking about a lot of money. And I was just a junior professor.'

The fact that Catlin was approached at all suggests a genuine will within the IOC – or among certain members – to tackle the drugs issue. 'Absolutely, yeah,' says Catlin. 'The Prince has always been committed. They had some serious issues. But drugs in sport was simply not a topic anybody knew anything about in the USA. Period. There was nothing written. There were a couple of congressional hearings ten years before, but no one paid much attention. The IOC learned from Manfred about what had gone on in 1972, and from Dugal about 1976, and 1980 is a lost year. The athletes were pushing, too, to build a lab. They wanted testing.'

The athletes wanted to be tested? 'Absolutely,' says Catlin. 'That's what drove the IOC over the top. Whether they would have done it on their own, I really don't know. But the Prince understood the problem and he really pushed it. Samaranch never understood.'

Once Catlin had said yes, he began researching, travelling and building a lab twenty times bigger than he had ever had before. 'I went from rags to riches.' As he says, he had a lot to learn. When Donike said casually at a meeting, 'We're going to do all the samples in LA by the T/E ratio,' Catlin had no idea what he was talking about. When he found out, he had to go back and order more mass spectrometers, the machines used for analysis.

In November 1983 Catlin's lab was approved by the IOC. A month later he was approached by the United States Olympic Committee, with a view to testing potential Olympians in the run-up to the LA Games. 'Those were our first official tests,' he says. 'But, uh, that programme didn't last very long… '

Indeed, the programme instigated by the USOC would come to be recognised as one of the most controversial episodes in the organisation's history – it would also raise the question of whether they were serious about preventing doping. Catlin may have been naive about the use of drugs in sport, but it didn't take him long to work out the real purpose of the testing programme he had agreed to run. As American officials would later admit, it was a 'screening programme', designed not to catch athletes, but to educate them.

On the face of it, that sounds laudable, and Catlin himself had tried to make a similar case to the Pentagon years earlier. Robert Voy, the USOC's chief medical officer, insists the original intentions were honourable. 'I took over three months after our athletes had walked out of the Pan-American Games,' Voy tells me, 'and that cost the Olympic committee a lot of financial support and sponsors, because no one wanted to sponsor druggies.' Voy was charged with ensuring that no American athlete tested positive in LA.

Catlin, however, concluded that the programme was indeed proving educational, but not in the way originally envisaged. Rather, it was teaching athletes and coaches how drug-testing worked; and it was telling them how to beat the system. He realised urine samples were being submitted with ever decreasing concentrations of drugs as competition got closer. 'I could sort them out on a big table and watch the doses coming down.' Much to the USOC's fury, Catlin refused to carry on.

After the LA Games, the committee's president, Colonel Don Miller, admitted that eighty-six American athletes had tested positive for banned substances prior to the Olympics. Ten had been at the Olympic trials. None were punished.

*

For the Games themselves, the organisation with which Catlin had to work most closely was not the USOC, or even the IOC, but the Los Angeles Olympic Organising Committee (LAOOC), which wielded more than normal power because no one else had wanted the event.

The organising committee was headed by Peter Ueberroth, a multi-millionaire businessman, who waived any payment for running the Games (helped no doubt by the fact that he had recently sold his business, First Travel Corporation, for $10 million). One of his right-hand men was Tony Daly, an orthopaedic surgeon and medical director to the Games, which meant he was, in effect, Catlin's boss. Uebberoth's stewardship was such a success that he came to rival Carl Lewis as the anointed hero of the 1984 Olympics. This was not quite how it looked from Catlin's lab. There were problems in the relationship from the start. Manfred Donike kept pushing for better testing; the organising committee kept pushing back.

The major issue seems to have been over Donike's T/E test. In April 1983 Daly said the test for testosterone would not be conducted unless there was convincing evidence of the science that underpinned it. More than a quarter of a century later, in his seminal book *Drug Games,* Thomas Hunt would translate that apparent statement of the obvious: 'Ueberroth had come to believe that the expensive doping regulations constituted a direct threat to the economic integrity' of the Games.

In other words, a multitude of positive tests would wreck LA's chances of a profit. Hunt says Ueberroth wrote to Samaranch, complaining that 'drugs and doctors are not only controlling the Games of the XXIII Olympiad, they are beginning to gain control of the whole Olympic movement'. While he conceded that 'the use of drugs must be curtailed,' Ueberroth added, 'Equally important, the dignity of the Olympic movement must be preserved.' And he may have had a sympathetic hearing. Dick Pound, at that stage vice-president of the IOC, once heard Samaranch moan about the scientists, 'All they live for is to find a positive sample!'

Donike's test was approved, but relations between the LA organising committee and the drug-testers grew, if anything, frostier as the Games approached. Officials were even upset when Donike and Catlin were spotted lurking at the cycling track. And Catlin claims the organisers tried to have the lab closed at the last minute. The reason? 'We were turning out positives at a pretty prodigious rate, and they didn't like that.' This was backed up by one of Catlin's colleagues in the lab, Craig Kammerer, who told the BBC that the organisers lobbied to have the testing programme scrapped entirely. It survived but by the end of the Games, in Kammerer's words, 'the integrity of the system had been destroyed'.

In the last couple of days of competition in LA, Catlin's lab detected nine positive tests – including five for anabolic steroids – and reported them to the IOC. Supposedly, the next move is to inform the athlete who can, and almost always does, request that the back-up or B sample is tested in the desperate hope that it might contradict the first finding. Yet, says Catlin now, 'those positives never saw the light of day'.

At 3 a.m. on Tuesday 14 August, as he talked to his wife on his terrace, Don Catlin was exhausted. His workload during the sixteen days of the Olympics had been immense. A total of 1,510 urine samples had been delivered to the lab with the numbers steadily rising as events reached their climax. It meant that, as the Games drew to a close, Catlin realised that he and his twenty-four-strong team, who were working up to sixteen hours a day, would have to carry on for several more days to clear the backlog.

'The big league events are the last two or three days, and most of the big-time track and field events were at the end,' explains Catlin. 'We were getting through the testing all right, but by then we were getting so many samples, we were so tired, and we started hitting these positives. We got positives that we had no idea were gonna be there. But we just couldn't finish by Sunday night.'

The day after the closing ceremony, Tony Daly told Catlin, 'We're all taking the day off – so close the lab. The Games are over, people are on their way home – just stop the testing.' 'Tony, look, we're under contract,' said Catlin. 'We're going to finish it.' His senior colleagues agreed, and Daly retreated. Then they found the nine positives.

He had no idea who they belonged to; the urine samples were identified only by a code. The only person who could match the code with the athlete was 'the Prince', Alexandre de Mérode. As he had done throughout the Games, Catlin handed de Mérode the day's documentation. The next day, de Mérode visited Catlin. 'The codes are missing,' he said.

Catlin says de Mérode (who could be 'somewhat oblivious,' says Catlin with no little affection) had returned to his hotel, the Biltmore, and placed the paperwork in a safe in his room. The next day the safe had gone and the papers too. 'The safe has been taken from my room,' de Mérode told Catlin.

The Prince's version was that he was at first told the safe had been taken to the LA committee's offices in Culver City. When he went there to ask for them, they said, 'We sent everything to you in Lausanne.' But nothing ever turned up in Lausanne. 'Those positives never saw the light of day, unfortunately,' says Catlin. 'I don't know what happened. But either the Prince or Tony Daly is lying, because they were telling completely different stories.' Since they are both dead, neither is available for comment.

The Biltmore is a large, old-fashioned hotel, with an air of faded grandeur rather than luxury, at least in the lobby. The drawing room upstairs is more opulent; the president's suite, where Samaranch stayed, even more so. Visiting the hotel, I asked at reception whether anyone was still there who had worked at the hotel in 1984. At least one member of staff was: Ken Battles, the head of engineering.

He, of all people, must have heard of the case of the stolen safe. 'Not to my knowledge,' he said when I asked. 'At that time we didn't have safety boxes in the rooms or even the suites,' he added – though it is perfectly feasible that the IOC would have brought their own.

'But we would have been aware of a stolen safe,' said Battles. 'Security would have been aware. That's a new one on me.'

The story gets ever more confused, because Arnold Beckett believed not that the safe had been stolen but that the contents had been shredded. This ties in with the notion of the Prince's obliviousness. But it seems beyond dispute that, as Catlin told his wife, something strange happened in the room at the Biltmore.

As Beckett told BBC investigators in 1994, 'In effect, the laboratory had been shut down by the order of someone to ensure that certain positive results never saw the light of day.' In private correspondence, though, Beckett later claimed that Daly admitted to him that the papers had been destroyed. And Catlin revealed to me an intriguing sub-plot: a plan for Daly to replace de Mérode as head of the IOC medical commission. He was reluctant to talk about this until I assured him that Samaranch – like Daly, de Mérode and also Beckett – had died. De Mérode had befriended the French chefs that the IOC had flown over to the Biltmore to feed them in their accustomed style. One of the chefs told him he had overheard Samaranch in conversation, discussing a plan to oust de Mérode from his role as head of the medical commission.

Catlin has further evidence of this. 'Tony actually came to me and said, "I'm gonna be the new Prince." He wanted me to help him. He said, "The two of us will handle everything." I said, "Well, let's see…" But the Prince was able to fend off whatever they were up to. He was a very, very clever politician, and he knew the IOC cold.'

For once, Samaranch and his rival from the IAAF, Primo Nebiolo, may have been in accord. The BBC reported a row between Donike and Nebiolo, who was trying to prevent the disqualification of the

Italian hammer thrower Giampaolo Urlando, after he tested positive for testosterone. He failed. Catlin also confirms that Daly's attempt to close the lab was preceded by late-night calls from Nebiolo urging him to stop the testing.

In the official report of the Los Angeles Games eleven positive tests are recorded. According to Catlin, there were actually twenty.

Catlin was keen, after the Olympics, to publicise what he saw as the faults in the system, and the mistakes, whether deliberate or accidental. 'I was going nuts,' he says. He wrote a scholarly article which listed the positives by day, together with the sample code – making it theoretically possible to match the code with the guilty athlete. When he sent a draft of his article to the IOC, they told him the document was confidential and could not be published. The paper was eventually published three years later, in *Clinical Chemistry*, but in an IOC-approved, watered-down version. It contained a summary table of the findings, but it was no longer possible to match the positive test with the athlete, or even the sport.

Yet it may, all these years on, still be possible to do this. 'I've still got 'em,' Catlin says.

Got what? 'The samples from 1984. When I left UCLA three years ago I had the urine samples still in my refrigerator.'

Would he still be able to match up the original positives with the athletes? 'Well, I don't know. Jim Ferstle and I talk about it. He knows what I have and he believes that with his information we could match them up, or, well, come close. I don't know… It's so long ago, and to open that door… I don't know.'

The 1984 Olympics represented a triumph for the capitalist world in more ways than one. They made a profit; something previously believed to be impossible. Montreal, which saddled itself with the Games only eight years earlier, spent the next three decades paying off the debt. Its stadium, originally nicknamed The Big O, became known as The Big Owe or The Big Woe.

The surplus in LA was $223 million, thanks in part to the record $225 million paid by ABC for broadcasting rights, and $4 million paid by each of the thirty sponsors. This established a model for future Olympics; a model created and constructed by Peter Ueberroth. He was even named *Time*'s Man of the Year for 1984 – ahead of Carl Lewis, and Ronald Reagan, who was re-elected president three months later in a feelgood 'Morning in America' campaign, which the Olympics helped make possible. 'Those who know him well say Ueberroth is a fascinating paradox,' the magazine commented, 'an idealist with a salting of cleverness, a man of high principle who is willing to go right to the edge of scruple to reach his goals.' Ueberroth went on to become commissioner of Major League Baseball, one of the highest profile jobs in the US, and was occasionally mentioned as a possible presidential candidate himself.

The mystery of the missing positive tests did not make the news at the time, and the whispers of drug-use certainly failed to detract from the aura of success. There were brief mentions of the issue in the papers, but they caused barely a ripple. Hardly anyone batted an eyelid when Robert Kerr, the doctor who – we know now – had secretly started to advise Charlie Francis's athletes, told the *Los Angeles Times* that the Olympians were laughing at Catlin's laboratory: 'I don't know one athlete who's been influenced by it.' Later Kerr said 'more than a dozen' of his patients had won medals while using the drugs he had prescribed. At the Dubin Inquiry in 1989 he would up that figure to twenty.

Surprisingly, Catlin did not just give up and turn to some more rewarding branch of medicine. In fact, he became even more committed. One senses, talking to him and to his ally Robert Voy, that this arose from their sympathy with the athletes rather than any faith in those running sport. For Catlin, there were parallels with his previous work with heroin addicts. He could see the athletes as victims, too. The biggest victims being the clean athletes robbed of their rightful medals by the cheats. Catlin used to display posters in his lab of some athletes he knew well and believed to be clean, including the hurdler Edwin Moses, the sprinter Evelyn Ashford, and the swimmer Janet Evans.

But Catlin and Voy also understood that the drug-takers were themselves in a bind, and felt forced to make a Faustian bargain. As Voy told me, 'Most athletes don't want to take drugs. But also, they don't want to be cheated. They believe that what makes sport different to a brawl is that there are rules and regulations and you want to create a level playing field. That's all they want. But when the Russians and East Germans are teaching them that you can cheat and win medals, what are you going to do?'

Both Voy and Catlin had a lot of contact with the athletes, and many of them talked candidly about what they were doing. You would expect Voy to have had that contact. It is more surprising in the case of the man in the lab, the drug-taker's ultimate enemy. But Catlin describes a surprisingly cosy relationship: 'If I find them positive, they come to my lab, and I get to see them and talk to them. And I've always had a pretty good relationship with them. They know I'm doing my job. Most of them will tell me privately what they've been doing.' With a shrug, he adds, 'You just have to follow straight and narrow rules and be fair and don't vary.'

In the spring of 1985, Catlin went to visit Manfred Donike at home in Germany. Catlin had become aware of a blind spot in his testing during the LA Games. There was a popular anabolic steroid, Stanozolol, that he realised could not be detected – and both men were certain it was being used.

They were discussing the problem and, 'Uh, he gave me some Stanozolol,' says Catlin.

He jokes that he did not feel able to run a sub-10-second 100m. In fact, he felt no effects at all. 'I only took one dose. But I took a big dose. Manfred couldn't find it in my urine, illustrating the problem. But he kept the urine, kept working on it, and Manfred did figure it out. It didn't take him too long, about six months.'

Donike's discovery of a test for testosterone had represented one major breakthrough. Now his test for Stanozolol could be seen as another small victory. That would be a modest verdict. Another claim might be that the Stanozolol test, and Catlin's own urine, provided the key to unlock the greatest Olympic scandal of all.

PART TWO
RIVALS

'This record is one of the best ever in athletics. I don't think
anyone will break it in the next fifty years... Other than me.'
BEN JOHNSON

8

LEWIS 8, JOHNSON 1

'I watch Roadrunner cartoons.'
BEN JOHNSON

Joe Douglas's predictions for Carl Lewis did not come true. Lewis did all he could at the Los Angeles Olympics, short of breaking an individual world record. But he did not become Michael Jackson, or even O. J. Simpson. The 'big one' – the multi-million dollar exclusive tie-up with an all-American corporation – failed to materialise.

Despite his four gold medals, Lewis did not break out of his sport, far less transcend the sporting world. He was merely the best at what he did. Whatever impact the 1984 Games had at the time, Americans still didn't love track and field. Far from walking from the LA Coliseum into the open arms of Corporate America waving multi-million dollar cheques, Carl Lewis returned to Houston to find that his home had been burgled, and his crystal collection smashed.

Where was Coca-Cola? Where was Pepsi, American Express, General Motors, McDonalds, Wal-Mart, or any of the other major corporations which Douglas thought he would be fighting off if his man delivered four gold medals? Lewis had kept his side of the bargain. So what went wrong?

Lewis claimed that Coca-Cola had shown interest in him beforehand: 'I had been offered a good deal but didn't want to sign until after the Games. Then came the negative publicity, and Coke backed off. I was disappointed because a company as big as Coke, with its powerful ads and positive image, could have helped turn things around for me.'

'People *love* Carl Lewis,' Joe Douglas told Rick Reilly of the *LA Times*. 'Madison Avenue must be playing hard to get,' commented Reilly.

One theory was that the gay question was putting off advertisers. 'It doesn't matter what Carl Lewis's sexuality *is*,' suggested Dwight Stones, the high jumper-turned-TV commentator. 'Madison Avenue perceives him as homosexual.'

Dick Patrick, then the athletics correspondent of *USA Today*, was mystified not only by the non-event of Lewis's corporate career but also his sport's inability to capitalise on his triumphs. 'I mean, four golds – it was a heroic performance. Why couldn't we get a really strong circuit going? Why couldn't track have had more presence on TV?'

Yet Patrick saw for himself that perhaps the corporations and networks had a point. 'I went to Houston to do a story on Carl, and I went to a workout of his. It was a brutally hot day. We hopped in his car, and en route we stopped at a 7-Eleven. He goes in the store without a shirt on. And I thought, my God, if this was done in Europe or Japan it would create a minor riot. He was like a rock star there. But here he is in Houston, his adopted home town, and it doesn't cause a ripple. The store clerk doesn't even say anything. It was like he was completely anonymous.'

Why was he unpopular? I ask Tom Tellez. 'Because he was progressive,' argues Tellez. 'He did things before anyone else did them. He wore tights, he wore his hair a bit different. He was before his time. That was the problem – he was too far ahead of everyone else.'

Douglas denies that there was any sense of disappointment about this. When I was in his lair, he walked towards a cabinet, and swung open the door with a flourish. 'He got so many sponsorship offers, many, many. They're all in those boxes, there.' But Douglas cannot or will not say what happened to all those offers. He points out that Lewis became wealthy and that he did have sponsors. But they were not the blue-chip backers who were expected. When the LA dust settled, Lewis could only count two corporate supporters – his long-time shoe and sportswear supplier, Nike, and the Japanese firm Suntory. There was an air of pathos surrounding Lewis in the months that followed.

During the winter, Lewis had breakfast in New York with Ira Berkow, the *New York Times*' star sports writer. Naturally, the article opens by describing Lewis's attire, 'black hip-length mink coat, black leather pants and a white shirt with a thin black tie.' Then there is an interruption from the waiter. 'First, I want to congratulate you,' he tells the athlete, bending closer and adding, 'And I think all the pressure put on you was unfair.' 'Thank you, I appreciate that,' replied Lewis.

Lewis told Berkow he had experienced similar reactions and support from ordinary people throughout the country. Yet Lewis had not been the 'ultimate popular star of those Games,' Berkow suggested. He seemed overshadowed by Mary Lou Retton, the gymnast who cavorted into the vacuum created by the missing Communists, his dignified and scholarly track colleague Edwin Moses, and Jeff Blatnick, who came back from cancer to win a wrestling gold.

'All those people were terrific,' Lewis replied, 'and they deserved all the accolades they got. They were basically new – even Edwin Moses, who hadn't been in the public eye that much – they were different. I had been Mr Olympics since 1981, and for the most part it was all on my shoulders. Then when 1984 came, it was like, "You've gotten us here, now goodbye."'

It had not all been negative, Lewis added. 'President Reagan invited me to the White House and he talked to me about the 100m race. I had the impression he watched it very closely on television. And Nancy, she was great. She hugged me.' And yet, as Berkow notes, 'For Jesse Owens, there were tape parades. There were none for Carl Lewis.'

He told Berkow he had briefly considered an offer to try out for the Dallas Cowboys; he had also continued his acting lessons at Warren

Robertson's studio and accepted a small part in a forthcoming movie. 'I make a statement in it against drugs and the wild life,' Lewis tells Berkow. 'I'm very religious and spiritual and I wouldn't take a role that has cursing and that kind of thing. I know it's hard to get movies that don't have that nowadays. But maybe we can bring back Mary Poppins.'

Nothing seemed decided for Lewis. Everything was up in the air, 'even the 1988 Olympics in South Korea,' according to Berkow, who picks up on Lewis's ambivalence, his restlessness, his stifled ambition, his overwhelming lack of certainty about what the future might hold.

But is it any wonder? As 1984 drew to a close, all Lewis could aspire to on an athletics track was repetition. The repetition of perfection may be more appealing than repetition for repetition's sake, but it was still repetition. Soon afterwards, Lewis hinted that it was only the prospect of no return from a showbiz career that kept him in sport, 'If I go to entertainment and succeed, I'll do that for the rest of my life. If I go and flop, I'll be right back to track in a year. So I may as well delay that year of fateful decision as long as I can, right?'

In the meantime, he thought he could combine his interests. Apart from the minor acting roles, there was his singing. If he couldn't beat Michael Jackson, perhaps he could join him. He released a single, 'Goin' for Gold', which, Lewis acknowledged, 'wasn't much of a threat to the charts'. He did live performances with a Houston band, Electric Storm, and in mid-1985 came a full album, *The Feeling That I Feel*, which 'wasn't bad,' said Lewis, 'It just wasn't good.' (The last time it appears to have been mentioned at all was by the *Independent* in 2003, who described it as 'execrable'.)

The album was financed by another company from Japan, the one place on earth where they could never get enough of Lewis: he featured in billboards for public transport ('When Carl Lewis is in a hurry, he takes the rapid transit line') on phone cards, and he was fêted wherever he went. Lewis had his own theory for his being so big in Japan. Whereas in the US 'being different usually means something bad, in Japan I'm only different because I'm black and an American. But they accept me as I am.' What he meant by 'different', he didn't say. But the love affair with Japan was clearly reciprocal. Lewis even made a donation of $10,000 to the country's version of the Special Olympics, for children and adults with learning difficulties.

He did not give up on his singing career and he returned to Japan, where a businessman put up $50,000 to allow him to record two songs with Quincy Jones, who produced Michael Jackson's *Thriller*. Another single, 'Break it Up', was released: it sold poorly in the States but was a minor hit in Sweden. The song begins: 'Let's all work together, you can't win on your own.' The video features Lewis in a gym and then in a jacuzzi, surrounded by scantily clad females with big, backcombed hair, with Lewis in a black leotard. This is interspersed with footage of him in competitive action.

'Break it Up' can be viewed on YouTube, where 880,000 have seen a video described by one on-line commenter as being 'so bad good it hurts'. This figure dwarfs the 65,000 who have watched the YouTube clip of Lewis's 100m victory in LA. However, more than 1.5 million have gone to his rendition of the national anthem. Read some of the cruel comments posted below these humiliations and it is impossible not to feel sympathy for Lewis. The 'Carl bashing' lives on, as does the homophobia. In his defence, in the case of 'Break it Up', it was the 1980s. All pop videos looked more or less like his.

When it came to his sport, Lewis seemed more animated, more exercised, by his battles off the track – with the national federation, the naysayers, doubters and those accused him of being on drugs, with the writer Gary Smith, the US sprint coach Russ Rogers, his sponsors Nike and their representative, his ex-friend Don Coleman. Nike initiated legal action against Lewis for failing to wear their branded clothing in some of his public appearances. It represented a new low: not only did Lewis fail to attract the blue chip, non-sporting brands, but even his most loyal backers were – as he described it – 'looking for ways to

125

dump me'. While Nike insisted it was a clear-cut breach of contract, Lewis claimed, 'Nike was no longer using me in advertising because company officials were still concerned about my public image.'

These feuds might have drained and distracted Lewis. But perhaps, in another sense, they also sustained him. They were things to rub up against, people to prove wrong. His critics and perceived enemies were opponents: the only ones he truly had. No wonder he was weighing up his options, no wonder he was drawn to off-track attractions and opportunities. On the track, Lewis had no competition.

At least not at that point. But the competition would come. And it would arrive in spectacular style at the most prestigious meeting on the European circuit, the Zurich Weltklasse, in August 1985.

In the summer of 1985 Lewis was nursing a hamstring injury, but he was still running, and running well, and he was still the man to beat. He proved that in a race in Modesto on 11 May, where he won in 9.98, with Ben Johnson fourth in 10.16. It was the eighth time they had raced each other over 100m. The score: Lewis 8, Johnson 0.

But Johnson was inching closer. Charlie Francis put Johnson's improvement in 1985 down to two major changes he made in his coaching. The first was emphasising speed over endurance, subverting the training doctrine that said conditioning based on endurance was essential, even for a sprinter. 'I now believed that stamina was important, but only at a given velocity,' said Francis. And it was velocity that was critical. He dismissed the traditionalists who stressed the importance of hours of low intensity, high volume training to acquire that endurance: 'If these people had designed the Great Pyramid, it would have covered 700 acres and topped off at 30 feet.'

Francis concentrated, instead, on honing the point of that pyramid – giving his athletes the edge in speed, not stamina. It is a philosophy that later became received wisdom. He also changed his athletes' weight training programme, following the same 'less is more' principle.

Not low intensity, high volume but high intensity, low volume. On the track that meant running shorter distances faster; in the weights room it meant doing fewer repetitions of heavier weights.

Though Carl Lewis did not discuss his training in the same detail as Francis would later do, for Tom Tellez the crucial word was 'biomechanics'. He remained low profile throughout his star athlete's career, partly because, as he told me, he had 'no interest in the business side of things'. He left that to Joe Douglas while he stayed in Houston doing what he knew and loved best: coaching.

For him, this meant zooming in on technique: breaking every movement down, studying it, perfecting it. As he pointed out, 'World-class male sprinters stride approximately forty-three times during a 100m race. If a mechanical error costs one one-thousandth of a second per stride, the total cost is .043 seconds at the finish line.' He would video Lewis's training sessions and then spend hours analysing them with him. 'The great thing about Carl was that you only had to tell him something once.'

His preoccupation with biomechanics was shared by Joe Douglas. But Tellez's style of coaching was perhaps as important as the content of his sessions. His modus operandi was to impart information, empower his athletes and step back: an approach that clearly suited Lewis. Would Lewis have thrived under the more authoritarian Francis? Would Johnson have excelled under Tellez? Probably not.

For Johnson, the benefits of Francis's new regime were startling. He was becoming the kind of athlete that Francis could only have dreamed of. It was his capacity for improvement that set him apart. In five years Johnson doubled the weight he could bench press, from 81kg to 165.5kg: he only weighed 72.5kg. No wonder he was able to up-end Lennox Lewis.

Francis also remarked on Johnson's 'immensely strong' grip. (I was relieved to find, when I met him in 2011, his handshake was firm but not knuckle-crunching.) The other ingredients in Francis's training cocktail, of course, were drugs. And the group's doctor, Jamie Astaphan, was also hitting his stride by 1985. He made changes after the LA Olympics, taking Johnson off human growth hormone, which he thought overrated except to hasten recovery from injuries. He began administering an injectable form of the anabolic steroid Dianabol, and he altered the timing of the steroid cycles, beginning Johnson's programme in the autumn rather than spring, reasoning that he would thus be physically stronger as he embarked on his hardest training phase.

But it was Francis's training programme that Johnson believes helped him, finally, to catch Lewis. It is why he says that steroids had little to do with his improvement. 'Drugs don't make you run faster. I took drugs to recover, not to run faster. Charlie got Astaphan to make sure everything was administered properly, that's all. We didn't go out there and do anything that we weren't supposed to be doing; we didn't abuse it, we didn't abuse drugs. We took what the body needs to train.

'Scientifically, it's not possible to take drugs to make you run faster.' And he repeats his mantra: 'A sprinter like me was born.'

By the mid-1980s Zurich was *the* meeting on the European circuit, unparalleled for prestige, money or atmosphere. 'The noise in the Letzigrund stadium was always extraordinary,' says the British athletics writer Neil Wilson. 'The fans were very close to the track and they used to bang on the metal advertising board and create a tremendous racket. We had to phone our stories in those days, and it was almost impossible.'

As the meeting's director Andreas Brügger put it to me, 'The question really would be, who wasn't in Zurich? Everyone was there!' Brügger was a pioneer of sponsorship, getting UBS bank on board in 1981. He had the advantage of being an insurance executive in the city, Switzerland's financial hub. As a former athlete himself (Swiss shot put champion in 1955) he had contacts in the sport. And he travelled extensively on business, trips he managed to combine with visits to other athletics meetings.

It was entirely fitting that Brügger's glitzy meetings would provide a focal point for the Johnson–Lewis rivalry. But at the 1985 Weltklasse Johnson still did not rank among the big stars, despite his Olympic bronze. It meant that, unlike Lewis, he had to run a qualifying heat, which, into a headwind, he won in 10.11. And in the final, he finally pulled it off: he claimed Lewis's scalp.

Johnson's winning time, 10.18, was not spectacular, though once again it was into a headwind, and it was a close race: he won by only a thousandth of a second. But the man who finished by Johnson's shoulder was not Carl Lewis: it was Calvin Smith. Johnson's clubmate Desai Williams was third, with Lewis trailing in fourth in 10.31. He clearly was nowhere near his best, but it was nevertheless the biggest and most satisfying victory of Johnson's career so far, and it was all the encouragement he needed. Now the score read: Lewis 8, Johnson 1.

Lewis played down the defeat. But Brügger, who had got to know the Lewis family well and says he liked Carl, remembers it differently: 'He was very disappointed, *very* disappointed.'

Brügger never did acquire the same closeness to the Francis group and says there was a similar pattern with the organisers of other major meetings, like Stockholm and Berlin. 'Francis and Ben Johnson separated themselves a bit from the organisers. They kept a distance. That was my feeling.' (Though in his book, Francis claimed that Brügger once told him, 'It was so nice to have your group here. Douglas and his demands make me want to vomit.')

'I know that Carl was suspicious about Ben,' says Brügger. 'That was the first time I heard these rumours – in Zurich in 1985. As a rule, if you follow the development of an athlete from a junior, you can follow his improvements and know exactly if he is doping or not. It's very rare that an athlete makes a huge jump. That's really suspicious.'

Johnson met Lewis again in Cologne four nights later, but both were below par, Lewis finishing second and Johnson third behind Marian Woronin of Poland. Johnson ended his season by winning at the World Cup in Canberra in October. Lewis, still troubled by his hamstring injury, opted not to go there. An alternative reason for his absence, offered by his long-time enemy Russ Rogers, was a fall-out over Lewis's reluctance to train with the relay squad. Johnson, starting to swagger, told a Canadian paper that Lewis was avoiding him.

Back in Toronto, Jamie Astaphan then made another change to Johnson's doping regime. He told Francis he had found a new and even more effective steroid to replace Dianabol. The latest potion – a milky white injectable substance that came in bottles – was introduced by Astaphan as 'Estragol'. It would be gentler on the athlete's system, and clear the body more reliably than Dianabol, he said, and it had another advantage: it was undetectable. Johnson began using Estragol in November.

But Johnson's emergence as one of the world's top sprinters caused some friction in his own group. Desai Williams, who had shown such early promise, left Francis as Johnson began to overtake him. There was no apparent acrimony. He still trained in Toronto. But, unknown to Johnson and Francis, in 1985 Williams made a phone call to Glen Bogue, manager of athlete services at the Canadian Track and Field Association, telling him that Johnson was using steroids, and that he was concerned about his health.

Williams added that he would tell him when Johnson commenced his next steroid cycle. Bogue said he would organise a random drug test, but he met with resistance from Wilf Wedmann, the CTFA president. Wedmann would later tell the Dubin Inquiry that he did not consider the evidence 'very substantial'; but then, Bogue, to protect Williams, had not revealed his source. In the end, no test was carried out. Dubin called it 'a significant missed opportunity', while questioning Williams's motives, saying, 'I do not think it was Mr Johnson's health that Mr Williams was concerned about.'

Lewis, meanwhile, began to be outspoken on the subject of drugs, calling for more testing. But he had been the target of innuendo and accusation himself. He had joked with Gary Smith about the rumours that he was taking 'gorilla hormones'.

'They're trippin'. They're up in the stratosphere... They say I take steroids. If I had it in my mind I needed steroids, I'd take them and tell everybody where they could go. But I wouldn't take them because subconsciously I would back off on working on my technique.'

'Gorilla hormone', supposedly reconstituted from the pituitaries of rhesus monkeys and gorillas, was believed to be widespread in the 1980s. It sounds like witchcraft, but was probably just urban myth. The evidence suggests that anyone who thought they were drinking gorilla juice almost certainly wasn't: neither the world nor the US has an infinite supply of gorillas.

However, human growth hormone was very much the undetectable wonder drug of the day and this was at the centre of persistent rumours about Lewis and his clubmates. HGH appears to have entered sport in the 1970s, when it was extracted from the pituitary glands of human corpses. Synthetic HGH began to be manufactured in 1981, and is used, medically, to treat dwarfism (Joe Douglas told me that he was administered it as a teenager, to treat his own lack of height). In a sporting context, it was believed to aid recovery, but was – and is – unproven as a performance-enhancer.

And there were said to be side effects. Dan Duchaine, author of *The Underground Steroid Handbook*, claimed that these could include elongation of the chin, feet and hands. HGH, he said, 'is the biggest gamble that an athlete can take, as the side effects are irreversible. Even with all that, we LOVE the stuff.' Duchaine was a Los Angeles bodybuilder who fed his cat Dianabol to help it survive the alleyways of Venice Beach. He later became David Jenkins's business partner and was found dead, aged forty-seven, in 2000.

'There's no way I'd let my athletes take drugs,' Douglas tells me, adding that Tom Tellez felt the same. 'We told the athletes: you do not take drugs. I would tell my athletes that drugs would shorten their lives, that they're not only illegal but they would hurt you physically in the long run.'

So for Douglas it is primarily a health issue? 'Absolutely correct,' he replies. 'According to the *LA Times*, steroids are gonna shorten your life. That's what I read. You only live to fifty-four if you use steroids. I don't know how true that is, but it's what I read. OK, there are situations the public doesn't understand. If you drink too much coffee, that's illegal. Or let's say you take vitamins, and there's a stimulant – aha, he's taken a stimulant!

'Are you married?' Douglas asks suddenly, but doesn't wait for an answer. 'If you're a woman, if there's this swelling here' – he indicates beneath his eyes – 'that's once a month. But we don't have periods, us men. So if you're swollen here, you're on drugs. When this is watery, right here' – he pulls at an eyelid, exposing the lower part of his eyeball – 'I know they're on drugs. I had two athletes in the 1990s. They were swollen here, under the eyes. And I turned 'em in. But they didn't do anything about it, the track and field people.'

When Douglas talks about drugs, he invariably means steroids. And he argued to me that the synthetic hormone EPO, which became fashionable in the 1990s, should never have been banned because he believed it was not dangerous. 'I don't give it to my athletes,' he said, 'because it's illegal, but philosophically? I'm not gonna condemn somebody for taking EPO.'

'But it's still unfair,' I protest. 'It skews competition. How do we know that what we're seeing is real?' I refrained from mentioning the 20 European cyclists thought to have died from EPO abuse in the early 1990s.

Douglas considers this argument for a moment. 'That's a good opinion. I can agree with that.' But he still thinks a greater threat to the integrity of sport is corruption in drug-testing: 'What angered me was the cover-ups.' We know now that Primo Nebiolo tried to suppress at least one positive test in LA. Did Douglas know of more cases?

'Of course I knew it went on,' says Douglas sharply. 'I said to Primo, "You gotta stop the cover-ups." He said, "Joe, positive drugs tests are gonna hurt the sport."

'I said, "What's gonna hurt the kids more is the cover-ups."'

As Johnson's stock rose, so did his earnings. As well as achieving an ambition on the track, by finally beating Lewis, he managed another. Johnson had always talked about having enough money to buy a home for his mother. Now he was able to acquire a large brick house in the Toronto suburb of Scarborough, for him, his mother, his three sisters, and his parrot.

Johnson carried his 1985 momentum into the following year, getting his season off to a flyer, indoors in Japan, with the world 60m record. 'In the future, I think I could maybe run the fastest 100m ever,' he said. He also met Lewis over 100m three times in 1986, a sequence that dramatically altered the dynamic of their rivalry.

In San Jose, at the end of May, right at the start of the outdoor season, he repeated his Zurich success of the previous year, beating Lewis convincingly, 10.01 to 10.18. The race saw two false starts, the second, interestingly and unusually, by Lewis. Was he trying to counter or pre-empt Johnson's explosive advantage? At the third time of asking, Lewis's start was legal, but sluggish; he passed several runners in the final 30 metres, but not the man he most wanted to pass.

There was, however, an off-the-track episode in San Jose that unsettled Johnson. Attempting to check in to the meeting's designated hotel, he was told he did not have a room. As the other athletes arrived and checked in, he cut an increasingly frustrated figure in the lobby. It also meant he was unable to eat or rest properly before the race, making his victory all the more impressive. But the incident troubled him.

Three weeks later Lewis was back to winning form, running a wind-assisted 9.90 in Eugene, at the national championships. He also won his forty-eight consecutive long jump competition, making it, he said, his 'best meet ever'. Then he fired a warning, 'People are going to have to run very fast to beat me.'

'People say Carl can't start and Carl can't finish and Carl is getting old,' he went on. 'People say I'm not willing to work as hard. I know what it takes to win. I can do what I have to do to win.' Then he suddenly veered into Ali-speak, 'In track and field, I'm the Prince, the Michael Jackson, the Lionel Ritchie, and all those put together.'

As a Canadian, Johnson was, of course, absent from the US championships. But two weeks later came the inaugural Goodwill Games in Moscow, an event designed by the tycoon Ted Turner to blow away the memories of the Olympic boycotts. And here Johnson lay down his biggest marker yet. There were two false starts, Johnson responsible for the first, Lewis for the second – an indication, perhaps, of how highly strung both now were. And Johnson was a sensation. He did not just win; he ran 9.95, the joint-second fastest in history, the fastest at sea level. Afterwards, Johnson claimed that, as he started, his blocks slipped 'a couple of inches, otherwise I might have done 9.90 or 9.91'.

Lewis finished third in 10.06, with Chidi Imoh of Nigeria second. Yet Charlie Francis was peeved that, in the aftermath of the Moscow race, the reporters clustered around Lewis, ignoring the winner. 'This seems to be really important to him,' said Lewis of Johnson. 'But I'm just biding my time.'

By now press reports were beginning to register, and relish, the needle that was developing between the two. Eventually, the journalists got round to Johnson, and asked if he, like his great rival, had other interests, such as acting or singing. 'I watch Roadrunner cartoons,'

Johnson deadpanned. Not everyone got the joke. Some seemed to interpret Johnson's sullen demeanour as a sign that he had no sense of humour, an impression not helped by his stutter and strong Jamaican accent. What Johnson said next was clear enough, though. 'The last time I beat Lewis, he had some complaints. Today, I beat him clear. I just wonder what he has to say this time.'

Lewis had already said it: 'I've already said this was going to be a relatively low-key season for me. I'm not too bothered.' Later, he added, 'I don't care about being number one in the world as much as Ben does.'

After Moscow, Johnson kept up a busy schedule, running in the Commonwealth Games in Edinburgh in late July, winning the 100m and 4x100m relay. From there he made the short journey south to Gateshead for a meeting with a sprinter nearing the end of his career. At thirty-four, Allan Wells had been overlooked by the Scottish selectors – who 'knew not too much about athletics and even less about the psyche of Allan Wells,' according to Doug Gillon – for a Commonwealth Games in his home town. The Games were a financial, organisational and public relations fiasco, caused by an African-led boycott and local mismanagement. Wells's omission was one tiny aspect of the prevailing stupidity, as was highlighted in Gateshead when he beat Johnson.

The race has a footnote in track history because Wells became the first high-profile sprinter to wear the knee-length cycling shorts that would later become ubiquitous (the 'Wells Wonder Pants,' as Gillon described them). Wells remembers not just the race but also a breakfast conversation he had with Johnson's teammate Angella Issajenko. 'I didn't really know the girl,' Wells tells me. 'But she was very friendly, and she was quite open, it seemed to me, about drugs, without actually mentioning anything illegal. She mentioned the doctor's name. She hinted at what they were doing. It seemed quite clear to me.'

Asked if he had his own suspicions about Johnson, Wells says, 'I think everybody had suspicions about everybody.'

From Gateshead Johnson travelled to Zurich, for his third meeting of the year with Carl Lewis. And for the third time, Johnson triumphed, this time in 10.03, with Lewis third in 10.25. As in Moscow, Imoh separated them. It was arguably this race that finally propelled the story of the Johnson–Lewis rivalry into the full glare of the public spotlight, not least because of Johnson's clear superiority.

And this time his winning gesture anticipated the finish of the 100m in Seoul two years later. Around 10 metres before the line he visibly slowed as he glanced to his left, towards Lewis, who was nowhere, then to his right, then back to his left, at the same time raising his right arm and pointing to the sky. Yet he still crossed the line two metres ahead of Imoh, Lewis and Linford Christie, the 26-year-old British sprinter who, having belatedly gone full-time, was starting to emerge as a force.

Now the story was no longer just about Lewis struggling to recapture his form, it was about Johnson, too. But, as ever, the sum was greater than the parts: it was the sense of an emerging rivalry – and antipathy – that captured the media imagination.

After five consecutive years at the top of the *Track & Field News* world rankings for the 100m, Lewis was toppled by Johnson at the end of 1986. Johnson had now won four of their last five meetings and, bearing in mind the altitude question, was arguably the fastest man of all time.

But Zurich, as well as confirming Johnson's coronation as the sprint king, was also the scene of two interesting off-the-track episodes, one alleged, one confirmed. In 2010, Johnson claimed that he had tested positive after the 1986 Weltklasse, but that Francis had managed to have it suppressed. In his tell-most-things book Francis made no mention of this, and Brügger is absolute in his denial. 'Dr Henry Perschak and doping expert Ernst Alder, who were supervising the test procedures, have no knowledge, even of any rumours, to confirm Ben Johnson's statement,' Brügger tells me in an email. 'If tests would have been positive or doubtful, the respective reports would have been sent to the IAAF. I could not find any correspondence on this subject.'

The other story is more convincing. The Francis group was well known for its macho attitudes, which sometimes irritated Angella Issajenko, who had to endure not just their disdainful talk about women but also their farting contests.

In some ways Issajenko's account confirms the prejudices of Joe Douglas, who was reluctant to work with sprinters because they were insufficiently monastic. As Douglas put it, 'Sprinters are flaky. Most of the people running around, going to bars and chasing women, were sprinters.' Carl Lewis, to Douglas's initial surprise and subsequent relief, was not flaky, nor was he interested in going to bars and chasing women. Ben Johnson, on the other hand...

'I ate whatever I wanted to eat and drank whenever I wanted to drink, throughout my career,' says Johnson, 'because I burned it off. And I liked to go out with the ladies, have a good time. That was one of my... my downfalls.'

Francis described Johnson's womanising as being characterised by the 'broken promise and forgotten obligation... He was always in trouble with the women he dated. On some days two or three of them would come out to the track at York University to wait for Ben while he trained. On more than one of these occasions I saw him end practice by hopping a fence, running to his car, and roaring off to avoid an awkward scene.'

One Francis story has Ben telling a girlfriend who was proving difficult, 'But you're the only one for me, baby. I don't care about *her*.' Whereupon, the girl glanced towards the parking lot and said, 'Ben, that would be a lot more believable if she wasn't sitting in your car right now.'

There are tales of Johnson being in nightclubs on the eve of big races – Frank Dick, the British coach, says he was surprised to see Johnson, late at night, heading into one the night before winning the 100m at the

World Cup in Canberra in 1985. Johnson insists he was always more interested in women than alcohol but, either way, it was little surprise that, as he sat in a courtesy car on the way to the track in Zurich, he reacted enthusiastically to the offer of a night out after the meeting.

The offer came from another man in the car, who Johnson had regularly seen on the track circuit that season, even though he wasn't – he didn't think – an athlete. He was a tall, good-looking, smiling African-American with bag-loads of confidence. 'He was very friendly,' says Johnson, 'and he loved to go out with the ladies. He was trying to show me how much he could get the ladies to come out with us and have a good time. We went out to the Ritz in Zurich. I wasn't going out to have a few beers, I was going out to see what he has... to meet up with ladies. I saw some champagne, and said, "Let's have some champagne." That was it. But he was charismatic, yeah. We had good times.'

The man's name was André Jackson. Or, as he prefers to be known, André 'Action' Jackson.

Today Jackson, born in the US, is a diamond executive and chairman of the African Diamond Council and divides his time between Angola and the United Arab Emirates. In 1986 he was just getting started in the African diamond business. So what then was he doing, that same year, in a nightclub in Zurich with Ben Johnson? And who, exactly, was he?

Well, in the early 1980s he had been a contemporary of Carl Lewis at the University of Houston. And the plot thickens when you type Jackson's name for an internet picture search. There he is sitting with Nelson Mandela in one. Even stranger, if you alter the search to 'André Jackson Carl Lewis', up comes a picture that appeared in *National Jeweler* magazine in 1999. It shows Lewis and Jackson together at the launch of 'A Cut Above', a diamond promotion fronted by Lewis.

What Johnson did not know in 1986 was that Jackson was friends with Lewis. He was also well known to Joe Douglas and the Santa

Monica Track Club. Douglas regarded him as a strong athlete and promising sprinter, if not of international standard. But Jackson had become a familiar face at major events. Lewis, who said that he got to know Jackson in about 1985, later explained, 'He loves to travel, so he often shows up for track meets.'

Johnson says Jackson neglected to mention the connection. By now the sprint rivalry was big news and becoming more rancorous with every meeting. And so it seems curious that Jackson, only a couple of hours after Johnson had defeated his friend for a third consecutive time, would spend the evening cavorting with the winner, acting – according to Johnson – as though he was his new best buddy.

And yet, in a nightclub in Zurich, amid girls and champagne, that's exactly what appears to have happened.

9

BIG BEN AND KING CARL

'The kid is back!'
CARL LEWIS

Did Carl Lewis and Ben Johnson really dislike each other? Or was there, as so often between heavyweight boxers, a hint of fakery, of playing to the galleries, all in the name of giving their rivalry an edge that would stoke public interest and inflate appearance fees?

It seems not. The antipathy appears genuine. Johnson can offer no plausible explanation for this. From Lewis's point of view, it is not difficult to imagine that he resented Johnson. After all, his self-image – not to mention his marketing plan – was predicated on the idea that he could transcend sport. Yet in order to do that he had to be the number one; it wouldn't work if he were just a contender. Johnson represented a significant threat to Lewis and not just on the athletics track. But in the view of the Francis camp, he treated his rival with disdain. Maybe that was fear. But Johnson interpreted his subsequent aloofness and stand-offishness as a lack of respect. He considered Lewis a sore loser.

The rivalry intensified in 1987, the year of the second World Athletics Championships in Rome, partly because their mutual dislike became more obvious, and partly because their meetings became so rare. Before the championships, Johnson and Lewis faced each other just once, in Seville on 28 May. It led to accusations that they were avoiding each other, though that charge came to be directed mainly at Johnson.

Now that he was acknowledged as the fastest man in the world, interest in him in his adopted country of Canada was also intense, to the point, as Francis would say, where, 'Ben's fame was beginning to encroach upon our training.' In 1986 he was awarded the Lou Marsh Trophy as Canada's outstanding sportsperson. He was starting to earn serious money, too – with appearance fees 'in five figures' – and he indulged his love of fast cars, eventually buying a Porsche and a Ferrari. In the meantime he drove a black Corvette (licence plate: BEN 84), a Mazda RX7 and a Toyota Supra.

By 1987, Johnson was Canada's best sprinter since Harry Jerome, a world record holder in several events in the 1960s, with the added bonus that the man whose crown he had inherited was an American. If Canadians love anything more than winning, it's beating their dominant neighbour – particularly someone who appeared to embody as many American traits as Carl Lewis. Lewis was confident, brash and outgoing; Johnson could seem humble, quiet, self-contained. Although it is interesting to note that, in different contexts – if you speak to Joe Douglas about the young Lewis, or Angella Issajenko about Johnson – these descriptions could be almost interchangeable. Lewis could be shy. Johnson could be a showman. But the image that began to form of Johnson was an awkward one.

Naturally, the press stoked the burgeoning rivalry, goading Johnson into saying derogatory things about Lewis. He didn't need much encouragement. Of their showdown at the Goodwill Games in Moscow, Johnson said of Lewis, 'He said he was going to fly in, kick my ass and go right home. Hearing that made me run faster than ever.' On his dealings with Lewis, Johnson said, 'Lewis talks to his few friends, that's all. When he's winning, he doesn't need any friends. When he's losing, he seems to need more of them. He and I just nod at each other, that's it.'

Interest was developing in Johnson off the track, too, and his personality began to be put under the spotlight. 'Big Ben, shy and silent,
seemed to burst out of his shell last year,' said the *Star* in another early
profile. 'He has heard the aspersions cast upon his intellect and felt their
sting, but remains amazingly calm. Never has Johnson refused to talk to
sportswriters who had unfairly fitted Ben with that slow-learner's label.'

'Sometimes nobody asked me anything, they just assumed I was
not intelligent,' Johnson told the paper. 'I don't really take it to heart.'

Later, the writer of the piece, Al Sokol, came to feel that he had
been insensitive for even raising the IQ-issue, and mentioned it to
Johnson, who said he was hurt but relaxed: 'You repeated something
I've been hearing all my life, but that doesn't mean I'm not going to
talk to you again because I want to let you know how it was. Teachers
said I was slow and I believed them. They didn't expect much from
me and I didn't give them much. Later Charlie told me I was a pretty
smart guy and I better start acting like one, so I did. No big thing.'

Francis said of Johnson that he found him 'a really bright guy who had
difficulty expressing himself'. The question of Johnson's intellect would
come to play a big role in the Dubin Inquiry. It was also addressed, fasci-
natingly, by Issajenko in her book. She had initially put the early shyness
of the athlete she calls 'BJ' down to embarrassment over the accent and
the stutter. Later she began to have second thoughts: 'I've concluded
that Ben is also astoundingly lazy… that if he can get someone to do
something for him, he will. He used to call me at all hours of the day
and night to look up things for him in the Yellow Pages.'

Yet for Issajenko, this anecdote seems to set off alarm bells even as she
relates it. 'Maybe there's more to it. People who are functionally illiterate
often exhibit manipulative behaviour; they resort to complicated, subtle
subterfuge to mask their illiteracy. Maybe BJ couldn't read very well.'

Early in 1987, Johnson ran an astonishing 9.7-second 100m in Perth,
Australia, though it was wind-assisted and hand-timed. A month later,

he would win the world indoor title in Indianapolis, lowering his own 60m world record to 6.41, and finishing so rapidly that he was unable to stop before careening into the restraining wall 20 metres beyond the finish. He toppled over it, landing on a concrete floor. But Johnson was unbreakable: he simply got up and walked away, unhurt.

Lewis was missing from Indianapolis, but the previous month, in East Meadowlands, New Jersey, the rivals had met over an unusual distance, 55m. Lewis kicked off the meeting by regaling the crowd with a rendition of the national anthem – by now he wasn't so much juggling his two careers as melding them – before he and Johnson got down to business.

But there was a familiar problem. 'Johnson burst off the starting blocks with such astonishing force… that his five rivals were left frozen,' reported *Sports Illustrated*. 'There was just one problem. The starting gun hadn't fired.' It wasn't his only setback. In an earlier heat Johnson had destroyed his shoes: the force of his push-off from the blocks sheared off most of the spikes. The image, or caricature, of Johnson was taking shape: he was a muscle-bound brute, a dark destroyer; too eager, too strong, on occasions, for his own good.

The final, when it got underway, also carried the whiff of a false start, this time by Lee McRae, who could almost feel the thundering feet of Johnson as he held on to win by a hundredth of a second, with Lewis a further five-hundredths down. 'Lee had an absolutely phenomenal start,' said Lewis. 'I'll leave it at that.' Only, Lewis – being Lewis – couldn't leave it at that. 'Lee jumped tonight,' he later told a reporter. Which, most thought, was probably true.

Johnson's reputation was by now growing in the US, too. *Sports Illustrated* dwelt on the different backgrounds and personalities of the rivals, depicting Johnson as raw, unpolished, unsophisticated. 'In private, Johnson is shy, but in public he appears cocky,' the magazine concluded. Lewis, in contrast, was 'so much more the veteran, so much more polished'.

Lewis's new-found vulnerability was leading to more sympathetic coverage. An arthroscopy, to clear a build-up of calcium on his left knee, had been carried out in September, after his defeat to Johnson in Zurich. And the US press accepted that he had competed in pain for much of the 1986 season. The message he wanted to convey was that in 1987 he would be back to his best – and that his best would be better than Johnson's. Despite finishing only third in the 55m race at Meadowlands, Lewis affected ebullience. After the race he sped to a TV camera, leaned in and announced, 'The kid is back!'

His self-belief certainly was back. But Lewis had endured other traumas throughout 1986. His left knee was the least of it, though the injury had been well documented. Less well known was that Lewis had also been coping with the deteriorating health of his father.

Bill Lewis had been diagnosed with colon cancer after complaining of feeling unwell during the family's Christmas celebrations in 1985. The cancer was aggressive and spread quickly. Yet Bill refused to yield, even going to Moscow to watch Carl at the Goodwill Games. He adopted the maxim that action was the enemy of negative thoughts. 'We should do everything we can, go everywhere we can,' he told his son. He died on 5 May 1987, aged sixty. Carl buried his 100m Olympic gold medal with him and reassured his mother, 'Don't worry, I'll win another one.'

Lewis's faith provided succour as he came to terms with his loss. He described himself as a born-again Christian, having been introduced to the Lay Witnesses for Christ, a group for Christian athletes, by his teammate Willie Gault six years earlier. The group's founder Sam Mings had by now actively started to recruit athletes, and had a big presence at the LA Olympics, by which time Lewis had introduced his entire family to the Lay Witnesses.

But Lewis's religious affiliations became more complicated when the music producer Narada Michael Walden – who would go on to success with Whitney Houston and Aretha Franklin – introduced him to Sri Chinmoy, a spiritual teacher from Bangladesh. Chinmoy, in his early fifties, was known as 'Guru' to his followers and disciples. For Chinmoy, sport and in particular running was a form of meditation – or 'continual transcendence'. He was balding, with a horseshoe of closely cropped white hair, and an open, usually smiling face. But he demanded absolute devotion. Among his disciples, he prohibited alcohol, caffeine, smoking, drugs, TV, radio, movies, music, newspapers, magazines, books not written by him, meat, dancing and pets. They were required to remain single, too.

Such rules did not apply to his celebrity disciple. According to a former devotee, Jayanti Tamm – who paints a disturbing picture in her book, *Cartwheels in a Sari: Growing up in a Cult* – Lewis was targeted by Chinmoy, 'who wanted nothing but the best around him'. It may have been smart tactics to encourage a famous music producer to reach out to him at a time when Lewis was seeking to get his singing career off the ground.

Lewis became a regular visitor to Chinmoy's spiritual centre in New York, where, says Tamm, he was 'lavished with attention and praise; he would drop in and have all the glory and blessings of the Guru'. But he was never a true disciple: 'He was never forced to surrender and obey in the ways that the disciples who were not celebrities were mandated. His connection was on his own terms. In fact, at one time, the Guru secretly offered Carl his choice of any of the female disciples to have as his personal escort, but he declined.'

In a ceremony witnessed by Tamm, Chinmoy assigned Lewis a name: Sudhahota. It means 'unparalleled sacrificer of immortality'.

SEVILLE, 28 MAY 1987

The only confrontation between Johnson and Lewis prior to their scheduled showdown over 100m at the world championships came in the Spanish city of Seville, and was significant in at least one regard.

According to Francis, it was the first time Johnson received a higher appearance fee than Lewis. It hammered home the point that Johnson was now the main man, Lewis the challenger.

Not that you would realise this if you watch the video. Lewis, in an all-white Santa Monica Track Club strip, and Johnson, in an unfamiliar white vest and navy blue shorts, line up alongside each other, Lewis in lane four, Johnson in five, with Calvin Smith in three.

The stadium is rudimentary, the track only six lanes wide. There is a large crowd, most of them standing rather than sitting, many shielding their eyes from the sun, squinting at the start as the six runners shake out their legs and bounce up and down to stretch their hamstrings. Adding to a rustic, slightly chaotic, atmosphere, a line of spectators flank the outer edge of the track. They can lean into lane six, and touch the athletes. It is a world away from the polished sterility of the Olympics: this bears more resemblance to school sports day, or bare-knuckle fighting. It feels raw and authentic. It will be the last time Johnson and Lewis face each other in such a low-key meeting.

Just before they are called to the blocks, Lewis does something that would become a habit. He steps forward and moves up and down the line, from lane one to lane six, shaking each of his competitors by the hand. It seems designed to establish him as the boss: the champion rather than the challenger. As they go through their last-minute routines, he and Johnson seem supremely aware of the other.

To see them run side-by-side is to appreciate the contrast in styles. Johnson powers out of the start, his arms flailing outwards as though he is using his hands as paddles, while Lewis takes a few paces to extend to full height, his arms pumping in smoother, straighter lines. But by then Johnson is half a metre up and the gap is widening. At halfway Johnson is running away with it. But after 60 metres, Lewis seems to suddenly shift gear. The gap narrows, then it starts to close. And as he homes in on Johnson, Lewis drifts towards his rival, running at the outer edge of his lane, and lunging for the line from three metres out, throwing his head forward. Johnson remains upright, chest out, head tilted back; he looks relaxed. Both think they've got it. Lewis throws an arm in the air, a gesture reminiscent of a boxer who suspects he's been defeated but celebrates in a desperate bid to influence the judges.

Johnson appears oblivious to Lewis's reaction: he casually decelerates before he reaches the bank of photographers camped beyond the line, then he turns, smiles shyly, and waves, acknowledging the applause. He knows he got it.

And he's right. The official times have Johnson at 10.06, Lewis at 10.07. But Lewis is furious and continues to insist he's won.

'Look, clown,' Johnson tells him. 'Let's run another one right now – then you'll know who won.' The atmosphere becomes heated, with Johnson and Lewis almost squaring up to each other until Mel Lattany, the retired American sprinter, intervenes, pulling Johnson away. 'Carl seemed to be confused over who won the race today,' Johnson said later. 'Next time I'll make sure he isn't confused.' The next time would be in Rome, at the world championships.

As well as the Johnson–Lewis showdown there was another hot topic in Seville. The news broke that David Jenkins had been arrested for his involvement in steroid smuggling. It was the talk of track and field.

'Jenkins sold his soul,' says David Jenkins, staring at the ceiling of his San Diego home. He is quoting Sir Arthur Gold, former chairman of the British Olympic Association. 'He's right. I did,' Jenkins adds. 'Sir Arthur said about me, "He was a very charming man, and he could be a very disturbed man" – and he was correct.'

The news of Jenkins's arrest, and the revelation of what this former athlete had been doing for the last few years, provided a jolt to the sport in both Europe and the US. Drugs and doping were by now regularly talked about in the media, but often in a way that suggested the issue was more hypothetical than real. There had been whispers, and the positive tests and mass exodus from the 1983 Pan-Am Games in Caracas caused a brief splash, but no big name from the West had been implicated, far less caught.

And that reinforced an important subtext to the debate: that doping was a foreign problem, specifically an Eastern European problem. For at least a decade suspicion had centred squarely on the Eastern Bloc, in particular the Soviet Union and East Germany. With good reason: the truth that emerged after the Berlin Wall fell was far more horrific than anyone imagined.

But there was an assumption that drugs were purely a Communist phenomenon. This was best expressed in remarkable comments made by Brooks Johnson, the US national track and field coach, in the official programme to the US indoor championships in 1984. 'It is evident that our country is gifted with the best natural athletes,' Johnson asserted. 'Others have sought to overcome this advantage with performance-enhancing drugs – and, to a very large measure, they have been successful in neutralising, even overcoming, our inherent superiority.'

The case of David Jenkins ought to have ended the complacency. Jenkins was different. He didn't come from behind the Iron Curtain; he wasn't some faceless product, with an unpronounceable name, of a ruthless sporting machine. He was a respectable, middle-class boy from Edinburgh, an Olympic medallist for Britain who now lived in California. As Jenkins says, his own use of steroids turned him into 'a liar, a cheat... immoral... self-centred... a mess'. Yet, as he also acknowledges, 'I had the benefit of an intellect, a great education, resources.' So what happened?

After running at the 1978 Commonwealth Games, Jenkins drifted in and out of the sport. Always a spiky, independent character, he also fell out with the British federation, and was suspended for running at an unauthorised meeting. He began working for Reebok, the sportswear manufacturer. And he kept running to keep in shape; and he kept taking drugs. He had moved on to small doses of another anabolic steroid, Stromba, in which the active substance is Stanozolol. It was

149

prescribed, he says, by a National Health Service doctor. In 1979 he stepped up his training and was reinstated for national competition, but still banned from international meetings. And then came a phone call from Andy Norman, British athletics' powerful promotions officer, asking him if he fancied racing in Houston.

Jenkins told him that he was barred from competing abroad. 'I'll take care of that,' said Norman. Jenkins ran the 400m in Houston and finished third. Then he called the British coach, Frank Dick, and asked to be considered for the Moscow Olympics. The following season he ran the Olympic trials and qualified. It meant he had to submit a urine sample for drug-testing. This did not bother him because he knew he had been off steroids long enough and was currently just taking testosterone, which was not a problem. He did not go back on steroids for Moscow, but came to wish that he had.

At the Olympics he was ill, 'shitting blood the day before the final', and could only finish seventh. Then, still simmering with resentment from his earlier feud with the British federation, he refused to run in the relay. It was a point of principle that Jenkins came to regret. 'In hindsight, I should have done the relay,' he says. 'My gripe was with British athletics, not these guys. They had a shot at a medal too. But I refused to run. So be it. That was it.' He was twenty-eight.

After retiring from athletics, Jenkins married an American woman and they moved to San Diego. In Britain, Jenkins had established a business installing gyms and health clubs: 'A lovely earner,' he says. But moving to America meant starting a new career. Soon he was selling protein tablets to trainers and coaches – strength coaches, mainly, looking after bodybuilders and gym rats.

But Jenkins was also in demand by athletes. It is often said that athletes know which of their competitors are using drugs, and so it may have been well known within the sport that Jenkins had used steroids. He says that, from about 1982, he spoke regularly and openly to athletes on the subject. 'By now it was open season,' says Jenkins.

'You'd sit down and talk over a beer. People would ask, "What's this, what's that, what's he using?" The conversation isn't about girls or music, or who you've fucked. It's just drugs. Questions like, "Who do you know?" and, "Jenkins, can you find me this?" And I was being approached by doctors, too.

'They're all coming at me. It's not the drugs they're wanting – they can go and get the drugs. It's the information they want: about the drugs, their half-life – how long they remain in the system – the testing.'

Thus did Jenkins acquire the role of steroids guru. But to fulfil that role, and the expectations of him, he had to learn. In those pre-internet days, that was a little harder than it might be now, but not much. 'I was just digging around. All that actually meant was going to the medical library, putting a word in the frickin' search facility and up come the papers! I'd get these, highlight bits, and put them in the mail to whoever had asked for the information.'

On one side of the fence, then, taking his own crash course in performance enhancing drugs prior to the Los Angeles Olympics was Don Catlin. And on the other was David Jenkins. (Although Catlin told me, with a resigned air, that he believed there to be many more David Jenkinses than Don Catlins.) Jenkins says he advised several athletes who competed at the LA Games. 'And a couple of them did very well in 1984. Very well. I mean, medals. Not in track, in field.'

'I realised there was a ton of this information out there,' explains Jenkins. 'And then I contacted Duchaine.' He met Dan Duchaine, author of *The Underground Steroid Handbook* and owner of the most muscle-bound cat in Venice Beach, in 1986. 'I'd been working on a book, about performance enhancement in sport. I wrote to Dan, he called me, and I told him what was going on. He said, "You gotta come and see me." So I went to meet him. It was like, frickin', meeting Hitler – or a visitation thereof. I went to see him in Venice for lunch. Lovely restaurant. Then he showed me his place; it was wacky. He was a radical guy.'

Soon after they met Jenkins got a call from Duchaine who told him, 'My connection just got busted in San Francisco.'

'OK, so?'

'Can you get steroids? I need Dianabol. Soon as you can get them.'

Again, Jenkins did his research. His search took him, almost inevitably, only a few miles from his home, to the Mexican border. He was driven to Tijuana in beaten-up cars by beaten-up guys to meet the lab-owner Juan Javier Macklis, who gave him a tour of the lab. Then he was served afternoon tea. Macklis told him, 'I can make anything. I won't make methamphetamines. But steroids, I can make.'

Jenkins immediately ordered 5,000 bottles, and called Duchaine to say, 'I need $25,000.' He paid Macklis $12,500 up front. Six weeks later the consignment was collected from the lab: $2,500 was paid to one of Duchaine's connections on the border, then Jenkins took possession and delivered the 5,000 bottles of Dianabol to Duchaine.

A week later, Duchaine called again, 'Can you get me 60,000 bottles?' It was a $300,000 order, the first of many. But, although Jenkins had provided athletes with advice, he insists he didn't supply them with drugs, or not directly. All his dealings were with Duchaine. And the steroids were bound for gyms, not just in California, but throughout the US. Duchaine had connections in almost every state.

But Jenkins did not merely organise the transfer of money and drugs. He also arranged for the raw materials to be delivered to the lab, where Macklis would turn them into steroids and bottle them. He was buying the ingredients from wherever he could find them, some coming from Morpeth in Northumberland. The raw materials would be flown in by British Airways, freight-forwarded to the Mexican border, then transported to the lab and back again.

Jenkins laughs. 'Morpeth! On BA flights! In ten-kilo drums, all sealed, with the chemical name on it.'

This was 1986. He was arrested in April 1987. So the business didn't last long. Jenkins says he suspected the authorities were on to him after nine months, around Christmas 1986. Jenkins had told his wife what he was doing, but no one else. What was it like living like that, I ask him. 'Well,' he says, 'there was the fear and there was excitement. The excitement was getting the orders, getting the money, running the cash machine.' He thumbs through wads of imaginary bank notes, making the sound effects, 'Trrrrrrrrr, trrrrrrrrr.'

'The fear,' Jenkins continues, turning serious, 'came from recognising the consequences. The fear is watching a movie and seeing people shot for $50,000, when I'm carrying $90,000 in the back of my car in a brown paper bag. Never mind the law. I would watch these movies and feel very fearful.' Jenkins shudders again.

At Christmas, 1986, Jenkins drove to Palm Springs, where his wife's family had a holiday home. He had told his in-laws – and most of his friends – that he was in the 'plastics business, producing plastic bottles in Mexico'. He pauses then adds, 'which was true, because we were making our own bottles. I just didn't tell them what they were filled with...

'I knew it was wrong. I was getting worried. I decided I wanted out. The operation was going to be shut down. The last deal was half a million bucks or something like that.' But at around this time, Jenkins answered a request to meet a bodybuilder from Ohio, who wanted to discuss proteins, minerals and multi-vitamins. Jenkins was running a legitimate business in supplements on the side. The bodybuilder brought an acquaintance with him, and they discussed protein, before moving on to talk about steroids.

But the men were not bodybuilders; they were federal agents. Shortly afterwards, the connections were arrested. Nothing happened for six weeks, which Jenkins spent in a state of rising panic: 'By now I'm surviving on sleeping pills.' He knew what was coming, as with a tsunami that is just over the horizon. But for six weeks: nothing, other than silent panic.

Later, Jenkins drives me to a restaurant in Oceanside, and, en route, he points out the spot where he was arrested, on the way home from running his legitimate protein business. He was in the federal holding prison, awaiting trial ('shitting myself, peeing myself'), for four and a half months. When news emerged of Jenkins's arrest it was reported that his steroid ring accounted for 70 per cent of the US market, and that it was worth £300 million. Nonsense, says Jenkins; had they had that much they could have lowered their prices and ensured a complete monopoly. 'The 70 per cent thing... that was just prosecutorial talk.'

It would be an exaggeration to describe the news as a wake-up call. It was a small shock, no more. Nevertheless, it is possible that David Jenkins's arrest nudged the drugs debate a little higher up the agenda in the build-up to the Rome world championships.

At the same time, another story emerged from Italy. Alessandro Donati, Italy's national sprint coach, gave an interview to *L'Espresso* and asserted, without naming names, that some leading Italian athletes were using drugs. Donati would later come to be hailed as an important whistle-blower. But at the time his claims seemed easily dismissed. *The Times* suggested that Donati 'raised the spectre of doping to deflect criticism of poor Italian performances in the sprints'.

Donati wasn't the only one concerned about doping. On the eve of the championships, the IAAF congress in Rome announced what looked like a serious move: the introduction of year-round drug-testing, instead of confining tests to competitions. The intention, said Arne Ljungqvist, head of the medical commission, was 'to chase the cheaters into their training havens and catch them red-handed... We are fully aware that people are working on substances which conceal the use of drugs. And we are equally aware that many athletes take drugs for a given period and then stop before official competitions so they can't be detected.' Actually, one country had been ahead of the game, at least in intent. An out-of-competition testing programme had been approved by the Canadian Track and Field Association, to be implemented in October 1986. However, it didn't get out of the blocks, perhaps thanks to Charlie Francis's opposition. In private he protested to the CTFA that it would be self-defeating unless other countries followed suit. In the end, it was implemented – but not till after Seoul.

Out-of-competition testing sounded like a positive step, and the timing – on the eve of a meeting that meant so much to Primo Nebiolo, the IAAF's Italian president – was perfect. It sent out a clear statement – that the governing body meant business. But, at least in the short term, nothing came of it.

Perhaps more significant was a less politicised, lower-profile, meeting in Florence, attended by scientific professionals interested in drugs in athletics. A Canadian delegate rose to demand that the IAAF stop the fixing of test results. This was Doug Clement, a former Olympic middle-distance runner who was both a coach and a doctor, and present as a representative of the Canadian Olympic Association. He admits now that his question was based merely on 'things I'd heard, rumours', rather than concrete evidence.

But Clement had his suspicions, some of them uncomfortably close to home. He says he got to know Charlie Francis when Francis was an athlete and found him, even then, 'more than curious about the effect of drugs. He was like a sponge, soaking up all the information he could. He asked a lot of questions.'

Yet Clement rejects the suggestion that Francis's methods were an open secret within the Canadian athletics community. After 1988, it was reported that Francis had been known by many of his peers as 'Charlie the Chemist'. Clement says that wasn't as widely known as was reported. Besides, Francis was hardly the only one implicated by rumour: 'When you saw anyone doing well the suspicion was there.'

Clement was an early advocate of out-of-competition testing and a staunch opponent of doping, and yet he says, 'I do understand very clearly why Charlie, in his own mind, could justify what he was doing. But it came with a huge risk. You're going to get caught eventually.'

But knowing – or thinking he knew – the extent of the doping problem put Clement in a difficult position. By 1987 he resigned as doctor to the Canadian team and reverted to coaching, in which capacity he travelled to Rome with his wife, Diane, a former Olympic sprinter who was the Canadian team's media manager.*

Ben Johnson was in their party too, and he arrived in Rome as many people's favourite for the 100m. The case for that seemed irresistible. There was his victory over Lewis in Seville, of course, but also his scintillating form since then. In Ottawa in early August he ran the fastest 100 of the year in 9.98; and two weeks later, in Koblenz, the second fastest, 10-flat into a headwind. 'If I'd had a nice tailwind, I could have broken the world record,' he said. He was on a roll. Two nights later, in Cologne, Johnson went even closer to the world record, clocking 9.95 to equal his personal best, and finishing so fast that he was unable to stop before hitting a photographer camped about ten metres beyond the line.

The collision sent Johnson sprawling on to the track and Francis into a panic. 'I thought ten years' work was in ruins,' said Francis. With Johnson grounded, the other cameramen rushed forward, crowding around to get pictures of the stricken athlete. Meanwhile, Francis attempted to reach Johnson – only to be pushed out of the way by another of the photographers. Johnson, seeing his coach jostled, sprang up and punched the aggressor. As *The Times* put it, 'Since Johnson is built like a brick outhouse, the argument ended there.'

At the US national championships in San Jose, meanwhile, the recently bereaved Carl Lewis was focusing more on the long jump, though he failed, once again, to break Bob Beamon's world record and had to be content, instead, with his fifty-first consecutive victory in the event. 'I've concentrated more on the long jump this year,' said

---

* Diane Clement, who competed in the 1956 Olympics, had stood for election to the IAAF ruling council in 1972, only narrowly losing. The man who scraped on to the council instead was Primo Nebiolo. Had Clement beaten Nebiolo, the sport's history might have been very different.

Lewis, 'and I will be doing so even more next season. I can still do it.' He meant the world record; though it never came.

After winning the 200m, Lewis felt a twinge in his hamstring, which threatened his participation in the 100m – unusually the 100 followed the 200. He ran, but in a compromised state, and finished second (in 10.06) to his six-foot-five Santa Monica clubmate, Mark Witherspoon. Both Witherspoon and Lewis wore black ribbons in memory of Bill Lewis. And a *Sports Illustrated* writer noticed a touchingly intimate exchange between Lewis and his mother. While Carl was talking to reporters after the 100m final, Evelyn drew him away, 'putting an arm around him, rubbing the small of his back, comforting and being comforted'.

Back in Europe, Johnson, unperturbed by the bruised shoulder and back suffered in the collision with the photographer, travelled to Zurich, winning the 100m there with yet another sub-10-second run: 9.97. That was good enough to beat the world record holder, Calvin Smith, who posted 10.07. Unusually, Johnson had a poor start in Zurich; he was also running into another stiff headwind. Some estimated his 9.97 equal to 9.87 in more favourable conditions.

Lewis, after winning the long jump at the Pan-Am Games in Indianapolis, was by now on his way to Europe, and he appeared in West Berlin three days later to take on Smith over 200m, winning in 20.09. Johnson ran in West Berlin, too. And he and Lewis did run the same event – but not together. In the 4x100m relay, Johnson ran the first leg for Canada, while Lewis ran the anchor leg for the USA.

This set it up nicely. Their only showdown would come in Rome.

'The Johnson–Lewis match has stirred the popular imagination and evoked comparison with Ali–Frazier and Borg–McEnroe,' wrote *The Times'* athletics correspondent Pat Butcher. The nearest comparison in athletics, reckoned Butcher, was the Jim Hines–Charlie Green rivalry at the Mexico Olympics. 'Hines proved the faster, but Green was the funnier. He ran in jet-black shades, which in the then new space-age terminology, he referred to as "re-entry shields". His first comment on finishing second was, "I decided to lose."'

Butcher described Johnson's gradual, year-on-year improvement, attributing it to Francis's four-hours-a-day training regime, including ninety minutes each day of 'lifting the heaviest weights'. The intention, Francis told him, was to improve Johnson's ability to sprint flat out for the full 100m, rather than the 60 he had managed at the Los Angeles Olympics.

'When he was younger he'd get as far as 40 metres, then have a heart attack. In the Olympics he got to 60 – and still finished third. Now he's ready to go all the way. The idea is to extend the energy package available, but working to higher and higher rates, and learning to tolerate them. If we pull this off, we'll send everybody back to the drawing board,' said Francis.

Lewis, meanwhile, insisted his four consecutive defeats to Johnson had not left him demoralised. 'I always intended to have a couple of low-key years after the last world championships and the Olympics,' he said. 'The strain of that completely drained me.' Perhaps it was foolish to write off Lewis. After all, in Seville, in his only meeting with Johnson prior to the world championships, he had finished only a hundredth of a second behind him. In Rome, said Lewis, 'with successive rounds – heats, semis, final – I'm just going to get better'.

Johnson responded by pointing out that at the previous year's Commonwealth Games in Edinburgh, in chilly conditions, he ran four rounds before claiming the title in 10.07. In his last five races, Johnson had averaged an astonishing 9.975 seconds. And in Seville, said Charlie Francis, Johnson had been nursing a calf strain. 'Lewis did not see the Ben you see today,' said Francis. He predicted that in Rome, Johnson – who claimed he abstained from having sex in the build-up to the championships – could run 9.85.

That sounded fanciful, on both counts: the abstinence and the time – 9.85? Impossible.

SATURDAY, 29 AUGUST 1987

In Rome's Stadio Olimpico, built under orders from Mussolini, it was a latter-day Italian dictator, Primo Nebiolo, who beamed with pride as the second World Athletics Championships got underway. These championships, bigger and bolder than Helsinki's, would reflect both Nebiolo's vision and the dark underbelly of his ambition. The major controversy in Rome involved a long jump that was falsely measured to get an Italian a bronze medal.

John Holt, Nebiolo's long-suffering general secretary at the IAAF, describes the incident, involving a blameless athlete called Giovanni Evangelisti, as the low point of Nebiolo's tenure. 'He had to have his finger in every pie, which is what got him into trouble eventually, with the Evangelisti case,' says Holt. Yet somehow Nebiolo survived the controversy, even as the Italian press pursued the truth of the rigged long jump with impressive doggedness. It was eventually resolved with poor Evangelisti's bronze medal being rescinded, and awarded instead to Larry Myricks.

On the eve of the championships, Nebiolo's big hope – apart from Italian success – was to see a world record in one of the blue riband events. The 100m would fit the bill very nicely. In a pre-event dinner, Nebiolo pulled Carl Lewis to one side, and told him, 'This is going to be the greatest meet of all time.' Then he told him how much he wanted Lewis to bless the championships with a new world record. 'A few minutes later,' said Lewis, 'I saw him talking to Ben Johnson, probably saying the same thing.'

Nebiolo was beginning to seem untouchable, not least because, as the championships got underway, he was poised to join the most exclusive club in world sport. He had been proposed by Ollan Cassel, the executive director of USA Track and Field, for membership of the International Olympic Committee, despite the fact that Italy already had its quota of one member, Franco Carraro, the former water-skier and future mayor of Rome. Juan Antonio Samaranch was keen to make an exception on the basis – as Nebiolo had consistently, if self-servingly, argued – that the man in charge of the biggest Olympic sport should sit at the IOC's top table. In bending so obligingly to Nebiolo's will, Samaranch may also have been guided by the old maxim: keep your friends close, and your enemies closer.

In Rome there seemed no end to Nebiolo's power and influence. But there is no doubt that he had also created a fantastic sporting occasion. After three successive Olympics diminished by boycotts, and some doubt as to whether the Communist bloc would attend Seoul the following year, here was an event for athletics to savour. 'Everybody who is anybody is here,' said the *New York Times*, adding that one event 'stands out by the sheer force and electricity of the two favourites, Lewis and Johnson in the 100'.

Johnson flew to Rome from Berlin, picking up an in-flight magazine which had a lengthy feature on his rivalry with Lewis. In Francis's view it was typical of many articles: pro-Lewis, anti-Johnson. (He obviously hadn't read the American press on Lewis in 1984.) Francis said that Johnson read, simmering with anger, that his 'greatest task lay not in realising his obvious sprinting ability, but in overcoming an almost debilitating stutter'. The article continued, 'It seemed almost symbolic: while Lewis was smooth and polished in every respect, Johnson was struggling and faltering.'

As they stepped off the plane, Francis asked, 'Ben, did you read that thing?'

'Yeah,' said Johnson.

'Are you angry?'

'Yeah.'

Later, Johnson told *Sports Illustrated* that this article 'became part of my race in Rome'. And so did Lewis's wooing of the international press, as word reached Johnson of his rival's champagne-fuelled media conference, held in the hills overlooking the Vatican, at the sumptuous Villa Miani.

Lewis's charm offensive formed part of Joe Douglas's latest marketing push for his man, pitching Lewis as friendly and accessible, as opposed to aloof and arrogant – the main charges against him at the Los Angeles Olympics. It seemed to work, with, as the days counted down, many in the media apparently dismissing the form book and backing the reigning world and Olympic champion. Lewis, not Johnson, was installed as the favourite, the rationale being that Johnson was fast but unproven in a major championship. *L'Equipe* went so far as to say, '*Tu ne peux pas le faire, Ben.*' (You can't do it, Ben.)

'Do you think Ben can become number one?' Francis was asked in one press conference.

'He's been number one for two years now,' Francis responded.

Heats for the men's 100m got underway on the second day of competition: seven qualifying heats began the process of whittling the fifty-six entrants down to the eight who would contest the following day's final. It was Lewis who made the more explosive start: 10.05 in his qualifying heat, a championship record, despite easing up in the final 10 metres and almost jogging across the line. Johnson was also fast out the blocks, easing up at the end: a comfortable victory in 10.24. He backed that up with 10.14 in the next round, finishing a close second to Ray Stewart, the promising Jamaican. Then Lewis reduced his record: 10.03. He was certainly running like a favourite. 'Lewis usually ran faster than he needed to in the heats,' claimed Francis, 'the better to intimidate the opposition.'

Or as Johnson later put it: 'The way Carl was runnin' the heats, he was settin' me up. But the time to do my running is in the final.'

The two favourites won their semi-finals on the Sunday afternoon, to set up their inevitable meeting in the final, just an hour-and-a-half later. Francis, nursing a tooth abscess brought on by the stress of the occasion, almost suffered cardiac arrest when he discovered Johnson lying, snoozing on the massage table of his physiotherapist,

Waldemar Matuszewski, in the ninety minutes between the semi and the final. 'You better start warming up,' Francis told him. 'Everyone else is out there.'

'It's hot out there,' Johnson said, slowly lifting himself off the table. 'It only takes a few minutes to warm up... Don't worry, I'm ready.'

SUNDAY, 30 AUGUST 1987, 6.40 P.M.

Johnson, in all-red, Lewis, in all-blue, line up in adjacent lanes, as they had done in Seville: Johnson in five, Lewis in six. And as they settle in the blocks the contrast between them is again apparent. Johnson low-slung, arms bent and set wide, resting on his haunches, head up, looking alert; Lewis upright, poised, arms straight, head down, staring at the track.

The start is astounding. When the gun goes, so does Johnson. ('Johnson reacted with such brutal suddenness that there will eternally be questions about this start' as *Sports Illustrated* would put it.) He is away quicker than the others – even the naked eye can see that. Francis said that Johnson's technique was to hold his breath in the final moments before the gun, creating absolute silence in his head, allowing no sound to distract him. Yet when I put that to him, Johnson shakes his head and says no: he was simply born with lightning reactions.

In Rome he appears to hear the gun before the others do. That's not quite the case: he flings his arms out and lunges forward, as his feet spring from the blocks, 0.129 seconds after the gun. Lewis reacts nearly seven-hundredths of a second later, in 0.196 seconds. As Francis would later say, 'The race is as good as over after the runners' first stride.' Johnson blasts out, Lewis follows, always a step behind. After 20 metres, just as Lewis is extending to his full height, he's a full metre down. He pursues Johnson, but raggedly, with a hint of desperation – style abandoned in favour of function. He surges in the final 20 metres – or appears to; in fact, the appearance is deceptive. They are all decelerating by now, but Lewis far less than the others. And although the gap shrinks, Johnson doesn't let up: he certainly doesn't die at 60 metres, he drives through the line, no celebrations this time.

The clock stops at 9.84. Then the time is adjusted: 9.83. A world record by a full tenth of a second, with Lewis chasing Johnson all the way to a personal best of 9.93, Calvin Smith's old world record, now history. Ray Stewart is third, Linford Christie fourth, adding an historic footnote to the world title race: three of the first four finishers had been born in Jamaica.

In the press area, Johnson's run is greeted by stunned silence. 'Normally the media are as infused with excitement as the general public by athletic excellence, if not more so,' says Doug Gillon. 'When Johnson did that, I can remember there was a silence in the press box. It's maybe too trite to say it was a silence of disbelief, but certainly there was open-jawed amazement at what we'd just witnessed. He had smashed the record and won by a street.'

After winning, Johnson kept running. It was as though the race continued, with Lewis pursuing him, eventually catching him and shaking his hand. He was gracious in defeat. Or was he? 'Carl wanted people to think he was congratulating me,' says Johnson now. 'But he looked me in the eye and accused me of getting a false start.'

Lewis would continue to pursue this argument, arguing that Johnson 'tricked' the starter and the electronic pads on the blocks, which detect changes in pressure, by throwing his arms and body forward before his feet left the blocks. He and Tom Tellez studied the start for months. 'Ben's hands are off the ground before anyone moves,' Tellez said. 'The naked eye says he's jumping, but he's not putting pressure on the foot blocks until after the gun. And it's the sensors in the blocks that detect a false start.' Charlie Francis described

Tellez's theory as 'preposterous, a physical impossibility – an affront to both Ben and Isaac Newton'.

When Johnson finally stopped jogging and celebrating he was interviewed by Dwight Stones for NBC. 'You said you'd run 9.85 and you ran 9.83,' said Stones, as incredulous as everyone else in the Stadio Olimpico.

'Yeah,' said Johnson to millions of viewers across prim middle America. 'I don't talk shit.'

Lewis, meanwhile, was fuming, and not only because of his belief that Johnson had got a false start. According to Joe Douglas, the Lewis camp's suspicion of Johnson's steroid use peaked in Rome. 'I knew,' says Douglas, 'that when his eyes are swollen and watery, he's on drugs. I knew Ben Johnson was on drugs. I can't tell you who told me, but one of Charlie's athletes told me. Plus, Ben put on weight and ran faster. You cannot do that. It's impossible, unless you take something to increase the force. But in Rome I heard he used a masking agent.'

Lewis recalled in his book being approached by Douglas on the track, minutes before the 100m final. 'He was a wreck,' said Lewis of his manager. 'He had heard something very disturbing, but he wouldn't tell me what until after the race because he didn't want to distract me.' It didn't work: Lewis says he was distracted. But, later, Douglas told him that that a US coach had overheard a conversation between Francis and another American track coach, in which Francis had said, 'I'm not worried, I'm just going to say that Ben had gonorrhoea.'

To Douglas, and the eavesdropping US coach, that suggested one thing: that he was using the in-vogue masking agent Probenecid, which was a treatment for gout or gonorrhoea. But Manfred Donike had established its steroid-masking properties earlier in 1987, prompting him to write to all IOC-accredited dope-testing laboratories, asking them to test for it. Two cases were discovered at the Pan-Am Games in Indianapolis, a month before the World Athletics Championships, but much to Donike's annoyance no action was taken. Probenecid was not yet banned, but Donike was pushing hard for its inclusion on the IOC list of prohibited products.*

But there is another, more important question. Was Johnson even tested in Rome?

After his celebrations and interviews, Johnson was whisked away by Primo Nebiolo, whose day had been made by the world record. He wanted to enjoy the moment with Johnson, and took him out for dinner.

Doug Clement recalls that his wife Diane, as part of the Canadian team management, received a phone call that evening, at around 11 p.m. It was from doping control, asking, 'Where is Ben Johnson?' 'Normally,' says Clement, 'dope control happens immediately the event is over. The athlete has an hour to report to the testing room. There's a drug-testing assistant – a chaperone – assigned to that person, to lead them to dope control, even while they're doing media interviews. But in Rome I believe Johnson had been taken away by Nebiolo to do a TV interview, and the chaperone seemed to miss the boat.

'Was Ben Johnson ever tested in Rome? I don't know.'

But he saw something that left a more indelible impression. Next to the Olympic Stadium was one of Mussolini's smaller excesses, the Stadio dei Marmi, the Stadium of the Marbles, filled with statues depicting athletes in classical poses, which during the championships was being used as a warm-up arena. 'Inside it was a catacomb-like area, lots of little rooms,' recalls Clement. 'They were dark and dingy, there were multiple caves. I was in there with some athletes and we went into one of these little caves. There were syringes everywhere. All over the floor. It was a like a drug den.'

---

* Probenecid was at the centre of controversy at the following year's Tour de France, when the overall leader, Pedro Delgado, tested positive. Although by then banned by the IOC, Probenecid had not yet been added to cycling's banned list. Delgado was exonerated and won the Tour.

It *was* a drug den – and a metaphor for the sport. In the sunshine of the Stadio Olimpico the triumphant championships were played out in front of 75,000 people; near by, in the shadows of the statues that adorned the Stadio dei Marmi, lay the dingy reality.

Yet the drug issue did get a public airing, and to a huge audience. It was provided by Carl Lewis. Three days after the 100m, as he prepared for the long jump, Lewis gave an interview to ITV in Britain. Broadcast on *News at Ten*, the channel's flagship programme, he gave the subject a public prominence it had never previously had. 'I feel a strange air at these championships,' said Lewis. 'A lot of people have come out of nowhere and are running unbelievably, and I just don't think they're doing it without drugs. It's worse than ever. There are gold medallists at this meet that are on drugs... We have always run away from the problem. We haven't been facing the issue... I'm not bitter or angry at anyone in this sport. But there is a problem, and it is a problem that we must resolve to clean up... '

Lewis's comments made headlines worldwide. And they were interpreted as a not-very-thinly veiled attack on Johnson. In fact, they would have been interpreted as a far more direct attack had the whole interview been broadcast. Edited out, on legal advice, was this comment, 'If I were taking drugs, I could do a 9.80 right away – just like him.' Charlie Francis, when asked to comment, stressed Johnson's decade of hard work, and his gradual improvement. 'Ben races so much and is tested so much, how can they say he is on drugs?' said an indignant Francis. 'I think Carl is lucky no one has sued him yet.'

Lewis was quizzed again as he returned to the stadium and success-fully defended his world long jump title. 'I don't think it's fair to point the finger or stab anyone in particular in the back,' he said when pressed for names. 'These people are definitely going to get caught. The time has come to step up the effort to stop drugs in sport. But it seems we aren't making any ground at all. The main culprits are the second-class athletes who do it to try and catch up.' The list of positives from Rome seemed to back him up: there were eight in total, two for the stimulant Ephedrine, six for steroids, but no big names.

If Lewis had won the 100m then his comments would have been less easily dismissed. But, given that they followed his defeat by Johnson, they sounded like sour grapes. Johnson certainly appeared untouched, and untouchable, as he looked forward to the riches ahead. Inevitably, it meant that he could look forward to earning millions. Equally inevitably, it meant that his entourage was expanding. He had a new agent, Larry Heidebrecht, a former coach who had earned notoriety the previous year when he was sacked by the University of Texas-El Paso for making payments to athletes. 'Anyone who knows anything about track knows that these things have been going on since 1970,' said Heidebrecht.

Still, it made him almost unemployable as a coach. Instead, he joined a private marketing firm in Virginia. And in Rome, within a year of launching his new career, he had the fastest man in the world on his books and a glut of endorsements, including a supermarket chain, an air courier, a vitamin company and Johnson Outboard Motors. Johnson was also beginning to rival Lewis's marketability in Japan, and after Rome he surpassed him, with sponsors including Visa, Johnson's Wax, Mazda and a Japanese oil and gas company. But Rome guaranteed him – and Heidebrecht – the biggest deal in athletics history: a four-year contract worth $2.3 million with Diadora. Gratifyingly, that was – so Johnson claims – twice what Lewis was paid by Mizuno, the Japanese sponsor he had joined after falling out with Nike.

Even if reporters shared Lewis's suspicions about Johnson they found themselves in an impossible position. There was plenty of what Doug Gillon calls 'informed scepticism' but that was nowhere near enough to enable them to write anything. The simple fact – the publishable fact – was that Johnson appeared to be a phenomenon. Now he wasn't just the fastest man in the world: he was the fastest man in history.

He basked in the acclaim in Rome, symbolically taking up residence on Monte Mario, in the plush retreat from which Lewis had looked ahead to the championships. In the immaculate hilltop grounds of the Villa Miani, it was now Johnson's turn to host journalists, even inviting them, in one stunt organised by his sponsors, to test their starting ability against his. Three British reporters – Gillon, Simon Turnbull and Mike Collett – earned bragging rights by achieving what Lewis had failed to do, beating the new world record holder out of the blocks.

Johnson was so relaxed and on top of the world that he could afford to indulge the hacks. But when he spoke about his run, he was serious. 'This record is one of the best ever in athletics,' said the 9.83-second man. 'I don't think anyone will break it in the next fifty years.'

He paused for a heartbeat, then added, 'Other than me.'

PART THREE
SEOUL

'The only people who will be caught for drugs
will be the careless or the ill-advised.'
SIR ARTHUR GOLD

10

DODGING

'All I know is that I'm running better than ever.
And Ben isn't running at all.'
CARL LEWIS

'I want to beat him in Zurich, then his mind is all screwed up.'
BEN JOHNSON

Ben Johnson, after winning the world title and becoming the fastest man in history, kept running. But not against Carl Lewis.

In the weeks after Rome, Johnson seemed to be running away from Lewis. He went to extraordinary lengths to avoid him. At a meeting in Rieti, just outside Rome, Lewis made an unannounced appearance and declared his intention to run the 100 against Johnson. He was apparently as keen for a Rome rematch as Johnson and his advisers were to avoid one. But the ambush didn't work. At Johnson's insistence, the meeting organiser staged two separate 100s – heats with no final.

In Brussels, with Johnson and Lewis both down to run the 200, the same thing happened – two separate races were arranged, one each. They travelled on to Lausanne, where Lewis ran in the 100, while Johnson took part in a specially arranged 60m. Lewis was scathing of Johnson in his book, and claimed the Swiss public were, too. 'After

Ben won his ridiculous little 60, the crowd whistled, and Ben took off, leaving the stadium without the traditional victory ceremony.'

Johnson freely admits that he was dodging Lewis, and says he had good reasons for doing so – but he will not say what they were. 'Carl had a lot of supporters,' he says cryptically. 'When I picked my races, and said, "I want to race here," Charlie said, "No, you're not going there." I said, "Why not?" Charlie said, "Because Carl and the promoter are friends." So we tried to get away from the rivalry. And people said, "Ben Johnson's afraid of Carl Lewis." No, I'm not afraid of him. I just know what people out there are capable of doing.'

Johnson says he felt plotted against. At whose instigation, he doesn't say. But he really felt people were out to get him? 'That's right, yeah.'

After Rome, relations were not just frosty; they were openly hostile. They had never really spoken, not normally, through all those years of competing alongside each other, waiting together in call rooms and warm-up areas, running in adjacent lanes, standing side-by-side on podiums. They never shared what could be described as a conversation, insists Johnson. Unless you count this one, in Brussels, when they ran their separate 200s. The promoter's son had a Porsche. Johnson said he came across a commotion outside the hotel lobby and discovered that Lewis had taken the Porsche for a test drive. Johnson asked if he could go next. 'No problem,' said the owner. According to Johnson, 'the car came back, Carl got out, and I said, "Carl, can I have the key so I can test drive it?" He said, "You'll have to ask the owner first."' Which was perhaps a reasonable and responsible answer. But as he relates the story, Johnson looks disgusted. 'Carl wouldn't give me the key. So I said, "Forget it."

'That's it. That's the only conversation we ever had.'

Apart from Johnson's fears about set-ups or sabotage, there was another reason for the pair to avoid each other. In the twelve-month build-up to the Seoul Olympics interest in their rivalry would intensify.

Larry Heidebrecht believed that the fewer times they met, the greater their value to sponsors and TV companies. Joe Douglas had similar thoughts, though he was not averse to post-Rome meetings. He thought they could only stoke interest, not dampen it.

Both men were raking in substantial sums for sponsorship and appearances but the notion of a pre-Olympic head-to-head had promoters salivating. As late as May 1988, with the Olympics four months away, the *New York Times* reported that promoters were close to agreeing a three-race deal worth up to $500,000 for each man. But that was likely to be Japanese money for races in Europe – Paris, Zurich and one other venue were being mentioned. There was no chance of getting the kind of money Douglas and Heidebrecht wanted from the US. 'As I see it,' Douglas told the paper, 'track and field has become a European sport. In the United States, interest is dying.'

In the end, there was no deal though Douglas was still hoping to arrange a lucrative post-Olympic 'revenge' match in Japan. In the meantime it was decided that the pair would meet only once, at the Zurich Weltklasse on 17 August, a month before the opening ceremony in Seoul. But just for the one race, reports suggested, they would be getting $500,000 between them – $25,000 each per second.

The demands on Johnson after his triumph in Rome gave Charlie Francis an insight into what Carl Lewis had dealt with before and after the Los Angeles Olympics. He even came to understand some of Lewis's excesses – his security guards, keeping the press at arm's length, staying away from the athletes' village – and reasoned that Lewis 'knew how to play the game, while we were still novices'.

According to Francis, he once got a call from Johnson asking whether or not to respond to a request from a supermarket in Toronto, reckoning the fee to be a little too modest. They had offered him $60,000.

'What do they want you to do for that?' asked Francis.

'Cut a ribbon to open it,' replied Johnson.

'Well get down there and take it,' Francis spluttered. 'Before they change their minds.'

Johnson does not seem to have been abnormally greedy, just ridiculously in demand. His commitments took him away from Toronto on a regular basis, most frequently to Japan. But the money he earned allowed him to buy the cars he coveted: a $108,000 Porsche and a $257,000 Ferrari Testarossa, for which he sought the number plate BEN 9.83. Ross Earl, who acted as his financial adviser, said that he tried to persuade Johnson to wait until after the Seoul Olympics before buying the Ferrari. He didn't listen. 'Ben was sure he was going to win the gold medal, and the world was going to come up roses.' Earl said.

Johnson claims that he met Enzo Ferrari in his factory near Milan in the days after the world championships. 'The fastest man on earth should have the fastest car on earth,' Ferrari is alleged to have told him. Johnson had his eyes on a black Testarossa with black interior. Ferrari told him it was one of only three in the world, but that he could arrange for one to be delivered to Toronto. The car did not arrive until the following summer, just before he left for Seoul. They did not have many happy days together.

Johnson had the money, of course, to be able to make such extravagant purchases (although trouble was already brewing in the shape of two years' worth of accounts that he had failed to file with the Canadian tax authorities). How he was able to access such funds might seem more of a mystery. The system of athletes receiving no money directly but applying to the national governing body for 'living expenses' from their trust funds was still notionally in place. In the case of the cars, Earl explained that Johnson simply applied to the Canadian Track and Field Association, who approved the purchases. The definition of 'living expenses' was clearly flexible.

At the same time, work began on Johnson's new home, all 7,300 square feet of it, to be constructed in the style of a Victorian mansion.

It would boast a separate suite for his mother, and a trophy room as big as the garage. 'It should be done by the fall, at the time of the Olympics,' Johnson told the *Star*. 'I've got it all organised. I just have to keep the money coming in to pay for it. It's a very nice feeling, to think how it will all be.'

Johnson was somewhat less generous on a day-to-day basis, and there are various stories about his reluctance to pay for even a pizza when out with his physio, Waldemar Matuszewski. According to Angella Issajenko, 'Someone else always paid the bill. We were still paying for his breakfast before the Seoul Olympics, when he owned a million-dollar house and drove a Porsche.'

He was obviously distracted, and there is a throwaway line in Francis's book that hints at the extent of that: 'Bowing to outside obligations, he resumed training three weeks late in the winter of 1987–88, missing half of his initial steroid cycle.'

Francis saw other changes in Johnson, but there was one he did not spot. Johnson still visited Jack Sussman, his family doctor since 1979. Sussman would later tell the Dubin Inquiry that he had been surprised at Johnson's transformation from skinny seventeen-year-old to muscle-bound athlete, and that he grew suspicious in October 1987, when his patient's left breast became unnaturally large. He knew that the condition – known as gynecomastia – can affect teenage boys, or users of anabolic steroids.

Like shrinking testicles, enlarged breasts can be an improbable side effect of testosterone-based drugs. Although testosterone is the male sex hormone, steroids can wreak all kinds of hormonal havoc, with too much artificial input effectively tricking the body into reducing its natural production. The consequence is that when the user stops taking it – as Johnson apparently did that autumn – the balance is altered. This is usually temporary, though, as some East German female athletes were horrified to discover, not always. When Dr Sussman examined Johnson's enlarged left breast, he asked if he was on steroids. Johnson said no. By January 1988, when it was examined again, the breast had returned to normal. Two months later Francis watched Johnson easily win an indoor 60m in Madrid in 6.46, close to his own world record of 6.41. From there he travelled to West Germany. But in a 60m in Sindelfingen he pulled up after 40 metres, and limped across the line. He had suffered a hamstring strain. Matuszewski travelled as a permanent member of the party by now, and, with Johnson remaining in Europe and receiving enormous fees just for turning up, he was able to give him intensive, three-times-a-day massages. What mattered now was how the injury healed. But the outside commitments did not abate. At one public appearance, in Karlsruhe, Johnson was overwhelmed by a stampede of schoolchildren; he was knocked over and further damaged his injured leg.

On returning from the European tour in April, worn out by the travel and frustrated by his injury, Johnson decided he needed a holiday. Francis was against the idea, but relented, and let him go to St Kitts, which happened to be the home of his doctor, Jamie Astaphan, who had returned to the island in 1986 while still retaining his connection with the group and making regular visits to Toronto. Desai Williams went too. He had rejoined Francis's group in autumn 1987, though obviously none of them knew about his phone call to Glen Bogue reporting Johnson's steroid use.

Two weeks later, when Johnson went back to Toronto, resumed training and started a new steroid cycle, the *Star*, greeting his return, referred innocently to the 'aspirin-type medications' he had been taking. The injured leg was still not right: he even had problems extending it fully. But he was contracted to meetings in Japan and felt he needed to start racing if he was to be ready for Seoul, so he went. On 13 May, he left the blocks in Tokyo at the start of his first 100m of the 1988 season and pulled up again, this time almost immediately. It was instantly clear to Francis that it was serious. This time it was a torn hamstring, the damage occurring – as it almost invariably does – in the vulnerable area surrounding the original injury.

Four months from Seoul, the fastest man in the world could barely walk.

'After I leave here, no one will know where I am,' Johnson told reporters during a brief appearance in Padua, Italy, on 13 June. He was fulfilling a commitment to his sponsor, Diadora, rather than competing: he was still injured. But where he had been, and where he was going, he would not say. Initially he failed even to tell Francis.

After the injury in Tokyo, Francis was anxious to avoid a repeat of the earlier mistakes. He wanted Johnson to receive daily treatment from Matuszewski, which meant he had to go to Europe with Francis and the others. Then it meant travelling from meeting to meeting: a prospect Johnson dreaded. Francis put his foot down: daily treatment was the only way to make a complete recovery. Knowing his man's predilections, perhaps Francis wanted to keep an eye on him too.

Johnson appeared to give way and said he would travel to Malaga to meet up with the others. But he never made it to Malaga. Instead, in an act of almost childish rebellion, he caught a flight back to his island paradise, to St Kitts. When he turned up at Astaphan's house, the doctor sent Francis a fax. Astaphan professed shock at Johnson's appearance. But he can't have been completely surprised. Shortly before this visit to St Kitts, Johnson visited Ross Earl, who kept his appearance fees – those he received in cash – in a safe in his house before transferring the money to the Canadian Track and Field Association. Johnson asked Earl for $10,000 in cash. When he arrived in St Kitts, he handed this to Astaphan, who later confirmed that he had requested it for the purchase of human growth hormone.

Johnson's relationship with Francis, strained beforehand, now appeared to be as badly damaged as the hamstring. And so when

Johnson did turn up for his engagement in Padua in mid-June – with Astaphan in tow – the pair had a showdown. It was the first time they had spoken in weeks. Indeed, one of Johnson's gripes was that Francis had not been in touch.

'I don't know how we can work together if you won't listen to me,' said Francis.

'Then I guess we can't.'

And that was it. Three months from Seoul, the fastest man in the world split with his coach (and he still couldn't run). The day after the argument, Johnson and Astaphan travelled to London and from there back to St Kitts, though, as he told reporters in Italy, his destination was confidential. 'I have to get in shape,' he said. 'I'm not in a panic about it, but I want to concentrate on my training.' He had just started gentle jogging, he told them. And he mentioned Dr Astaphan: 'A specialist in sports medicine,' as the *New York Times* described him.

When news of the split reached the press it was reported, accurately, as acrimonious. In London, *The Times* said 'Johnson is alleged to be upset that Francis did not take better care of him after he tore a muscle in his first race of the season in Tokyo in mid-May.' But the *Toronto Sun* had a fascinating take, hinting that Astaphan's role in the split may have been more significant than merely providing a base for the Caribbean holiday. The paper quoted Astaphan as saying, 'Charlie's been dropping sly innuendos about Ben juicing up on steroids, and if it doesn't stop there'll be a massive law suit.'

That comment was widely reported, but timing, and the identity of the source, is everything. Hardly anyone knew who Astaphan was. It was still months before the world tuned into the Olympics. And so it created barely a ripple.

But Astaphan's increasingly central role began to be reflected in his remuneration, which went well beyond the $10,000 in cash he received from Johnson. He insisted later that he originally worked for Francis's athletes for nothing, even subsidising their drugs out of his own pocket. But in Rome he received his first significant bonus: $25,000, paid by Larry Heidebrecht from the Mazda sponsorship.

By mid-1988 he wanted his fair share of the spoils. With Francis out of the picture, he also sought to revamp Team Johnson, talking to Matuszewski about whether the physio would be interested in working exclusively with Johnson for $5,000 a month and a $250,000 bonus if he won gold in Seoul. That never happened, and the two later had different opinions as to which of them proposed the idea.

But Astaphan did negotiate his own deal. In early July, when Johnson finally returned to Toronto, the Canadian Track and Field Association received a signed agreement between the athlete and the doctor stating that Astaphan was to be paid $10,000 a month, plus medical and travel expenses, for the 'maintenance of his physical and psychological integrity and well being'. The first invoice was backdated to May. The money was to come from Johnson's trust fund. And it was approved.

Later, speculation would centre on what exactly Johnson – and Astaphan – got up to in St Kitts. Did the doctor put him on a drug programme that even Francis knew nothing about? Johnson maintains he did not, though he also says that Astaphan, 'started giving me all the pills, all these different coloured pills, and I just took them'. (Presumably they weren't aspirin-type medications.)

Mainly, though, Johnson relaxed in St Kitts. 'I never had a break until I had my injury,' he says. 'For almost eleven years I was running, like a horse. I missed practice once in two years. That's how dedicated I was. But I was very, very tired. I was drained. Burned out. My body was dying. My body was saying to me, "Ben, it's time to take a break."

'I said, "Charlie, I need a rest." He kept saying, "Come to Europe with us and travel with us." I said, "I don't want to travel with my injury, and with all my luggage, all over Europe. I want to go somewhere and just relax." I went to St Kitts to relax. That's all. I didn't go there to take drugs. I gained about 25 pounds. It was the first time I ever enjoyed my life. Just eating, drinking and having fun.'

And this was less than twelve weeks from the Olympics. 'Yes, but I had the best fun I ever had in my life there,' says Johnson. 'It was like back home in Jamaica. I didn't have to train for seven weeks. Seven weeks I was there. Enjoying myself.' His description of himself as a racehorse is intriguing: the implication was that he was not in charge of his own destiny, but surrounded by a group of people whose only concern was to maximise his speed and profitability.

Racehorses will happily go out into a field and graze for a while if allowed. But Johnson's ability to switch off was unusual in a top-class athlete. Francis had witnessed it in Rome when he fell asleep in the ninety minutes between the semi-final and final. Yet it hints at something else. Francis's desire and intensity was apparent to everyone around him but how driven was Johnson? Did it matter to him as much as it did to his mentor? 'It mattered to me after a while,' he says, not entirely convincingly. 'I wanted to be the best I could be.'

'But not everybody has the same mindset,' shrugs Johnson. 'I can have problems and still perform.'

Did he not think, as he was lying on the beach, this could be the life for him? Why bother with the demands and hard work of training, and the endless travel? 'Well, yeah,' says Johnson. 'But I thought I would do that after I won the gold medal.' And with that, he laughs. A rare, unrestrained, guffaw.

It was not all rest and relaxation in St Kitts, Johnson adds. Initially he trained in the sea, doing water-resistance exercises designed to strengthen his leg without straining the injury. Then he began jogging. And he did some weight training. The regime had its effect: his leg began to heal.

There is another fascinating aspect to Johnson's stay in St Kitts, which may also have proved significant in his recovery – or, if you are a conspiracy theorist, in his eventual downfall. While there, he was attended by yet another mysterious figure, an American athletics coach called Jack Scott. Scott had developed a 'myomatic' machine that used micro-currents to stimulate the nerves and blood flow to the injured area, thus speeding recovery.

Scott had gained a following in the athletics world for his two books, *Athletics for Athletes* and *The Athletic Revolution*, but more so for his radical coaching ideas, and his vocal opposition to drugs and to racial and gender barriers. When he was appointed athletic director at Oberlin College in Ohio in the early 1970s, Scott tripled the budget for women's sport and employed three black head coaches – at a time when such figures were very rare, even in all-black colleges. What's more, they included Tommie Smith, the 1968 Olympic 200m champion, whose black power salute on the podium in Mexico had made him a pariah. Yet Jack Scott was far more famous for something completely different, nothing to do with sport at all.

In 1974 the Patty Hearst case transfixed America. Hearst, the nineteen-year-old heiress to her family's publishing empire, was abducted by a left-wing urban guerrilla group, the Symbionese Liberation Army, whose goal was 'proletarian revolution', to which end they committed bank robberies, murder and one of the most famous kidnaps of the twentieth century. Two months after she was taken, Hearst was caught on camera taking part in a raid on a bank in San Francisco and sent messages announcing that she was now committed to the cause.

Scott, whose politics were as radical as his ideas about sport, got involved, though it remains unclear in exactly what capacity. He was talking about writing a book about the SLA and implied he was sympathetic to the cause but opposed to the group's methods. His exact role, like Hearst's, remains highly equivocal. At one stage Hearst was in his keeping, though it is now anyone's guess whether he was trying to save her from the SLA or the FBI. (He alleged just before he died, in 2000, that the victim was complicit in the kidnap from the start. She said Scott was only interested in money.) Patty Hearst was jailed for thrity-five years but served only twenty-two months and eventually received a presidential pardon. Scott was never charged with anything, though this was not for want of trying by the authorities.

And fourteen years later, it was the same Jack Scott, with his new machine, who popped up in St Kitts. On the one hand, it seems little more than a footnote. Except that the previous year Scott had worked and become friendly with Carl Lewis. And a few months later he travelled to St Kitts to work with Johnson, at the invitation of Larry Heidebrecht, and without the knowledge or approval of Francis.

I mentioned his name to Joe Douglas. 'Yes, Jack Scott,' he says, a little vaguely. 'I had a good relationship with Jack Scott. He came up with a machine – I have one. I used to have a bunch of them, I don't know where… ' Douglas then disappeared for some time before returning empty-handed. 'I think my athletes took 'em all. The electric currents would go back and forth, and it's supposed to help you heal. It was the best machine I've ever used.

'But Jack Scott?' he muses. 'I think Jack Scott was a good man. I had a lot of respect for him. But Jack Scott was not involved in drugs. No way.'

Jack Scott was only fifty-seven when he died. And the mystery of his loyalties in 1988 remains as elusive as the mystery of his loyalties in 1974.

While Johnson was in St Kitts, Carl Lewis was injury-free, training hard and running fast. In March he had one of his regular meetings with Sri Chinmoy, who told him that, when he meditated – which he ought to do three times a day – he should imagine that he possessed 'bullet speed'. On another occasion he offered more specific sprinting advice. 'Imagine that a ferocious tiger is right behind you and at any moment is going to devour you. You know how fast a tiger can run! So you will run for your most precious life, and you will run the fastest.'

Chinmoy was by now attracting attention for his own superhuman feats, lifting objects – a light aircraft on one occasion – animals – elephants were a favourite – and people. Muhammad Ali, Nelson Mandela and Richard Gere were among those lifted by Chinmoy as they stood on a specially made platform. His official photographer's revelation that he was asked to airbrush some of the pictures did undermine his credibility. But Lewis remained an admirer.

Over the winter, he had taken part in several indoor meetings, stopping off in London en route to Stuttgart for one race, and giving a lengthy interview to Steve Rider of the BBC. He said he had not yet decided whether to defend all four Olympic titles. 'My coach doesn't want me to run the 200,' he said. 'But he didn't in 1984, either.'

For his TV interview, Lewis's familiar flat-top hairstyle had become long, almost bouffant, and he was dressed casually, in a white sweatshirt. The main topic of discussion was, of course, the 100m, and whether he could reclaim his position as fastest man in the world. What will it take, asked Rider, to become the first man ever to retain the Olympic 100m title? 'Well, the main thing is being healthy,' replied Lewis. 'If I can stay healthy I believe I definitely have the opportunity to run a lot faster than last year.'

So you won't be avoiding Johnson? It was a question designed to get a reaction, which it did. 'Well, if I recall correctly, it wasn't me.' Lewis sat up in his seat and raised a finger in mock-admonition, and laughed, opening his mouth wide enough to reveal metal braces on his teeth. 'Over the last six years, seven years, I've run against everybody, I've taken on all challengers, probably more than anyone else in history... I'll always be ready.'

The interview moved on to drugs. 'Of course I think the drug issue is a very, very big problem,' said Lewis. 'I know Seb Coe was speaking out very strongly against it. We have to realise that we have to get an independent agency to handle the drug-testing because it is not being dealt with fairly in our sport. People are on drugs, they are in competitions on drugs, and they're not getting caught. There is a problem there.'

Although the IAAF had promised to introduce out-of-competition testing, there was indeed no sign of significant progress. 'We know that many athletes are on drugs and we know there are many athletes who are afraid to address the issue... ' said Lewis. 'A lot of people who are against me are in many cases on drugs. I've always been very outspoken, but never in a negative sense... They say, "Oh, but he says all these gold medallists in Rome were on drugs." They were, and, uh... '

'All of them?' asked Rider.

'No, it's not all of them, that's not true,' replied Lewis. 'There was a substantial amount. The problem is people are afraid to address the issue because they're afraid of the backlash.' And he added his belief that positive tests were being covered up. 'All these cases are happening right now, today, where people are being caught in major meetings and their tests are being destroyed. This is all happening.'

Shortly before the interview, *The Times* had run a three-part investigation into the problem of drugs in athletics. The paper alleged that athletes selected for supposedly random tests frequently knew in advance, that samples were indeed sometimes destroyed and never tested and, most damaging of all, that at some meetings clean urine samples could be supplied for athletes caught in 'embarrassing situations'. The paper claimed that the all-powerful Andy Norman had arranged a clean sample for the hammer thrower Martin Girvan at a meeting at Crystal Palace in 1984.*

This outspoken interview was emblematic of Lewis's renewed self-assurance. By mid-July, at the US Olympic Trials in Indianapolis, he was, in the words of one report, 'a swift against sparrows', as he recovered from his customary sluggish starts to fly past opponents.

---

* A British Athletics Federation investigation into this affair, chaired by Peter Coni, QC, cleared Norman, though he appeared to incriminate himself by claiming: 'I wouldn't put myself in jeopardy for an athlete of his standard.' This, said Coni, left 'open the glaring corollary that for an athlete of a very different standard, very different considerations might apply'.

But nowhere – and never again – was his astonishing speed so evident as in the Indianapolis final, in which he ran the fastest 100m yet seen. A strong following wind (measuring 5.2, well above the legal limit of 2.0) meant that his time could not count as the world record. But it was still breathtaking. Lewis ran 9.78 to win the race, with Dennis Mitchell running 9.86 for second, and Calvin Smith third in 9.87. Earlier, Lewis had twice posted 9.96 – with a slight tailwind in his qualifying heat, but into a headwind in the quarter-final.

In the final, Lewis got a poor start. But, watching the video, one can see an immediate contrast with Rome the previous year. It can be detected just by watching his face: though he has ground to make up in the closing stages, he appears relaxed, his jaw loose, as he breezes past the opposition. In Rome he had seemed acutely aware of Johnson, his eyes swivelling to the side to check his progress, his jaw clenched. This was different. 'Smooth as glass,' said Tom Tellez.

Wind or no wind, the figure 9.78 sent shockwaves around the athletics world. Only Ben Johnson, who watched the race on TV, claimed to be underwhelmed: 'Lewis ran 9.78 with a 5.2 wind. So what?' He claimed Lewis would have run 10.05 had it been calm. 'If I was there, I would have run 9.2… His first 40 metres were bad. Like always.'

Journalists at the US trials – more of them than usual, it being Olympic year – found Lewis relaxed, accessible and very different from the exasperating character of 1984. Neil Wilson, then athletics correspondent of the *Independent*, recalls Lewis going well beyond the call of duty to accommodate him and two British colleagues, Colin Hart of the *Sun* and John Rodda of the *Guardian*. 'When we arrived we approached Joe Douglas and asked if the three of us could have a private interview with Lewis,' explains Wilson. 'He said that would be OK, but not during the meeting, because he was competing in three events.

'On the Sunday, the last day of competition, we were beginning to panic. Nothing had been arranged. And we'd all travelled to the US to interview Lewis. So we approached Joe again, but he told us he had a dope test, then he was seeing his mother, and then he was taking a private jet to appear on the David Letterman show. "But he'll be having dinner with his sister Carol this evening, if you'd like to join them," said Joe.

'This dinner finally took place at midnight in a mall in Indianapolis. Just Carl, Carol and the three of us. And he talked for two hours, then went straight to the airport to catch his flight. This was just for the British press, remember. And he was absolutely sensational.'

Usurping Lewis as the sensation of Indianapolis, however, was another sprinter. While the wind gusted throughout the meeting, and changed by the minute, the blustery conditions produced one moment of apparent calm, and one aberration. Even though the flags told a slightly different story, it was absolutely still – at least according to the wind gauge – for a women's 100m final that saw Florence Griffith-Joyner blaze to an extraordinary 10.49 – more than a quarter of a second better than Evelyn Ashford's world record.

At the time, the questions over Griffith-Joyner's astonishing new mark centred on the possibility of a faulty wind-reading – the gauge by the triple jump read 4.3, while the one by the running track read zero. But the questions that never went away concerned what might have transformed her, at the age of twenty-eight, from a decent 200m specialist to the greatest female sprinter the world had ever seen. She was also the most flamboyant, 'Flo-Jo' earning almost as much attention for her appearance as her speed, from her garish, full-length Lycra suit to her six-inch-long painted nails and extravagant mane of hair. The more serious questions and innuendos of drug use dogged Griffith-Joyner until, and well beyond, her abrupt retirement a few months later, immediately after the Seoul Olympics. She died ten years later, aged just thirty-eight, suffering an epileptic seizure in her sleep. Her 100m record survives to this day.

But the new star of women's athletics did not test positive at the US Olympic trials. Among others, Carl Lewis did.

*

'Dear Mr Lewis,' began the letter dated 26 August, and signed by Baaron Pittenger, the executive director of the US Olympic Committee:

On behalf of the United States Olympic Committee and relative to my earlier letter of 6 August, 1988, I must confirm that the analysis of your Specimen B for sample #2383 and for sample #2356 was positive for Pseudoephdrine [*sic*], Ephedrine and Phenylpropanolamine... Documentation is forthcoming. By policy of the USOC, this finding is cause for disqualification from the Olympic Team for the 1988 Summer Olympic Games in Seoul, Korea.

Lewis, Joe DeLoach, who had beaten Lewis in the 200m at the trials, and Floyd Heard, all of the Santa Monica Track Club, were among eight athletes whose samples were found to be positive. This letter would have rocked the athletics world had it become known at the time. But it didn't.

The athletes were told they had ten days to appeal. This would be heard by a three-man committee, comprising Pittenger, Dr James Betts, a surgeon at a children's hospital in Berkeley, and Don Catlin, whose lab had analysed the tests. Yet Catlin had only an advisory role; he was not involved in deciding whether or not sanctions should be applied.

The stimulants found in Lewis's urine carried an automatic three-month ban under IOC rules, which would have knocked him out of the Olympics. The only way he could avoid that was if 'inadvertent use' could be determined. It is unclear what form the appeal took. But within days, when a second letter was sent by the USOC, he and the others had been let off, with 'A warning rather than a suspension,' wrote Pittenger.

At the foot of his letter to DeLoach, beneath Pittenger's signature, there was a hand-written scrawl, which read, 'Joe – this is the formal notification which I must send according to the testing protocol. As you know, this case has been excused as inadvertent use. Good luck.' And with that, Lewis and DeLoach and all the others were cleared to compete in Seoul.

These cases finally came to light, fifteen years later, when a Californian newspaper, the *Orange County Register*, was handed 30,000 pages of documents detailing 118 doping positives, all ignored, between 1988 and 2000. The source was Wade Exum, who had succeeded Robert Voy as chief medical officer of the US Olympic Committee in 1989.

Pittenger responded to the revelations by saying the athletes were not punished because the committee's rules specified that there had to be a 'sole intent' to dope. 'I thought without question that it was inadvertent use and didn't meet the "sole intent" criterion,' Pittenger told the *Los Angeles Times*. 'I am not the least bit defensive about the decision that was made.'

James Betts proved uncontactable. Don Catlin, the third member of the appeals panel, recalls the case well and remembers his frustration: 'My role was simply to say what I found, not to say what I thought about it.' Which doesn't mean Catlin didn't – and doesn't – have an opinion. 'I disagreed with their finding,' he says. 'Because essentially they overlooked it.'

The traces of stimulants found in Lewis's urine were small, Catlin acknowledges. But there was, in 1988, no threshold: the mere presence of any of the three banned stimulants carried a three-month suspension, according to IOC rules. But according to Catlin, 'athletes knew they could say that they had taken something they'd bought over-the-counter and get a reduced sentence. And that happened fairly often.'

Later, Lewis would explain that the culprit for the positive tests was a herbal dietary supplement in pill form, reportedly containing the Chinese remedy *ma huang* used in the treatment of asthma, hay fever and the common cold. 'I took all kinds of different herbs,' Lewis told the *LA Times* in 2003. Had he known ma huang contained Ephedrine, he would not have taken it. 'It didn't say it on the bottle,' he said.

The levels detected in Lewis's urine ranged from two parts per million to six parts per million for combined amounts of the three stimulants. These are levels that, under today's anti-doping rules, would be considered OK: the threshold established in 2000 is 10 parts per million for Ephedrine, and 25 parts per million for the other two.

But under the rules of the day, it was a punishable offence. And with the affair coming to light just a month before the Olympics, it must have caused Lewis stress. But he did not think the incident worth mentioning in his autobiography. Given how outspoken he is in his book and elsewhere about drugs that might seem curious. Lewis had even featured in a US Olympic Committee campaign the previous year to highlight the risk of inadvertent positive tests through poorly labelled over-the-counter supplements.

Douglas says that, when he heard about the positives, he asked Lewis for 'all the vitamins you've been taking'. He told me that, as part of Lewis's appeal, a member of Catlin's lab took Lewis's ma huang remedy, then provided a urine sample that contained the banned stimulants. Catlin denies this, insisting, 'I always advised my staff never to get involved in such things.' But Douglas bats the whole thing away: 'Carl wasn't worried. He knew what he did. He wasn't cheating. Carl never cheated in his life.'

It did become known that there had been positives at the Olympic trials. Robert Voy mentioned the affair during a press conference in mid-August, although he gave no names. Voy had been the USOC's medical officer for four years, starting in early 1984 when they introduced the controversial pre-Olympic screening programme, which Don Catlin insisted on getting stopped.

Since then he and Voy had become close allies. Voy was not just committed to the anti-drugs cause, he was also unusually candid about the scale of the problem in the US, a little too candid for some of his colleagues. 'The East European countries don't have a corner on the market for drug abuse,' Voy told *The Times* in August 1988. 'Our drug abuse is a little worse.' He thought Eastern Bloc athletes beat their Western counterparts because they were better coached and better trained, not because they used more drugs.

Despite the cover-ups, the issue was getting more and more attention. In June 1988 Voy and Catlin attended the first World Conference on Doping in Sport in Ottawa, a three-day meeting involving twenty-six countries, including East Germany and the Soviet Union, chaired by 'the Prince', Alexandre de Mérode of the IOC, whose zeal against drugs in sport was almost matched by his fury when the Canadian hosts banned smoking in the conference hall. The chain-smoking de Mérode 'went wild' when told to stub out his cigarette, recalls Catlin.

In one of the breaks, Catlin and Voy got talking to the head of the Soviet delegation, a man with a large anchor tattoo on his arm, Vasily Gromyko. Catlin said to him, 'You know, the US and Soviets are the star performers in drugs in sport, why don't we get together and run a programme?' Gromyko replied, 'Yeah, sure, let's do it.' So they developed a plan for each side to test the other. An agreement was signed in November 1988 and actually came into effect, though it would of course be meaningless unless both sides were operating in good faith.

But this outbreak of détente was symptomatic of a consensus at the conference about the gravity of the problem. The Norwegian representative, Hans Skaset, called for out-of-season testing worldwide, saying, 'The future of sport is at stake. If the present problems in international top level sport are not countered with more vigour and determination than today, top level sport will emerge as a completely commercialised entertainment industry, stripped of its educational value, during the next decade.'

The British scientist Arnold Beckett issued a similarly grave warning about human growth hormone, the use of which he believed to be rampant. There was 'not a cat in hell's chance' of detecting HGH, said Beckett. He mentioned that a supply worth £50,000 had disappeared from Great Ormond Street children's hospital the previous year, and was believed to have reached the black market in California. And he warned of a new wonder product: the blood booster Erythropoietin (EPO). 'There are some serious problems emerging,' said Beckett.*

Voy says that he returned from the conference newly aware of the scale of the problem, but encouraged by the Soviet Union's apparent support, and with his resolve to tackle doping reinforced. 'But something very profound happened to me between this conference in Ottawa and the actual Olympic Games,' Voy wrote in his book, *Drugs, Sport and Politics*. He meant the fate of the eight positives from Indianapolis. Voy did not buy the inadvertent-use defence, and still feels the same. 'The athletes in question were not new to the testing process,' he tells me. 'They had been tested before, many times. They were well aware of the rules regarding ma huang and other herbs.' For Voy, the relevant fact was that 'they may have competed under the influence of a performance-enhancing drug'.

The exonerations were not the problem for Voy. It was what happened when he mentioned the eight positives to the press, at a pre-Olympic 'open house' event at the USOC headquarters in Colorado Springs, attended by about a hundred journalists. Voy gave a two-hour presentation and, as he told me, 'I was very up front with the press. I had a reputation with them, and I'm a very direct person.'

Which meant that when he was asked, 'Were there any positives at the trials?' he replied 'Yes, there were eight positive tests at this event.

---

* Beckett was right about HGH: a test was not developed until 2008, with only a twenty-four-hour window of detection. Another new form of doping discussed at length during the conference was 'abortion doping'. Delegates alleged that some female athletes had been artificially inseminated and then had the foetus aborted after three months to receive a hormone boost. De Mérode said he had heard of a Swiss doctor who performed this service.

The athletes in question were positive, and the appeal process – to determine if it was truly doping or whatever – is in the works'.

This, says Voy, earned him 'permanent membership on the "shit lists" of both the USOC and TAC, the American track and field governing body. He summed up the response as, 'Dr Voy should learn to keep his fucking mouth shut'. Subsequently, Voy was told not to speak to journalists about drugs, an order that also applied in Seoul.

In early July Ben Johnson returned to Toronto from his St Kitts paradise. He would run in the following month's Canadian Olympic trials, and then head to Europe, for his showdown with Carl Lewis in Zurich.

Charlie Francis, meanwhile, had been stewing over his split with the athlete he had coached for eleven years, but also reflecting that Ben's grievances were perhaps not so much personal as stemming from the inevitable pressures of his celebrity. Perhaps he needed to make more allowances.

Yet Francis's failure to understand his star's needs, however demanding they might have been, could have owed something to the aspects of Johnson's personality that made him so well suited to the extreme pressure of high-level competition. To this day, Johnson appears laid-back, imperturbable. But the Zen-like calm that he conveys can perhaps be misleading, an unreliable guide to his pent-up feelings.

Francis returned to Toronto from Europe two days after Johnson. He had started to focus on reconciliation, his determination hardening as he watched Lewis run 9.78 in Indianapolis. He bristled as he listened to more brash comments after Lewis dipped below 10 seconds again in Paris on 27 June, the meeting originally slated as a showdown between the two. 'All I know,' said Lewis in Paris, 'is that I'm running better than ever. And he isn't running at all.'

Johnson and Francis got together at Ross Earl's house, a meeting brokered by Larry Heidebrecht. According to Johnson, Francis laid into him 'for not wearing his Diadora tracksuit, and on, and on. He was talking to me like I was a spoiled child.' But he hit back, 'I criticised him for not checking on me while I was recovering in St Kitts, for Waldemar's failure to prevent my second injury in Tokyo, for not listening to me, for making me feel guilty for wanting some time off... '

With their respective gripes off their chests, they shook hands and agreed to begin working together again. In mid-July, talking to the Toronto *Star*, Johnson was back in full Ali-esque flow. Francis had said he was on target for 9.78 or 9.8 by Seoul. Johnson said, 'I think I can run faster than a 9.8. My leg is 100 per cent. I think, in my own mind, I can run a 9.76 by the Olympics.'

The Canadian Olympic trials in Ottawa, from 5 to 7 August, served as a major test for Johnson. He passed with flying colours, and that reassured Francis that he could recapture his form in time for Seoul, six weeks away. 'Big Ben' – as the *Star* had taken to calling him throughout their reports – won his first heat in 10.38, running 'at 80 per cent', before taking the final in a wind-assisted 9.90. It wasn't as breathtaking as Lewis's 9.78 (then again, neither was the wind), but the headline was obvious: 'Big Ben is back'.

The trials were well attended by the world's media – 120 journalists turned up, keen to see how Johnson was looking, and running, and whether his rivalry with Carl Lewis might live up to its gargantuan billing when the two finally met, first in Zurich, then in Seoul. The press pack included Dick Patrick of *USA Today*, and for Patrick, as for most others, the meeting brought confirmation that Johnson was in shape. But for him it also confirmed something else. It was the moment, he says, when his suspicions about the Francis athletes hardened into certainty.

In Ottawa, Patrick encountered Jack Scott, the man with the magic machine, who was now working with Ben. 'Jack invited me back to the warm-up area. And I remember seeing a hurdler, Mark McKoy, take off his shirt. Now Mark used to be a little guy who was always knocking on the door of the podium, but maybe not quite making it. I was aware he'd joined Charlie's group a couple of months before. He takes off his shirt and his physique has changed so much that I thought, "My God, there can be no doubt." And when I saw Angella Issajenko warming up, and she was so thickly muscled, to me, that was the equivalent of a positive drugs test. They were positive on sight.'

Not that Johnson could have tested positive in Ottawa. Unlike Carl Lewis, he was not tested at his national trials.

Back in Europe, in Sestriere, Italy, Johnson ran 9.98 to win the 100 a week before his meeting with Lewis in Zurich. And two days later he spoke to the Canadian journalist Randy Starkman. Johnson was sitting by the pool of his hotel in Cesenatico, on the Adriatic Coast, but his mood seemed at odds with the relaxed setting. Starkman recalls him bubbling with frustration, simmering with anger. 'I want to say it plain out: I just can't take it any more,' Johnson told Starkman. 'He's always saying this, saying that.'

'He' was, of course, Carl Lewis. 'I can't keep up with this crap any more,' Johnson continued. 'Whenever he's running against me, my intention is to kick his butt. That's the way it's going to be from now on. I want to beat him in Zurich, then his mind is all screwed up.' Starkman recalls now that, as Johnson spoke about Lewis, his stutter overcame him. 'When he said he was going to kick Carl's butt, he could hardly get the words out. I think he was trying to get under Carl's skin. But Carl was the master manipulator.'

Starkman detected a change in Johnson, one that took effect in the immediate aftermath of Rome. 'I had been covering sport in Europe for an agency since 1984,' says Starkman, 'so I'd hung around these guys a lot, but after Rome, boom! Ben hits it big. When I went to see him in Cesenatico there's suddenly an entourage. It had always been Charlie and his athletes, but suddenly there are all these other people on the scene – Larry Heidebrecht, and it was the first time I ever met Jamie Astaphan. It was this big entourage.'

A late threat to the Zurich meeting had emerged when Heidebrecht hinted that Johnson might withdraw. A post-Olympic clash in Japan would be more lucrative, Heidebrecht reasoned, and a meeting in Zurich could reduce the million-dollar pot believed to be on offer. But Johnson insisted he didn't care about the money. 'The money will come late on, after the gold,' he said. 'I want to run against Lewis in Zurich.' 'What burns Big Ben,' wrote Starkman, 'is the lack of respect he has received from Lewis since ending his rival's five-year reign atop the sprinting world.'

But yet another threat to the Lewis–Johnson grudge match emerged on the eve of the Weltklasse. Andreas Brügger was in his office in the meeting headquarters, the Nova Park Hotel, when he was approached by Kim McDonald, the London-based manager of some of the world's top athletes. 'Andreas,' said McDonald, 'there's something going on downstairs in the conference room. There are sixty athletes there – and they want to boycott Zurich.'

'What the hell is going on?' asked Brügger.

'They don't accept that Ben Johnson and Carl Lewis are being paid these monstrous sums, $250,000 each.'

The complainants included Linford Christie, who would later express his displeasure at being named as one of the instigators. He claimed that it was the American contingent who called the meeting. Christie named Harvey Glance, the experienced sprinter who was no friend or fan of Lewis, as the main protagonist.

But the athletes were mistaken, says Brügger now. They had fallen for the 'propaganda' of Joe Douglas and Larry Heidebrecht about their runners getting so much money. 'When people hear that Johnson and Lewis are competing against each other in Zurich, they think that Zurich is paying this amount,' says Brügger. 'But the rumour was, of course, maintained mainly by Joe Douglas, I believe. Joe was the one who kept that story alive, because he was thinking that would help him organise the meetings in Japan.' Brügger laughs. 'He is not dumb,

Joe! But, of course, everyone believed what they read in the newspapers.' Which was that Lewis and Johnson were getting $500,000 and Christie $5,000.

Until the rebellion, Brügger was not unhappy to read that the fiftieth Weltklasse would stage 'the world's richest ever race'. Such publicity could do no harm. And the charade was maintained until the eleventh hour by Douglas and Heidebrecht, who refused to confirm or deny the fees bandied around in the press. 'It's a substantial amount, and we are pleased,' Heidebrecht told reporters. 'We're very happy,' said Douglas. 'We think it's good for athletics.'

But with so many of the other athletes up in arms, Brügger was forced to set the record straight. 'I went down into that meeting and told them, "You should know me well enough that I wouldn't make such a deal. I would feel ashamed to pay them as much and you maybe a fraction."'

Brügger then offered to show Johnson's and Lewis's contracts to three representatives of the athletes. It confirmed, he says, that each was paid a flat $25,000. He was being a little disingenuous. Brügger acknowledges that both Johnson and Lewis would in fact have earned far more than that, because he had agreed to give them a share of any additional TV money. In the event, several broadcasters paid to show their race, including Canadian TV. 'But the figure of $500,000,' says Brügger, 'that was propaganda to try to make Japan sign a contract!'

Douglas smiles and shakes his head slowly at the idea that he could ever have pulled such a trick. 'I could see people thinking that way,' he says breezily, as though the idea has just occurred to him. 'The truth is, it wasn't that much money. It wasn't $500,000 – that's true. But it was a lot. I've already told you: Carl, when he ran at any major meet, got a minimum of $100,000. I met with some of the athletes in Zurich, and said to 'em, "Carl and the athletes on my team stood up for you so you could make more money." That was true, too.'

ZURICH, 17 AUGUST 1988

The old Letzigrund Stadium, now demolished, was a small arena capable of eliciting unusual passion from the supposedly phlegmatic Swiss, giving the Weltklasse the tension and drama of a local football derby rather than an athletics meeting. ·

The place is full with 23,000 spectators, banging on the metal advertising boards around the perimeter of the track, creating a mini-cauldron and a frenzied, claustrophobic atmosphere. Tonight it is charged in anticipation of a contest that has all the build-up and hype of a heavyweight title fight.

They arrive at the same time, in separate cars. They warm up in separate corners of an adjoining field. They don't exchange a glance, never mind a word. Even in their warm-ups they present a contrast in styles. Johnson prefers gym-type exercises: he does push-ups and sit-ups. Lewis moves more slowly, like a large cat, stretching and shaking out his limbs.

The line-up for the final anticipates Seoul a little over a month later: it is almost identical. Dennis Mitchell, the wiry young American sprinter who had been coached by Bill Lewis as a teenager; Ray Stewart, confident, cheeky, a raw talent from Jamaica who had won bronze in Rome; Linford Christie, his muscle-bound physique accentuated by a garish, tight yellow and turquoise full-length warm-up suit; Johnson's clubmate Desai Williams, at twenty-nine the veteran of the field; and the previous world record holder, Calvin Smith, are all there, further underlining the prestige and importance of the Weltklasse. The only runner not destined for the final in Seoul is the Nigerian, Chidi Imoh.

Johnson and Lewis are in adjacent lanes: four and five. When they are introduced, the Letzigrund crackles and fizzes. The brief eruption is followed by an eerie silence.

Lewis adopts a familiar routine as he settles in the blocks. He stares up the track and rests his left arm on his left knee, sitting back briefly on his haunches. Johnson, beside him, is absorbed in the task of placing his hands in the peripheral corners of his lane – a strangely delicate, measured act. He squats low, close to the track. Lewis is more upright and looks down. Johnson looks up. But as the starter shouts, '*Fertig*' ('Set'), a photographer snaps, his flash ignites, and Johnson breaks the line, moving a fraction before the others.

It's a clear false start. But Johnson is furious, arguing with the officials, complaining that he had been distracted by the flash. They repeat the same routines, Johnson still shaking his head, and settle again. This time, they get away, Johnson cleanly, but not as rapidly as in Rome. Still, he stretches his lead over Lewis in the first half of the race. The gap appears to open even more by halfway, and Johnson is still ahead with 20 to go, but Lewis engages that other gear; with 10 to go he draws level and, in the blink of an eye, he surges past a fading Johnson. In lane eight, Calvin Smith, in an appropriately understated all-black outfit, finishes rapidly, stealthily, to claim second, confirming that he has finally recaptured his world record form of 1983. Lewis's winning time: 9.93. Smith is second in 9.97, Johnson third in 10.00.

It ends Johnson's five-race winning streak against Lewis. And, as he is lifted into the Zurich night by his sister, Carol, and launches into the kind of celebrations worthy of an Olympic title, Lewis believes that he's broken a spell, removed a hex. As he tells reporters, 'I will never again lose to Ben.'

11

THE GLASNOST GAMES

'This is the ultimate moment of my life.'
BEN JOHNSON

Two years earlier, it was Ben Johnson who had a strange encounter in Zurich – with Carl Lewis's friend, André 'Action' Jackson. But in 1988 it was Lewis who had an interesting exchange with someone who, like Jackson, seemed to have manoeuvred himself into a position whereby he straddled both camps: Jack Scott.

A few days after the Zurich meeting, claimed Lewis in his auto-biography, Scott offered 'some information from inside Ben's camp'. Whether it was solicited or not, Lewis did not say. Scott said he had travelled to St Kitts after an invitation from Jamie Astaphan, who told him he was fed up with Ben and wanted to work with Carl. Alleg-edly, Astaphan said much else, too. He said Ben was talented, yes, but only great because of drugs. 'If I could get Carl on drugs,' Astaphan supposedly said, 'he would run 9.5.'

Between Zurich and Seoul, Lewis discussed this with Joe Douglas. They mulled over the questions: 'Why would Astaphan tell Jack Scott all this? Why would Jack tell us? Why would Astaphan be so eager to work with me instead of Ben?'

Further questions about Astaphan's motives at this time would surface later, during the Dubin Inquiry. There, it emerged that, by

1988, Astaphan had taken to recording his phone calls with Johnson. Angella Issajenko had by now grown wary of Astaphan, suspicious of both his motives and the extent of his personal ambition. 'Jamie was in there for one year,' she said in a later interview with the BBC, 'but he wanted to take over the whole kit and kaboodle.'

Bob Armstrong, lead counsel at the Dubin Inquiry, came to believe that, during the *froideur* between Johnson and Francis, Astpahan began to regard himself no longer as just the doctor. 'When Charlie and Ben had their falling out he saw himself as Ben's coach. He didn't have Charlie's knowledge – nobody did. So that was really the height of stupidity.'

Perhaps the height of hubris, too. Indeed, one gets a sense of the doctor developing a God complex. Its roots could perhaps be traced to Rome. As Astaphan watched his patient sprint to the world title, did he fancy himself in the role of Frankenstein, with Johnson as his creation?

What Randy Starkman says seems to reinforce the idea. He recalls, from 1988, being in one 'mixed zone', where journalists interview athletes at the big meetings, waiting to speak to Johnson. 'But Larry keeps pushing Ben past, saying, "Interview Dr Astaphan, don't forget Dr Astaphan." I thought maybe Heidebrecht was thinking that if Astaphan doesn't get enough attention, he isn't going to be a happy camper. It was only afterwards that I realised all the things that were going on with all the egos in the entourage.'

'Astaphan,' says Starkman, 'was kind of a weird guy, very nice and very friendly, but he did this curious thing: he would sniffle all the time.'

Whether it was a clash of egos, or something else, a divide seemed to open between Astaphan and Charlie Francis during 1988. Given Johnson's sudden wealth and fame, it would be normal if those around him sought a greater share of the pie. And, given Johnson's disappearance to St Kitts, and the even more mysterious arrival of Jack Scott, Francis had reason to be uncomfortable.

Francis seemed to have no time for Scott. And his role was also played down by Astaphan, who insisted he had not been much help. Yet Scott stuck around. According to Francis, he 'appended himself to our group without invitation', in Ottawa, Zurich and again in Seoul.

'The talk with Jack Scott was the last piece of evidence I needed,' said Lewis in his book. 'Before this, I had pretty good information that Ben had been doing drugs. Now I knew for sure… To win the 100 in Seoul, I would have to beat a druggie. I still didn't know what I could do about it. Probably nothing.'

Douglas looks vague at my first mention of Scott. He does one of his disappearing acts, then returns to mount a staunch defence of him as an anti-doping coach. Dick Patrick is intrigued at the notion that Scott might have been spying on Johnson on St Kitts. 'I hadn't thought of that,' he writes in an email, 'and I consider myself a sceptic. My first reaction was no way, but I'm reconsidering that. Jack had a conspiratorial side, as his involvement with Patty Hearst attests. But I think he had a sense of fair play and ethics that would have prevented him from being a spy.

'Then again, maybe Ben cheating offended him. I'm getting a headache trying to assess this information.'

Four days after Zurich, Johnson raced once more in Europe. On a cold, wet night in Cologne he was third again, this time behind Calvin Smith and Dennis Mitchell. The conditions were slow and so were the times: Smith won in 10.16, Johnson eased off to a 10.29 when he saw he was beaten. But Smith, who had flown past Johnson 25 metres from the line, was resurgent. After four injury-ravaged seasons, he was finally fit, healthy and fast, registering his victory in Cologne despite stumbling out of the blocks.

Having failed in 1984, Smith had qualified for the US team for the individual 100m in Seoul. He was Allan Wells's tip for the gold medal, but Smith knew what stood in his way. Though he didn't see eye-to-eye with Lewis, he shared his suspicions about Johnson. 'I mean, there was no doubt to me that he was on drugs,' says Smith now. 'It was just a matter of proving it.'

It wasn't just Johnson he suspected, 'There were many I figured were on drugs and stuff.' There was the physical evidence first and foremost. 'Also, most normal athletes are going to have their bad days and good days. When it comes to the major meets, guys on drugs don't. And there's a lot of different stuff that goes on with them as far as their attitude goes. They act like they're not worried about you or anybody else, because it's not natural ability that's going to work, it's the drugs that are going to work. They have that over-confidence about what they're going to do.'

Smith says that athletes were divided into two camps: clean and dirty. 'I knew who the drug coaches were, as well as the drug athletes. There was no secret. It was just never talked about in the media.' Surely he must have encountered drugs during his career? 'No, I didn't. I guess I didn't associate with those particular coaches.'

A more nuanced perspective comes from Ray Stewart, the Jamaican whose coach Glen Mills would later go on to work with Usain Bolt. He had won the bronze in Rome and would travel to Seoul with big ambitions. He was only twenty-three and still improving, though he had yet to break the 10-second barrier.

What Stewart says now might be coloured by his more recent experiences. After retiring, he went into coaching until, in 2008, the *New York Times* published a story alleging that he had purchased human growth hormone, anabolic steroids and testosterone for his athletes. Stewart ended up being banned from coaching for life, though he denies all the allegations, and angrily protests his innocence, saying his tormentors had 'no physical evidence'.

He does, nevertheless, appear to hold a less black-and-white view of the drugs issue than Smith. Stewart says, 'The world is always, "This guy's on drugs and that guy's on drugs," but it comes to a point where I look at it this way: if the guys that were in charge are not doing what they need to do, then why talk about it?'

Stewart is exuberant: he talks quickly, breathlessly, and his conversation is punctuated with bursts of laughter. So it was the system that was at fault? 'Right. It's the whole system. So whenever people keep saying stuff, I just say, "Hey man, listen up – whatever happened, happened. That's the past. We can talk as much as we want to talk but nothing is going to change, so just leave it alone."' As a runner, says Stewart, his attitude was, 'I just got to go out there and compete the best way I can with them guys.'

If the system was at fault, and athletes could get away with taking drugs, then why not take them? Stewart doesn't exactly answer the question. Instead, cryptically, he says, 'The thing with me, from growing up as a kid, I have this tendency that when people give me something, I would think that it might be worth trying – but I'll smell the thing before I eat it, right? If I ask them what it is and they can't tell me exactly, I'm not going to take it.

'You know,' continues Stewart. 'I look like I'm still in my thirties. People look at me every day and say, "Raymond, what are you doing, man? You don't age! What do you do?" 'I say, "Just water the plants and they grow a new leaf."'

Even though Smith had rediscovered his best form, Cologne was a race that Johnson should have won. And he and Francis knew it. They withdrew from the next meeting, in Berlin, and returned to Toronto on 22 August: thirty-two days before the final in Seoul.

Johnson had been drug-tested in Zurich – his nineteenth test since 1986: the nineteenth he had passed. Now he began a final, mini-steroid programme, designed to bring him to peak condition, but also to clear his system before Seoul. Timing was everything. Normally, Astaphan recommended twnty-eight days' clearance, though he knew that was a generous allowance. He believed eleven days to be a safe clearance time, and claimed to know of one athlete who sailed through an IOC test just three days after taking steroids.

This time he was cutting things a little finer than normal, but only just. Astaphan drew up the programme for Johnson, Issajenko, Williams and McKoy, which included the milky-white injectable substance he called Estragol, and growth hormone. He later described it as 'a very quick programme. They had just completed a strenuous trip, and they needed a little bit of rehabilitation and rebuilding.' As had become the norm since Astaphan's return to St Kitts in 1986, it was Francis, in his own bedroom, who administered Johnson's injections. It was all part of the blurring of roles: if Astaphan had started to see himself as coach, Francis was acting as the doctor. He gave Johnson Estragol injections on 24 August, and then two more up to the 28th: twenty-six days before the Olympic final (taking into consideration the time difference between Toronto and Seoul).

Astaphan also took an extra precaution, making arrangements for all four of the sprinters to received diapulse treatment, which helped to flush the drugs from their system. On 6 September they left for a holding camp in Vancouver, and on 14 September they flew out to Tokyo. Johnson had started to perform well in training, his times over 80m suggesting to Francis that he was capable of running 100m in the high 9.80s. In fact, he was in similar shape to Rome the previous year, and he would improve.

Johnson arrived at Kimpo Airport in Seoul on 16 September, seven days before the 100m heats. His arrival was chaotic, even crazier than his stop-off in Tokyo, where he had been mobbed by autograph-hunters at the airport. In Tokyo the police had been efficient, and kept the media and fans at bay, but in Seoul the pictures of Johnson arriving at the airport eerily foreshadowed the scenes that accompanied his departure just ten days later.

The atmosphere was as frenzied, the sense of unruliness the same. Johnson was jostled by a mob of reporters and TV crews and forced to move at snail's pace through the terminal, a small speck at the centre of a maelstrom. Johnson was not comfortable with this, particularly because he was being crowded by real people, rather than the egos of the entourage that normally formed a cocoon around him. As he negotiated the crowd, Francis might have been forced once again to conclude that he and Johnson were 'amateurs' at this game. Lewis, it later transpired, flew into Seoul under a false name.

It got worse. The mob that greeted them on arrival at Kimpo had been just the local media and a small number of fans. In the main terminal building all hell broke loose. Johnson's police guard was swept away as he found himself in a stampede: in front of him, an old woman was knocked to the ground, her trolley overturned and bags scattered. Francis, fighting to remain close to his athlete, feared a repeat of Karlsruhe, where Johnson had been knocked over and kicked by schoolchildren. Francis recalled the frantic scene as he 'struggled to stay close behind Ben, keeping my body between the mob and his legs'.

In the mêlée there were some angry words from Johnson, aimed at the photographers in particular, and the bad feeling spilled into his first media conference. It was an inauspicious start to his Seoul campaign. There were now parallels with Lewis in 1984, not least in the expectations surrounding Johnson, especially in Canada. He was arguably the biggest sports star the country had ever produced. Great ice hockey players like Bobby Orr and Wayne Gretzky were little known across much of the world and only middle-sized stars in the US, but they were the most famous men in Canada. And only a few weeks earlier, Gretzky had been traded by the Edmonton Oilers to the Los Angeles Kings, an event treated as a national catastrophe by the Canadian media, a devastating indication that they could never beat the US, even at their own game.

As the journalist Al Sokol put it, Johnson provided 'a wonderful story for Canadians, and we needed heroes. We certainly needed heroes who beat Americans.' But that desire, he and others later admitted, perhaps affected the nation's judgement; no one wanted to ask difficult questions and break the spell.

Although 386 athletes made up the Canadian team, it was over-whelmingly about one man – to such an extent that there was huge disappointment when Johnson announced that he would not take part in the opening ceremony. Like Lewis in 1984, he opted out of the athletes' village – 'a zoo,' said Francis – checking into the Hilton. Francis assumed the role of Joe Douglas, taking full responsibility for both decisions.

Daily, in the void between the desire for gossip about the Olympics' biggest star and the supply of actual facts, rumours swirled around Johnson, including the story that his father had been killed by Hurricane Gilbert, which was ravaging Jamaica. He hadn't: but the storm damage meant that Ben senior couldn't abandon his telephone engineering duties, and was prevented from flying to Seoul to watch his son.

Another distraction was the news – which Francis kept from Johnson – that the IAAF, apparently bowing to pressure from the Lewis camp, had agreed to investigate whether Johnson had false-started at the previous year's world championships. Francis was incandescent at this diversion. He believed the loss of his world record could 'psychologically destroy' Johnson on the eve of the Olympics. It would also effectively nullify his greatest weapon: his start. But Francis need not have worried. Three days before the heats got underway in Seoul, Lewis's appeal was rejected and Johnson's time of 9.83 seconds was confirmed as the world record.

Amateurs they may have been in the fame game, but at least Johnson and Francis avoided one of the mistakes made by Lewis and Joe Douglas in Los Angeles. They made no attempt to present Johnson as a rival to Michael Jackson. Which was lucky. Jackson's recently released album, the long-awaited follow-up to *Thriller*, was called *Bad*.

*

Lewis had his own problems. They centred, not for the first time, on his relationship with the US sprint coach, Russ Rogers, and his involvement – or lack of it – with the relay squad.

Before the Olympics, the American team based themselves in a luxury resort in Japan. The Nihon Centre was a retreat for some of Japan's wealthiest citizens: a secluded complex hidden behind barbed wire, with luxury chalet accommodation, a 400m running track, swimming pool, gym, jacuzzis and a golf course. Annual membership was said to cost £200,000. But it was isolated: the security guards and barbed wire as effective at keeping the athletes in as the public out.

The British stayed at Nihon, too, which meant that Linford Christie, Calvin Smith, Dennis Mitchell and Lewis – all 100m contenders – could keep an eye on each other in training. Christie had heard Allan Wells's tip for Smith, so he paid close attention to him. And he gained encouragement: watching Smith practise his starts, he didn't think he looked that sharp.

But much to the annoyance of some athletes – the prickly Christie in particular – members of the British and American media also stayed at the Nihon Centre. This gave the press an unusual degree of access. 'I had breakfast, lunch and dinner with the US team every day, I went to their workouts,' remembers Dick Patrick. 'There wasn't anywhere else to go.' It meant, too, that Patrick and his colleagues picked up on the tension in the American team, in particular the feud between Lewis and Rogers.

In some respects this was merely the latest manifestation of a war that had waged for several years between the Santa Monica Track Club and TAC, the national governing body. Before they had even arrived in Japan, Lewis had been angry that two of his clubmates, Joe DeLoach and Mike Marsh, were not automatic picks in the relay squad, and he accused Rogers of favouring 'his' athletes – athletes to whom, Lewis claimed, Rogers acted as agent as much as coach.

From Rogers's point of view, the problem was Lewis. Their enmity seemed to have its roots in the Far East in 1985, when, according to

Rogers, 'we really had our big dispute'. Rogers had selected Lewis for the relay at the late-season World Cup in Canberra, and, en route to Australia, they competed in Japan. 'He hadn't qualified at the nationals, though I selected him for the relay,' says Rogers, 'and I took him to Japan, but he showed up with his band. He was some kind of singer by now. I didn't care, as long as he came to practise. But after the meet in Japan he told me he had to go back to the States, so he didn't come to Australia. I wanted to kick his ass.'

Prior to Seoul, Lewis had failed to attend a Rogers-organised relay squad training camp in Switzerland – though Lewis said he knew nothing about the camp. The conflict had flared into the open at Sestriere a month earlier, where Lewis claimed to be surprised to see members of the US relay squad warming up: he had no idea they were competing. Lewis hurriedly assembled a Santa Monica team, including DeLoach and Marsh, entered the relay at Sestriere and won as the national team dropped the baton. Even Dennis Mitchell – coached as a teenager by Carl's father – called it a cheap stunt, and accused Lewis of selfishness.

In Nihon, Lewis spent much of his time, according to Patrick, lobbying for DeLoach to be included in the team, so the presence of the reporters was not unhelpful to him. He spent less time with the relay squad. Rogers said he refused to practise with the team and he eventually issued his own salvo: 'If Carl continues to disturb the team, I will have to take him off. The next incident he does to disrupt the team, he's got to go. I have no choice. He's at the end of his rope. The only thing he can do is hang himself.'

Rogers tells me, 'My rule was that if he doesn't train with us, we don't want him on the team.' The incident when Lewis was excluded from the relay team was a misunderstanding, he adds. 'He said I'd kicked him off the team. I didn't kick him off the team! I told him I couldn't pick him because he hadn't practised with us. And that's when the stuff really hit the fan.'

There was even a threat not just to take Lewis off the relay team but also to send him home. 'But still Carl caused a lot of problems,' says Rogers. 'We got into a big debate between us, about who was the head coach. But then it kind of eased off. The competition was close and he eased off. I don't know how he was able to focus with all that going on. But that was Carl.'

The other figure involved in this controversy was, inevitably, Joe Douglas. In the midst of it, Douglas was banned from attending the US team's training sessions in Seoul. 'Yeah,' Douglas confirms, 'but I got in anyway.

'Look,' he adds, 'that situation with TAC, there's a lot to that story. It went back to when they made it legal for athletes to take money. They said, "We're gonna take 25 per cent." So, when I made up a contract with a meet promoter, let's say an athlete is making $10,000, then I would say, "OK, $9,900 will be paid to me for my technical advice, $100 to the athlete." So the federation gets $25. Now, I can do what I want with my money, so I give it to my athlete. It was legal.

'They knew what I did, but they didn't deserve any of the athlete's money,' Douglas continues. 'They've never supported the Santa Monica Track Club. Never.' The rift between the federation and the club, and its athletes, grew ever deeper. And in Seoul, relations reached rock bottom.

Coincidentally, the British sprinter Linford Christie was embroiled in a not dissimilar dispute with the British head coach, Frank Dick. Like Lewis and Rogers, Christie and Dick had never got on, and the focus of their dispute was again the relay.

Theirs was a feud that had intensified at the previous year's world championships, when, during a practice session in Rome, Dick asked Christie to run the first leg. When he refused, Dick ordered him off the track. At that, Christie told Dick what he thought of him and the pair began shouting at each other, at which point Christie clocked some press photographers 'hiding behind the bushes'. Then, as he admitted in his autobiography, he lost his temper and they kept clicking.

That also sealed Christie's spiky relationship with the British press, which deteriorated further in Seoul and persists, for a variety of reasons, to this day. In fact, more damage was inflicted before Christie had even touched down in Japan, when a reporter approached him during his flight and asked, 'Are you on drugs?'

Christie, whose late blossoming had put him in contention for a medal in Seoul, was something of an enigma. He was a combination of dour and flamboyant; at times 'boorish' – as Sebastian Coe later described him – at others relaxed, with a big smile and infectious laugh. The paradox continued: he could seem as brooding and introspective as Johnson, while some of his outfits suggested another, more extrovert side to his personality, more like Lewis.

Christie was an early adopter of the knee-length Lycra shorts first favoured by Allan Wells, the attraction of which owed as much to their aesthetic appeal as their possible aerodynamic qualities. Christie admitted this in his autobiography. Never mind putting Lewis in the shade: some of his warm-up outfits and garish one-piece racing costumes could have been taken from Florence Griffith-Joyner's wardrobe. They were so revealing they garnered Christie – or rather his bulging 'lunchbox' – attention that he claimed to find disgusting.*

Johnson hit it off with Christie. They had much in common: both were born in Jamaica, though Christie had left for London when he was seven. And they had warmed up together at the previous year's world championships in Rome, with Johnson proving generous in his encouragement. 'There are not many athletes with whom I will warm up, but Ben is one of them,' said Christie. 'He doesn't take rivalry

---

* Two decades later, he fronted an advert for Kleenex pocket tissues using the line: 'I've got a tiny packet.'

with him off the competitive track.' With one exception. After their warm-up in Rome, Johnson said to Christie, 'Let's go and beat Lewis.'

With Lewis, on the other hand, Christie's relations were less good. They had clashed in Sestriere, a few days before the Zurich meeting, exchanging what Christie described as 'harsh words'. Though they shook hands and publicly made up at Nihon, there was little warmth, which only mirrored Lewis's relationship with most of his fellow sprinters – except those who raced in a Santa Monica vest.

Christie put his late development down to his coach, Ron Roddan, and to the ubiquitous Andy Norman, who encouraged him to give up his job at the Inland Revenue and try to fulfil his potential as a sprinter before he was too old. In Seoul, Christie was making his Olympic debut but was already twenty-eight – fifteen months older than Lewis, twenty months older than Johnson. He hadn't even made the relay team in LA.

Christie's arguments with Frank Dick cast a shadow over his time in Nihon. Their relationship was not quite as corrosive as Lewis– Rogers, but it wasn't good. 'Tensions were high,' Dick admitted to me. 'He had his job to do; I had mine. There was a fair bit of respect as well. But the chemistry between him and me was not good in these situations. There was a bit of arrogance with Linford. That is the case with the top sprinters; they are very like that. A bit of posturing, like the heavyweight boxers.'

Christie arrived in Seoul after the opening ceremony, which he had been denied the opportunity to attend, with Dick deciding – like Francis – that it was too close to the 100m heats. Christie, in his first Games, would have liked the choice. Then again, in his opinion the British team's opening ceremony uniform was 'tatty', so perhaps it was a blessing in disguise. 'Looking good means feeling good,' said Christie.

'Doping equals death,' said Juan Antonio Samaranch, the IOC president, as he opened the 94th Session of the IOC, held in Seoul on the eve of the Games of the XXIV Olympiad.

Samaranch meant death in several different ways. In a physiological sense, 'with the profound, sometimes irreversible alteration of the body's normal processes,' but also, he explained, 'physical death, as in certain recent tragic cases,' and 'death of the spirit and intellect by the acceptance of cheating' and, finally, 'moral death, by placing oneself outside the rules of conduct demanded by society'.

Samaranch followed these doom-laden words with some positive news. It was becoming traditional for sporting bodies to reveal an impressive new anti-doping initiative on the eve of a major championships, even if it would only come into play at a later, often unspecified, date. In Seoul, Samaranch announced a new anti-doping charter, the product of the Ottawa conference.

More immediately, a £3 million anti-doping laboratory, equipped with the latest technology, and the capacity to test 1,600 urine samples over the sixteen days of the Olympics, was ready to begin work in Seoul. Don Catlin, after his experience of running the lab at the 1984 Games, had been charged with helping the IOC find an appropriate facility. He could only find one with a mass spectrometer, the instrument used to analyse urine samples, and it was in the suburbs of Seoul, at an institute devoted to the study of ginseng. So the IOC helped fund that, while establishing the main doping control centre near the Olympic stadium.

Samaranch's 'doping equals death' speech didn't make enormous headlines, but in Britain it was covered in *The Times*, which had led the way on the drugs story, largely through their sports news reporter, John Goodbody. This was exactly the kind of story he was in Seoul to cover. The sports news beat was a relatively new one, prompted by the realisation that sport wasn't all fun and games. Goodbody was a popular figure amongst his colleagues, partly because he knew about obscure subjects like steroids – as a weightlifter in the 1960s, he had sampled them himself – and he was generous in sharing his knowledge.

'There were three main stories at the time,' says Goodbody. 'Football hooliganism, sporting links with South Africa and drugs.' Drugs had moved up the agenda in the twelve months leading up to Seoul thanks mainly to Lewis's comments on the subject and the arrest of David Jenkins, who, as the celebrations in Seoul began, was in California awaiting sentence.

Despite Samaranch's acknowledgement of the gravity of the issue, it could seem at times that Goodbody was ploughing a lone furrow. One of Goodbody's contacts was Arnold Beckett, the British member of the IOC medical commission, and so he was familiar with Beckett's general pessimism about the task confronting the testers. On the eve of the Games, Goodbody forecast that less than one per cent of the drug-takers would get caught. 'That has been the success rate at previous Olympics and there is no reason to suppose it will improve here.' He also quoted the British administrator Sir Arthur Gold, 'The only people who will be caught will be the careless or the ill-advised.'

Nevertheless, on 17 September, the Olympics opened with a flourish, and in a spirit of optimism. Samaranch invited 'the youth of the world' to come together in Seoul, and asked the global audience to rejoice in the celebration of sporting excellence. The speech about drugs had been made to IOC colleagues behind closed doors. Speaking to 70,000 in the Seoul Olympic Stadium, as well as a television audience of a billion-plus, Samaranch was wholly upbeat as he welcomed a record 160 nations – a figure that, pleasingly for the IOC, trumped not only Primo Nebiolo's World Athletics Championships but also the United Nations.

As the five Olympic rings were displayed by parachutists at 12,000ft, who then landed in the middle of the stadium, the athletes marched on to the track country by country, Carl Lewis among the 700-strong American team (not standing apart, as he had been in Los Angeles). In his team-issue blue blazer and tie, he marched around the track, gesturing enthusiastically, bouncing up and down, waving a miniature US flag.

The opening ceremony was hailed as a triumph, not least because of the number of nations involved. With Seoul adopting the motto

'Harmony and Progress', the era of Olympic boycotts seemed consigned to the past. For the first time since Munich in 1972, it was almost unblighted in this respect. Only North Korea – whose bid to share the events with its southern neighbour had been thwarted – boycotted the Games, along with its allies Albania and Cuba.

The 'glasnost' that was sweeping the Eastern Bloc, gradually blowing away Russia's hegemony, breathed fresh life into the Olympic Games, too. It started with showcasing once-benighted South Korea to the world. The Games would be the country's 'coming-out party', as the government acknowledged, and they hoped they would do for South Korea what the Olympics had done for Japan following the Tokyo Games in 1964.

Who knew, perhaps Seoul could come to be recognised as the Glasnost Games, defined by a new spirit of openness, transparency and candour.

Ben Johnson did not venture far from his suite in the Hilton as the Games got underway. He had his mother, Gloria, and his sister, Jean, with him in Seoul, his mother planning to see him race this time. In Rome, Gloria Johnson had admitted, 'I closed my eyes; I said a prayer. The gun went off and it was over. I didn't see it, but I knew he'd won.'

With Charlie Francis in the village, looking after another eight athletes, Johnson spent a lot of time on his own in the week between the opening ceremony and the 100m heats. Mainly, he rested. On the Tuesday, three days before the heats, he had his last proper training session. On the Wednesday he didn't leave his room.

Johnson was suffering from a minor injury: an inflamed Achilles tendon, and so Astaphan gave him a shot of cortisone. Johnson says there was now growing tension between Astaphan and Francis. Astaphan was irritable, anxious – which was out of character, thought Johnson, who had originally found him placid and friendly. Now he was acting very strangely. He and Francis had been having regular arguments, and in Seoul these became volcanic.

Johnson knew nothing about the source of the friction – just as he knew nothing about the review of his Rome world record, which was concluded only on the Tuesday. Francis acted as a buffer between his athletes and the outside world. However, when Johnson lay on Waldemar Matuszewski's treatment table two days before the heats started, and Astaphan administered the cortisone, the doctor dropped a bombshell. According to Johnson, Astaphan, currently on $10,000 a month, told him he wanted a million dollars or he would reveal everything. The response was that they would discuss it after the race.

Anyone else might have been totally thrown by this. But Johnson had a wonderful ability to compartmentalise. One of his greatest strengths, as his sister Jean acknowledged, was 'the way he's able to block out the entire world if he wants... It's natural. That's him, that's Ben.'

At his press conference, Johnson exuded self-belief. 'I guarantee this time no one is going to beat me out of the blocks. I want to win that Olympic gold medal. He could beat me a thousand times, but as long as I win this one it wouldn't matter. I feel exactly as I felt before Rome last year. Carl Lewis has got to run my race. He's got to come and catch me. But he won't.

'This is the ultimate moment of my life. I'm in my prime. I haven't run my best race yet. When I'm at my best, no one can beat me.'

On the Thursday, Johnson left his room to do an hour's light training. Leaving the gym, he bumped into Sherri Howard, an American 400m runner. They started talking and Johnson asked her out. And so at 9 p.m. that evening, less than twenty-four hours before the heats, less than forty-eight hours before 'the ultimate moment' of his life, Johnson went on a date. He had always had an eye for Howard, he says by way of explanation, but had never previously plucked up the courage to speak to her. In Seoul, amidst all the other pressures, it somehow seemed easier.

Johnson says he became suspicious when Howard excused herself after just forty-five minutes. And he claims he subsequently learned that she was friends with Carl Lewis. But Howard has a different recollection of the evening. 'I remember being in the mess hall, eating. Then we went for a drink, a walk, a talk – Ben walked me back to my room. I had a feeling he might be interested in me. I didn't know it was a date. But men probably remember what they could never get.'

Howard, now an actress in LA, tells me that she was, and still is, a friend of Lewis. She had no qualms about being out with his bitter rival. She was bemused by the animosity between them, and felt it was stoked by Lewis. 'Carl was running an anti-Ben campaign. It was like he had a vendetta. He was fixated on Ben, saying, "He's positive! He's positive!" But Ben didn't get involved in that so much. I thought he was a nice guy, very respectful.' She also recalls the rumours around the men's 100m, even before the heats started. 'It wasn't just Ben. Everyone said it was a "loaded" field, and they weren't talking about their speed: they were talking about what everybody had taken.'*

News of the date with Howard reached Francis, though he heard Johnson had been in a bar, drinking beer, with two women after midnight. He was neither shocked nor alarmed. 'Ben liked beer and he loved women, but his nightlife never seemed to hurt him.'

Johnson maintains that Francis's version is incorrect on two crucial points, however. 'It was one woman. And it was champagne, not beer.'

When he had arrived in Seoul, Carl Lewis had tried to check into the athletes' village – which in Seoul were a series of high-rise blocks – in an attempt to avoid the bad publicity he received for his aloofness in 1984. Once again, he had no intention of actually staying there. He had rented a house that was part of a Baptist mission, a deal arranged by the Lay Witnesses for Christ, the group of Christian athletes Lewis

---

* Rob Woodhouse, an Australian swimmer at the Seoul Games, recalls a popular joke among the athletes when 'Testing, Testing', was announced over the public address system in the canteen in the athletes' village. 'When they said "testing", the 100m sprinters couldn't be seen for dust.'

had gravitated towards as a young man. However, Lewis failed to get in to the village, denied access by over-zealous security guards, maybe confused by his fake travelling name. Two days later, with his accreditation finally approved, he checked in. And then checked out again.

Lewis kept a low profile. He didn't have much choice. 'He has so much difficulty moving around,' Joe Douglas told reporters. 'People want to touch him, take pictures of him, ask for his autograph. Even with all the precautions we've taken, people still find us. Carl has had trouble walking just 20 metres.' He did hold a press conference, at which he seemed preoccupied by his rival. 'No matter what, Ben is going to take the lead, because that's where his focus is. But what I like to do is come out of the blocks and accelerate continually all the way until I can no longer accelerate, somewhere between 50 and 70 metres. Then I just try to relax and maintain. That's my objective, to run all the way through. Ben's objective is to run as hard as he can for 60 metres and then hold on.

'Ben's going to make a move the first 10 or 20 or maybe 30 metres. But after that, during my acceleration phase, he shouldn't really move any more, and at the end I can continue and just maintain. So it isn't that I'm running faster than the others, it's that I'm decelerating slower than the others. It isn't me coming from behind; it's me continuing the momentum and the other athletes coming back.'

In his house at the mission Lewis had plenty of company. The family was there as well as Joe Douglas and his clubmate Joe DeLoach. There was also Sri Chinmoy, his spiritual coach, who would come and go, along with assorted disciples.

And, finally, there was another houseguest, described by Lewis in his book as 'a family friend'. It was Ben Johnson's drinking partner from Zurich in 1986. It was André 'Action' Jackson.

12

SWEATING IT OUT

'They were trying to sabotage me.'
BEN JOHNSON

FRIDAY, 23 SEPTEMBER 1988

In front of half-empty stands, the thirteen heats for the men's 100m got under way at 9.50 a.m. Johnson and Lewis, from heats eight and thirteen, were easy qualifiers, Lewis posting his trademark fast heat, 10.14. Like a dog whistle, it sent out a message that could be discerned only by the intended audience.

The intended audience watched this race in his tracksuit top, chewing gum and looking impassive – bored, even. Others swooned. 'He's a magnificently built athlete,' said the BBC commentator Ron Pickering. 'Broad shoulders, very slim hips. This is the man you'd want to take pictures of. The immaculate Mr Lewis in fine sprinting form.'

Johnson had run at full throttle for only the first 30 metres of his race before he visibly eased, and coasted to the finish in 10.37. In the stadium the small crowd, with a heavy concentration of school-children, shrieked and laughed at the spectacle of the world record holder jogging the final 10 metres, and still winning easily. Other-wise, throughout the heats, they clapped and cheered and chattered, generally at the wrong moments. 'They didn't cheer when they should have, and they were loud when they should have been quiet,' Lewis complained.

Johnson's first run underlined his strategy, which was to expend only as much energy as was required to qualify. No more. Not for the first time, it put the approaches of the two favourites in sharp contrast: Johnson unconcerned about what others would read into his performance, Lewis seemingly intent on sending out a message that he was sharp, confirming his status as champion and favourite. Johnson was focusing inwards, Lewis outwards.

Since Zurich, Lewis had become most people's favourite. There were too many doubts about Johnson: the injury that had disrupted his season, his questionable form generally and his defeat in Zurich. And there had been stories about him in the week leading up to the finals, too. That he was injured. That his father was missing, presumed dead. That he had been out on the town – a Korean newspaper heard about his Thursday night out from a security guard at the Hilton. Lewis, on the other hand, was uncharacteristically – but very deliberately – low-key. His final week's preparation, surrounded by family and friends, had been incident-free, serene.

When the draw was published for the quarter-finals, which got underway two hours after the heats, it seemed likely that Lewis would make serene progress to the following day's semi-finals too. While Johnson found himself in a high quality race, up against Dennis Mitchell and Linford Christie, Lewis only had to worry about the Brazilian, Robson da Silva. Two would go through automatically, plus the four fastest losers from across the six races.

Prior to his quarter-final, Francis pressed upon Johnson the importance of not repeating what he had done in the morning. There could be no cruising over the final 10 metres: he could take no chances. Christie was to his left, and then there was Mitchell, wearing a one-piece suit complete with hood – an aerodynamic outfit inspired by Florence Griffith-Joyner. There was a problem at the start, caused by Mitchell rocking in his blocks, interfering with the false start sensors. The other runners had to break while Mitchell was spoken to by an official. He shrugged in response, as though he couldn't make out what he was being told. 'Well, why not take the headgear off?' asked an exasperated David Coleman on the BBC.

When they got away, much to Francis's delight, Johnson blasted out of the blocks. He was quickly upright and sprinting with his customary wide gait and paddling hands. In the next lane but one Mitchell pushed him hard, almost drawing level. In between the leading pair, Christie had the same problem as Lewis. At six foot two, it took him longer to unfold, to pick up and get into his stride. But then, in contrast to the lithe Lewis, he was all brute force and strength. There was nothing relaxed about Christie's sprinting: his eyes popped, the veins on his neck throbbed. At 50 metres, now fully extended and playing catch-up, he lagged about half a metre behind Johnson and Mitchell.

Then, inexplicably, and to Francis's mounting horror, Johnson started to ease up. Or was there a problem? Christie thought so: 'It appeared to me that he had nothing more to give.' Christie did have more to give; he continued to surge through the middle. When Johnson became aware of him on his left shoulder, he couldn't respond. Once he had started to decelerate, he couldn't re-accelerate. And as Christie burst through to win in 10.12, and Mitchell held on for second, Johnson, third in 10.17, slowed to a jog. Then he turned and tugged casually at his vest as he made his way off the track, bowing his head as he disappeared into the bowels of the stadium. His expression betrayed no disappointment or anger; he gave nothing away.

But others were panicking on his behalf. 'Johnson made the novice's mistake and relaxed too soon,' said a surprised David Coleman. 'From 50 metres out Christie was always mowing them down... Johnson's got to sweat it out now.'

Johnson had missed out on automatic qualification. With five heats remaining, his fate was out of his hands. Francis was furious, though he bit his tongue as Johnson traipsed to the warm-up area, where Matuszewski had set up his massage table. He lay on the bed as he had his rubdown. Johnson was a little annoyed with himself, but he was a lot less worried than Francis; he couldn't imagine that 10.17 would not make him one of the four fastest losers. On the massage table he was so calm and relaxed that he drifted off.

Until, around half an hour later, he became aware of a figure nearby. It was Lewis, having just run 9.99 to qualify fastest. He strolled towards Johnson's massage table, a crowd of schoolchildren following him on the other side of the barriers, pestering him to stop and sign autographs. Six feet from Johnson's prostrate form, Lewis stopped, the schoolchildren clustered around him, and he began signing their programmes and scraps of paper. 'Yet another of Lewis's mind games,' was the Francis verdict.

But by now he was too relieved to be irritated. With Lewis having completed the final heat, Johnson's time had survived – he was the fastest loser, and safely into the semi-finals.

SATURDAY 24 SEPTEMBER, 9.50 A.M.

Dick Pound, former Olympic swimmer, lawyer and the International Olympic Committee vice-president credited with masterminding the Games' increasingly lucrative marketing programme, arrived at the Olympic Stadium early on Saturday morning. He wanted to watch his fellow-countryman Johnson, as his challenge for gold reached the semi-final stage.

Surprisingly, Pound had never met either Johnson or Charlie Francis. He had been president of the Canadian Olympic Association when he was first elected to the IOC, but stepped down from the domestic job as he ascended the international hierarchy in the early 1980s. By Seoul, Pound was Juan Antonio Samaranch's right-hand man, his fixer, even if they did not always see eye-to-eye. Pound had distanced himself from his roots. 'I made a point of not getting too close to the swimmers, or the Canadians,' he explains. 'You've got to be pretty even-handed, otherwise they think there's an inside track.'

But Pound had been following Canada's sporting hero with great interest from afar. He was hardly naive. 'I do remember being a little concerned about whether he was being tested often enough,' he tells me. 'They were notorious enough, the sprinters, that they were using these things. I remember thinking, I hope someone's looking after him, and making sure he's OK. And then, we're in Seoul.'

No Canadian could be entirely Olympian as the great day approached. Pound was inevitably swept up in the frenzy around the possibility of a Canadian victory. So he quietly went to the stadium for the semi-finals with his wife Julie and set aside his privileges. 'Sometimes at the track I like to go to the very top of the stand and get a different view from the one in the IOC seats.'

This time, Johnson had again been drawn against both Mitchell and Christie, and also Robson da Silva. And now there was a new problem: he had been up much of the night with stomach cramps: 'It was like I wanted to throw up, but I couldn't throw up.'

Johnson was at the track by 7 a.m and spent forty minutes warming up with Desai Williams, who had qualified for the other semi-final where he would face Lewis, Calvin Smith and Ray Stewart. Johnson still had some pain in his Achilles, so Matuszewski applied some anti-inflammatory creams, and used an electro-stimulation machine – it is not clear if this was Jack Scott's contraption. Perhaps not, given Francis's scepticism.

Lewis's race was first. There was a false start – Lewis and Francis both felt that the Korean starter was inconsistent in the length of time he allowed between 'set' and firing the starting pistol. Second time, Lewis got away cleanly and smoothly, and won with almost embarrassing ease. His time was 9.97 – an Olympic best for anyone at normal altitude. Second was Calvin Smith, but a street behind, in 10.15. Stewart was third, with Desai Williams scraping through in fourth. Francis would have one athlete in the final, at least.

As Johnson and the other semi-finalists lined up, Francis watched from his usual position, at 30 metres. Once again he felt a parental sense of care, responsibility and even fear, though the hulking figure that settled into the blocks, splaying his arms out, with even the slightest movement sending ripples through his muscles, did not look vulnerable. Johnson wore his all-red Canadian kit, his thick gold chain, his black, yellow-laced Diadora spikes. He crouched low, eyes focused on the track ahead, ready to pounce.

When the gun went, Da Silva lurched first. A second shot rang out. False start. The eight shook their limbs out and once again resumed their positions. The gun went again; they were away. But a half-second later the gun fired again. False start. Dick Pound, sitting in the top row in the stands, was stunned to see the red-blazered, white-trousered officials telling Johnson that he was the culprit.

'Goddamn it, that's not a false start!' protested Pound. 'The fucking starter doesn't understand how quickly Ben reacts,' he continued to no one in particular. As Pound vented, his wife turned to him and asked: 'What are you going to do about it?'

'What do you mean, "What am I going to do about it?"'

'Go down there,' she said. 'Tell them. Do something!'

Johnson had been false-started on sight – it had not been detected by the sensors attached to the pads. Pound thought the starter had second-guessed the device out of sheer surprise at how quickly Johnson reacted. 'They're taking his start away from him,' Pound continued to protest. Even if it were not some sinister plot to neutralise Johnson's greatest weapon – or a consequence of the lingering suspicions over his start at the world championships in Rome the previous year – the effect would be the same. If he was forced to hesitate, his advantage was lost.

Julie Pound elbowed her husband sharply in the ribs. He left his seat and made his way down to the track as Johnson's heat re-started, with a clean start this time and Johnson winning commandingly in 10.03. When Pound reached the track, by now very much making full use of his vice-president's accreditation, he sought out Artur Takac, the experienced Hungarian athletics official acting as a technical consultant to the IOC in Seoul. 'You know, Artur, this really isn't fair,' Pound told him. 'You know our guy wins his races at the start and Lewis wins his at the end. You can't deliberately take the start away from him – and that's what happened there.'

'No, no,' said Takac. 'That is not possible. It's electronic. The officials can't call a wrong false start.'

'That was not a false start,' said Pound. 'If you've got your read-outs from the machine, can you get them and explain them to me. Show me the tape.'

Pound says that Takac disappeared 'for about twenty minutes or so and came back and said, "Well, sometimes mistakes happen." He said the tape had been inconclusive.

'And I said, "Don't do this again. Don't let it happen in the final, or I'll call for an examination."'

Francis was also enraged by what he considered a 'false' false start. So was Johnson. Before he won the restart, ahead of Christie, Mitchell and Da Silva, he remonstrated furiously with officials, eventually waving them dismissively away – the kind of gesture that would earn a footballer at least a yellow card. Yet he had characteristically managed to regain his composure quickly enough to win comfortably. 'I didn't false start,' he says now. 'I was too fast for the gun. They were trying to sabotage me.'

Did it weigh on his mind afterwards, and compromise his start? 'I just made sure that, in the final, I wasn't gonna move a muscle,' he says. 'When they fire, I go. I don't move before that. The race they called back would have been my fastest start.

'But it did slow me down for the final, yeah.'

THE DIRTIEST RACE IN HISTORY

SATURDAY, 24 SEPTEMBER 1 P.M.

Lunchtime in Seoul – before dawn in London, late at night on the US East Coast, mid-evening on the West Coast.

All of which was significant. Traditionally, athletics finals had always been held in the late afternoon or evening, and, when the IAAF produced their provisional timetable for the 1988 Games, the men's 100m final was scheduled for 5 p.m., Seoul time – the middle of the night in the USA.

With the American audience in mind, or more particularly the money American TV would pay for the broadcasting rights, Juan Antonio Samaranch of the IOC immediately put pressure on Primo Nebiolo, the IAAF president, to shift the finals to US prime time. But Nebiolo stood firm. He said he couldn't interfere with the athletes' schedules.

There would only be one circumstance in which he would be prepared to compromise: if athletics received a bigger slice of the TV pie. It was Nebiolo at his most calculating, realising that he – or his sport – held the key to the deal the IOC could make with their biggest single source of income: American television.

In the IAAF's in-house magazine, *Review*, Nebiolo insisted, 'Finals in the morning would not allow athletes to realise their potential. We are governed by the interest of the athletes.' Up to a point. The stand-off continued for almost two years, until, eventually, members of the Korean organising committee travelled to Rome to meet Nebiolo. A series of meetings followed, claimed the investigative journalists Andrew Jennings and Vyv Simson, with the Koreans finally asking, 'What do you want in return for changing your finals' times?'

'$20 million dollars,' replied Nebiolo.

Though the Korean organising committee later denied that they paid $20 million to the IAAF, John Holt, then the federation's general secretary, confirms the story. 'With the money from Seoul, Nebiolo created a foundation to do good work in the underdeveloped countries. There was a windfall from the Seoul Games and the foundation lived off the interest, which brought in about $2 million dollars a year.'

The final was moved.*

And so it was soon after midday when Nebiolo took his seat in the royal box of the Seoul Olympic Stadium, and prepared to enjoy the most eagerly and excitedly anticipated race of the Games – and arguably the most hyped of all time. There were no empty seats now, and no noisy schoolchildren. Instead, there were 70,000 spectators, buzzing, transfixed by the eight small figures who appeared in one corner of the track: stretching, bouncing, strutting, preening, staring; looking anxious, intense, nervous, confident, terrified.

---

* At Beijing in 2008, the swimming finals were held in the morning but not the athletics, reflecting the US team's changed strengths and the audience's changed priorities.

13

THE HUMAN BULLET

**'He was so far in front he could have
sent a postcard to the other guys.'**
CHARLIE FRANCIS

SATURDAY 24 SEPTEMBER, 1.20 P.M.

The men by the blocks, going through their routines, are Robson da
Silva, Raymond Stewart, Carl Lewis, Linford Christie, Calvin Smith,
Ben Johnson, Desai Williams and Dennis Mitchell: the finalists for the
men's 100m.

'When people see us on the track,' says Ray Stewart, 'we might be
putting on little games and they think, "this guy is a little conceited".
But put yourselves in our shoes, man, and understand that this is part
of our game plan – as a competitor, we've got to psyche ourselves up.

'It's part of our motivation as well as trying to drive fear into the
other person. It's not to look cool. People don't know. They're not in
our position.'

Stewart felt he was lucky to qualify. He had suffered cramp in the
semi-final, and the Jamaican team was so under-resourced that he
didn't have a dedicated physical therapist. Every other team had a
massage table; Stewart didn't. Before the semi, he had asked Johnson
– with whom he hung out regularly, playing dominoes during quiet

evenings on the European circuit – if Waldemar Matuszewski could help out. 'Of course,' said Johnson.

Later, before the final, when he finally found one of the Jamaican physiotherapists, Stewart asked her for a massage. She rubbed baby oil into his legs. 'She had to borrow the baby oil from someone else,' says Stewart, 'and I just kept my fingers crossed hoping I'd be able to go out there and do my best race.'

There couldn't have been a greater contrast between Stewart and the Americans. Frank Dick, Britain's head coach, recalls, 'In the warm-up area, between the semi-finals and the final, the Americans had their sprinters standing in ice baths – giant bins filled with ice. It was the first time people had seen them. All this stuff was going on, a lot of it for show. You were watching and listening to see the giants coming in. Johnson and Lewis, in particular, were like prizefighters, gladiators.

'Twenty minutes before the race, I left the warm-up area. I had worked out that in the NBC enclosure you could get free hamburgers. So I took a little tour around there. And then I found my spot to watch the race.'

Another scene that played out in the warm-up area, in the minutes before the athletes were called, was a familiar one. At some point in the final moments each athlete paused, closed his eyes and bowed his head; some even appeared to be muttering to themselves. 'It was funny,' said Linford Christie, 'because everyone was praying. Even the atheists were crossing themselves. It's all, you know, "Help me, God, to win."'

A more unfamiliar spectacle was also observed in the warm-up area, which might have unsettled Lewis. He and Tom Tellez watched Johnson practising his starts. But he was holding nothing back. 'All the other sprinters are sitting around relaxing, and Ben was doing these flat-out starts,' recalls Tellez. 'That was weird so close to the race. I thought, is there something I don't know about sprinting?'

When Johnson finished his starts, he quickly settled into his usual calm. Then Williams handed him a full plastic bottle. It had been given to him by Mark McKoy, who said, 'Jamie told me to give this to you guys for after the 100m.' It was another of Astaphan's precautions: a masking agent, albeit an unsophisticated one, made with large quantities of honey and vinegar. Johnson did not know what it was. He took one small sip and discarded the bottle, leaving it in the warm-up area.

At 1.20 p.m., eight minutes before the start of the race, the runners are on the track, bent over their starting blocks, carrying out adjustments to the pedals. Lewis takes longer than most to get them right. While Lewis is in an all-white warm-up suit, Johnson wears the red and white Canadian tracksuit. 'In the old Westerns they had the guy in the white hat and the black hat,' Lewis would say, years later. 'I felt like the clean guy going out and trying to win, I was the guy in the white hat, trying to beat this evil guy.'

Johnson settles into the blocks, holding the set position, bursts briefly forward and almost immediately slows down – a controlled explosion. Lewis walks up the track, turns, walks back, hands dangling by his hips. Johnson removes his tracksuit top to reveal a pale yellow T-shirt. He walks 10 metres up the track, exchanging a high-five with Desai Williams. Six-and-a-half minutes before the race starts, Johnson peels off his T-shirt. It's warm, but not too hot – 25 degrees Centigrade, high 70s Fahrenheit. And there's a slight breeze blowing down the track, on the backs of the runners.

Now Lewis is sitting down, stretching his hamstrings. He gets up, walks along the track, turns, wanders across to lane eight, shakes his teammate Mitchell's hand, then approaches Johnson from behind. Johnson turns and Lewis offers his hand, which is accepted. A couple more handshakes with the others. Now, with three-and-a-half minutes to go, Lewis takes his tracksuit off. Standing, after pulling awkwardly at his trousers, he removes his top and fidgets with his number. Lewis hates wearing numbers: he finds them cumbersome, off-putting.

Johnson prowls his lane, pacing slowly up and down. Finally, the eight runners, stripped and ready, gather behind the line, waiting to be called. Johnson and Lewis linger a step behind the others. 'I try to dictate the race,' Johnson says. Dictating the race starts now: before the race starts. 'So I am about six, seven metres behind the line. I feel very strong, controlling everything. The night before, I put everything in my mind: it's locked up, ready to go. Everything is planned out in my mind. I'm not guessing or thinking. I know what I'm going to do.'

Now Lewis shoots the briefest of glances at Johnson, then, almost in the same movement, scratches his ear. There is a self-conscious-ness about Lewis, a self-containment about Johnson. Between them, Linford Christie wipes his mouth with the back of his hand and Calvin Smith stares ahead and bounces up and down on the balls of his feet. Johnson breathes deeply, shakes his arms and legs, and stares down the straight.

In the stands, Charlie Francis can't sit in his usual place in the athletes' section – no space. He has found a spot in the press area. Standing, craning to see the start, he is nervous and sweating profusely. Elsewhere in the stadium, Gloria Johnson sits with her daughter on one side, Jamie Astaphan on the other. And in another part of the stadium, Evelyn Lewis closes her eyes, swallows hard, screws up her face; this time it's Carl's mother who can't bear to watch.

They're called to the line. Johnson and Lewis hang back, but Lewis concedes and steps forward, followed by Johnson. An eerie hush descends: the kind of silence that can only be made by 70,000 people. It endures for all of the eighteen seconds that it takes the runners to settle in the blocks. In the set position, they hold for two very long seconds. And then it takes Johnson 0.132 seconds to react to the starting pistol.

'And it's a fair start!'

'When the gun go off, the race be over,' Johnson liked to say.

His strategy was not to listen for the sound of the gun; it was to concentrate on what he would do upon hearing it. On the line, he focused on his left hand – his lead hand, which he drove forward and upward as his right foot, his back foot, pushed so hard that it had been known to rip the block out of the track. As he starts, the appearance is of Johnson leaping: his four limbs being propelled forward. Then he lands like a cat, on his feet, fully erect, perfectly balanced. Lewis, in his first few strides, is bent at the hips and slightly off-balance as he picks up and drives forward.

Johnson's start is astonishing. And yet it is a blink slower than it had been in Rome. There, he was away after 0.129 seconds (any reaction below 0.100 is deemed a false start). Here, it is 0.132, only marginally quicker than Lewis's 0.136. In Rome, Lewis's reaction time had been 0.196. This time Lewis, who had been working all year on improving his start, almost matched Johnson out of the blocks.

And yet, Johnson was right. 'When the gun go off, the race be over.'

But, contrary to appearances, this is not a race that Johnson has won with his start alone: it just looks like it. At 10 metres he leads by a foot. Stewart also makes an excellent start, Lewis and Williams lag just behind, Da Silva, Christie and Smith are a little adrift, the usually fast-starting Mitchell is trailing.

Apart from the sight of his gold chain being tossed violently from chest to chin, Johnson is a picture of muscular grace. After 10 metres, he is six-hundredths of a second up on Lewis. Over the next 10 metres it expands to nine-hundredths. At 20, Lewis steals his first, furtive glance towards Johnson.

Between 30 and 40, Johnson gains another three-hundredths on Lewis, whose face is beginning to betray the first signs of panic.

Johnson continues to accelerate between 40 and 60, and the gap to Lewis and the others expands to its maximum: now there is two metres of daylight between the leader and the pack, except for Stewart, who has pulled up injured. Johnson appears to be floating above the track, his feet dabbing the ground – the merest contact for maximum velocity, as Francis preached, like spinning a wheel. Then Lewis begins to emerge from the group, hunting down Johnson, and almost imperceptibly drifting towards him.

In the last 20 metres, to Francis's horror, Johnson relaxes a little, and stops pumping his arms. Now Lewis looks across at him again, for a third time, wide-eyed with the anguish of what's happening. He has fifteen-hundredths of a second to make up. It's impossible. Five metres from the line, his arms relaxing by his body, Johnson finally looks at Lewis, and, with his head cocked to the left, his right arm shoots straight up in the air, finger pointing decisively skyward. Take that.

The clock stops: 9.79.

'He was so far in front he could have sent a postcard to the other guys,' said Francis later, though he was annoyed that Johnson had relaxed at the end. 'It's still painful to me,' he would say three years later. Meanwhile, the other two medallists, Lewis and Christie, had also recorded personal bests, with 9.92 and 9.97. And Smith, in fourth, his head flung back in the closing stages in his trademark style, had also dipped below 10 seconds, with 9.99. It was the first time four men had broken 10 seconds in the same race. Opinion seemed unanimous: we had just witnessed the greatest race of all time.

The analysis of the race spoke of Johnson's superiority. He wasn't just a fast starter. He was the quickest man in the field over seven of the ten 10-metre sections. Lewis, Christie and Smith were quicker than him between 60 and 70 metres; and Lewis was fastest of the whole field from 80 to 90 and over the final 10 metres. At their fastest, from 50 to 60 metres, Johnson and Lewis hit exactly the same speed: 26.961mph. As Johnson once said, he was like a racehorse.

As they finished, Lewis hardly broke stride; he chased after Johnson. But when he caught him, Johnson seemed oblivious to his presence – the ultimate insult. Lewis had to turn him around forcibly and grab his hand. Johnson patted his rival on the lower back, briefly clasped his hand, then turned to embrace Desai Williams, before catching a Canadian flag as it was thrown to the track, and he began to jog a lap of honour, and Lewis stomped away, wearing a look of thunder.

In the stands, Astaphan embraced Gloria Johnson's mother. Waldemar Matuszewski kissed them both. Then he said to Astaphan, 'Our dreams are OK: now we get the houses, the cars, the money that will cover everything!'

'Did you sign any contract?' asked Astaphan.

Matuszewski told him no, he didn't.

'Then this is not for you, Waldemar,' said Astaphan.

This, according to Matuszewski, within minutes of the race finishing.

Evelyn Lewis, a glamorous woman with a permed, bobbed hairstyle and dangling earrings, looked distraught, but also puzzled. She was fixated by Johnson's start. 'You see that?' she asked, her eyes filling with tears as she stood up to clap her son, the silver medallist. 'He shot out like a bullet. See that?'

And in the press area, where Francis stood rooted to the spot, Simon Barnes of *The Times* turned to a neighbour and said, 'Fuck me.'

'Fuck me,' replied his colleague.

'I don't know about anabolic steroids,' said Barnes to John Goodbody, when he had regained his composure. 'I reckon that's rocket fuel.'

It was extraordinary. The most hyped race in the history of the Olympics had achieved something utterly remarkable: it had surpassed its billing. It was magical, thrilling, the stunning denouement to one of sport's most compelling rivalries. The race to end all races. A race that – we instinctively knew – would be remembered long after the rest of Seoul had faded in the memory.

But we didn't know how long. Or exactly why.

Carl Lewis seemed to have no idea what to do, where to go. For a few moments he stood with hands on hips, staring blankly at the big screen in the stadium, waiting to study the replay. He looked lost. 'I don't feel it was the best race I ran here,' he told NBC. The race contradicted that: his start had been fast, he had just run a personal best: 9.92.

Had he not been aware of Johnson's explosive start? 'Well, no. I didn't see him until about 60 or 70 metres. He must have really caught a flyer; he was out there in front like he was in Rome. I just tried to run the best race I could and I'm pleased with my race,' Lewis went on, contradicting himself somewhat.

'I thought Carl ran a very good race,' says Joe Douglas now. 'Carl concentrates only on what he has to do. He doesn't come up too quick, he comes up at a 45-degree angle and he drives every step. I thought he ran a great race. I was very, very happy with him. Johnson's run; I knew what it was. I was unhappy about that. But that's life. Carl, I thought, handled it well.'

When Johnson had finished his long, frequently interrupted lap of honour, he stopped to give a brief interview to the TV reporters. He was asked what he cherished more: the gold medal or the blistering world record. 'The gold medal,' said Johnson. 'It's something no one can take away from you.' Had he not relaxed near the finish, he thought he might have run 9.75, 'but I'm saving that for next year'. Around him, a crowd of people had gathered, a larger-than-ever entourage of hangers-on, all trying to get close to the new champion.

The medals ceremony followed just half-an-hour after the finish. But, as the medallists were called, Lewis was nowhere to be seen – he was showering. To the side of the track, Johnson and Christie line up anyway, Johnson in his team issue white tracksuit top and red bottoms, one trouser leg tucked into his sock, giving him the air of a naughty schoolboy. Lewis, in his all-white tracksuit, eventually appears and falls in line as Johnson and Christie begin their march to the podium. Lewis, expressionless, tugs at his sleeves as he walks out, and at his collar, pulling it up around his neck.

For the highest-profile event of the Olympics, the medals are presented by the two most powerful men in attendance: the grey-suited

Juan Antonio Samaranch and blue-suited Primo Nebiolo. As the three medallists wait behind the podium, Johnson turns to Christie and they appear to share a joke, while Lewis stares straight ahead, biting hard, the muscles in his jaw twitching. When, finally, he is called, Johnson trots jauntily up to the top step of the podium. He doesn't smile as 'Oh Canada' is played; he squints through the sunshine as the flag is hoisted, then he looks down, lost in his thoughts, or perhaps just unsure how to react.

After the presentation, Johnson is led into the stands, to receive a phone call. It was the Canadian prime minister, Brian Mulroney. 'My congratulations on behalf of all Canadians,' Mulroney told him. 'You were just marvellous. There is an explosion of joy here in Ottawa.'

'Thank you,' said Johnson.

Then, engulfed once again, unable to move more than a few yards without his entourage expanding, Johnson slowly makes his way to doping control. Lewis, Christie and Smith – the first four finishers were automatically tested – were either waiting or had been and gone. Johnson was the last of the 100m men to report. The centre was located behind double glass doors beneath the stands of the Olympic Stadium. A discreet slate grey sign by the doors read, 'Doping Control Centre. *Controle Anti-dopage*.' There was a single sheet of A4 taped to one of the glass doors, its instruction scrawled in a black marker: 'No one is allowed to enter without Pass'.

Inside, there was a waiting room. Also in this restricted area was a small adjoining room where the paperwork was completed, and a toilet where, under the gaze of a lab staff member, the athlete would fill a bottle with a urine sample. Then he would divide his urine into two smaller bottles, labelled A and B. Then he would sign forms to indicate that he was happy with the procedure.

In the waiting room was Arne Ljungqvist. It was his job to monitor the athletes as they waited to give their sample, to ensure the correct protocol was followed. 'Normally we had someone from the IOC and someone from the IAAF supervising,' explains Ljungqvist. 'But I fulfilled both those rules: I was on both. So it was just me.

'When Johnson appeared it was chaotic,' he continues. 'There was such excitement, of course. And there was a huge group around him, people shouting with joy and enthusiasm. There were a lot of people, I don't know how many. It was difficult to get things in order: we had to calm them down and let people into the doping control station in some reasonable order. In those days there were no rules relating to who could be in the waiting area, and who could not be. It's different now.'

But on this Ljungqvist appears to be mistaken: the rules in Seoul were that the athlete was allowed into the waiting room with one accredited member of his support team. Johnson was accompanied by his therapist, Matuszewski.

Johnson had to wait and Ljungqvist watched him carefully. 'I had been at a reception a few days before the final, and Johnson was there,' he says. 'I saw his yellow eyes. I was not happy with what I saw. Those yellow, jaundiced eyes are a sign of steroid use. But it doesn't count; all that counts is a positive analysis.'

Johnson recollects something that Ljungqvist apparently missed, though. There was someone else in the room: a familiar figure, though he couldn't, at that point, recall his name.

It was André Jackson: the man with whom he had enjoyed a night out in Zurich in 1986, and who he had seen, sporadically, around the track circuit; the same André Jackson who was staying in Seoul with Lewis. Jackson was not involved with the US team – or with the Olympics – in any official capacity. But, nonetheless, Johnson recalls, 'André was sitting right in front of me the whole time, on the ground, back against the wall, with the refrigerator on the other side of him. We were just talking and joking around about the races and other things. Waldemar was working on my Achilles, which was very sore.

'I was in there almost two hours,' continues Johnson, 'and I said, "Man, this is taking too long."' Johnson had emptied his bladder before the race; now he was dehydrated and couldn't go to the toilet. So he drank beer, not just because he liked beer, but to speed up the process. 'But it was taking a long time to go to the washroom,' Johnson recalls. 'I said to André, "Pass me another beer." Some other people were coming and going, but André was there the whole time. And Waldemar is not paying attention; he's working on my leg.

'I had about eight beers.'

Eight beers?

'Yeah.'

Did he know at this point, as he sat chatting, that he was with a man so close to Lewis that he was actually staying with him?

'I knew he'd run with Lewis's group back in 1984 and '85 but he never made it as a sprinter. But I thought him and Lewis would not be associated all these years later on. He was very friendly. He loved to go out with the ladies. He was talking about how much he could get the ladies to come out with us and have a good time... '

Johnson laughs: a deep, deep laugh.

'In the dope control room, André said, "Congratulations on your victory." I said, "Thanks." Then I said, "You're not supposed to be here; you're supposed to be on the outside." I guess he didn't like that very much. He said, "I'm just here to wish you good luck, take some pictures." We talked about other things. It was friendly.'

Although Ljungqvist was there too, he says he can't recall seeing the tall, handsome black man in a white T-shirt, stonewashed jeans and Mizuno trainers. Yet Jackson was certainly there. There is a photograph of him, sitting on the floor alongside Johnson, with two cans of beer.

Elsewhere in the stadium, the journalists were waiting, impatiently, for Johnson to appear for his post-race press conference. When he got there and took his seat – after Lewis and Christie had done their stuff – he was buzzing. He sat beside Francis, and discreetly told him, 'I'm shit-faced.'

'But I was able to speak properly,' says Johnson now.

That was not the impression of some of the journalists. They thought Johnson was monosyllabic at best, incoherent at worst, though there was one surreal moment of clarity, when he announced, 'I'd like to say that my name is Benjamin Sinclair Johnson junior, and this world record will last fifty years, maybe a hundred.'

As well as the fact that Johnson was now drunk, another factor might have contributed to the strange atmosphere. It was that some of those present now found themselves unable to suspend their disbelief any longer. If there had been widespread scepticism about Johnson a year ago in Rome, now his 9.79-second run – and the margin of his victory – produced outright cynicism. Journalists often have to write less than they know, or think they know. There is often an air of suppressed rebellion when they attend press conferences. This was an extreme case. When Johnson finally appeared, there were nudges and winks. At least one journalist mimicked the act of injecting his arm with a syringe.

'But you could not write,' says Doug Gillon, 'that Johnson was the gold medal winner subject to the results of the drugs test.' There was also the fact of history. Suspicion outweighed positive tests by a factor of at least a million to one; no big name had ever tested positive. And nobody thought that was about to change. But there was something else, too. As well as scepticism and cynicism, there was awe.

Johnson's run had been scintillating, no matter how it had been achieved. In some, a head-versus-heart struggle played out: the head said that everything about Johnson and his run invited suspicion, the heart thrilled at what it had just witnessed. It was the heart that governed the emotional response, which was the only response in the aftermath of the race. And it could be summed up in one, three-letter exclamation: Wow!

Something that had not significantly changed, four years after Los Angeles, was the prevailing attitude towards Carl Lewis, at least from

240

his own country's media. He hadn't won the race, and it seemed that he still couldn't win with some sections of the media. Four years ago he had been accused of showboating, and of being too calculating. Then he showed too much. Now he showed too little. 'In his aloof manner,' wrote the *New York Times*' columnist Dave Anderson, Lewis 'spoke as unemotionally as a talking computer about how he was "pleased with his performance" of 9.92 although the Canadian set a world record with 9.79. Pleased? When he didn't win history's best 100m race? Performance? When he was a relatively distant second banana?'

Johnson had abandoned social niceties – 'The important thing was to beat Carl' – which Anderson respected: 'That's the way a real competitor should talk. No clichés. No avoiding the issue. No memorised lines. Throughout his comments, Lewis was so cool he was cold. His only words of praise for Johnson were a quick, "He ran a great race, he ran a great time." Other than that, while Johnson took nearly two hours to reach the interview area, Lewis's only deference to Johnson's victory occurred when he momentarily started to sit down at the gold medallist's microphone, then moved to the silver medallist's microphone.

'At least outwardly, Lewis never seemed to understand what was at stake... This wasn't just another Olympic 100m dash. This was the Olympics' answer to Ali–Frazier III, to Nicklaus and Palmer in the 1967 United States Open, to Borg and McEnroe in the 1981 Wimbledon final,' wrote Anderson.

Simon Barnes of *The Times*, attending his first Olympics, had a quite different take on the press conference, and on his American colleagues' attitude towards Lewis. He paid a tribute of sorts to the 'magnificent certainty' of Johnson, 'the Human Bullet, with eyes of flame. A brick wall would have slowed him up a little – he would have lost maybe a couple of hundredths blasting through it.'

But mainly Barnes seemed concerned with – and perhaps a little bit *for* – Lewis:

A thousand or more journos pressed for deadlines, yelling questions, exploding flashlights, a shoving mass desperate for a quotable line. And no longer do we have the three fastest men on earth, basking in their pride. We have three shifty, defensive, edgy characters. Johnson, not a great wordsman, kept his answers as brief as possible to disguise his stutter. Christie, the fastest European ever, played a dead bat to everything: not what pressmen want...

And Carl Lewis – well, everybody hates Carl Lewis. 'He's just so arrogant,' American journos say vaguely. They say he is phoney, that he is only in it for the money, that he never smiles. As Lewis set out to win his four gold medals in Los Angeles he seemed on the verge of becoming the Great American Hero. He failed. It is hard to understand why. He does everything right, shakes hands with everybody before a race, professes born-again Christianity, does laps of honour with the Stars and Stripes – but he is still hated.

True, he seems to feel no joy in his achievements. He is blank, cold, arrogant. But then enough Brits have found Sebastian Coe the same at times – yet Coe does not lack love as Carl Lewis does. Lewis is pursued by rumours of alleged homosexuality. I care nothing for his sexual tastes myself. But the American press have cruelly nicknamed him 'The Flying Faggot', signifying a dislike of Lewis more than a dislike of homosexuality.

'Yeah, and he makes so much money, that doesn't help,' said another representative of the land of opportunity.

What keeps Lewis from the love of the media, and thus from the love of the great American public? Is it his arrogance? His humourlessness? His joylessness? The rumours? The money? I think it is all a lot more simple than that. I think that at the heart of the Lewis Problem is the fact that Lewis is black... You get the idea that, unconsciously, a lot of people are waiting for black athletes to show some kind of human failing. You also get the impression that black athletes come out on the defensive right from the start.

Black athletes come into a press conference and are faced with a sea of white faces, all apparently hostile, waiting for them to say something stupid. This is not necessarily a fair assessment – but it is certainly how it must look. Small wonder they take refuge in 'arrogance' or monosyllabic 'unhelpfulness'.

Now, when he recalls the Seoul 100m, Barnes says it still thrills, still takes his breath away. He lists it among his top three sporting moments. He has no regrets about introducing the race angle, and stands by his comments. 'Lewis was an indigestible person in some ways, but if there's a problem affecting a black person, there's going to be racism involved somehow. Even if a black person is hugely popular, there's still a racist element. Not just in America; here in Britain, too.'

On the evening of his triumph Johnson returned to the Hilton and changed into an all-white suit. Then he went downstairs and headed out to a nightclub in the Hyatt Hotel, where he bumped into Russ Rogers, the American coach. Rogers had mixed feelings about what had happened in the final. Actually, Rogers didn't have mixed feelings at all. He was ecstatic. It's not something he readily admits; but it's obvious. And there's the fact that, when he bumped into Charlie Francis, in the immediate aftermath of the race, Rogers congratulated him and quietly said, 'Thank you.'

'I was shocked,' explains Rogers. 'I was shocked that Ben won by such a distance. I thought it'd be much closer. But when he came out the blocks, after five yards I knew he'd won. He jumped out the blocks; he didn't run out the blocks.'

And was Rogers pleased that Johnson had beaten one of the athletes in his team, even one he had been battling with almost from the moment they touched down in the Far East? 'Well,' says Rogers, 'with all the things that had taken place with Carl, with his attitude, I wasn't surprised that he was beaten. You've got to be focused. That day, I knew he'd get second.

'After the race Carl was in total shock. He was wide-eyed with shock. He could not believe that Ben had beaten him. He was in a daze. He knew he was going to win that race. He *knew*.'

When Rogers bumped into Johnson at the nightclub he was greeted enthusiastically. 'I was there already and Ben came in and grabbed me. We sat there and had some drinks. We must have had about twenty-five drinks. I got to bed at four o'clock; I had to get up at seven.

'Ben had a white suit,' continues Rogers, 'and he was signing autographs, "Ben Johnson, fastest man in the world." There was a queue of people – fellow athletes, no matter what country – waiting to see him.

'Most of them were saying, "You showed him."'

14

DENY, DENY, DENY

'Have you taken anything?'
DICK POUND

'No.'
BEN JOHNSON

In his rented house in Seoul, Carl Lewis reflected on his defeat with his guru, Sri Chinmoy.

Chinmoy reassured him that Johnson's world record would be beaten. But he also reprimanded him: 'Now, please tell me, why did you have to glance to the right side after 75 metres? Even a beginner, a novice, would first and foremost be advised not to do that. It is such a deplorable mistake! I was so sad when I saw you looking at him. Originally your goal was in front of you, but then you changed your goal. He became your goal instead of the tape.'

'You are right,' said Lewis.

'I am telling you, until the very last moment nothing is decided,' said Chinmoy. 'In boxing there are twelve rounds. Even if someone is leading in points after the eleventh round, still you can knock him out in the twelfth round.'

Tom Tellez was in Seoul, though he was not staying in the same house as Lewis. 'In sixteen years coaching Carl, I never had a bad day with him,' he says. Which only made him more puzzled by what he had just witnessed. 'I was annoyed at the way Carl ran the race. He looked at Ben right at the start then again twice, three times. I had never seen him do that before. I was surprised. If he hadn't done that, I'm not saying he would have won. He might've won, I don't know. But it would have been close.

'I don't know if he was too caught up in the rivalry,' adds Tellez. 'It was more like he lacked a bit of confidence. That wasn't like Carl.'

SUNDAY 25 SEPTEMBER, 6 P.M.

Twenty-eight hours after Johnson's victory, Dr Jong Sei Park, the director of the Seoul anti-doping laboratory, analysed his urine.

Not that he knew it was Johnson's urine. Park had found two positives in the first week of the Games, both Bulgarian weightlifters: Mitko Grablev and Angel Guenchev, and both gold medallists. The disgraced pair were followed by the rest of their country's weightlifters out of Seoul, but the exit of the Bulgarians hardly overshadowed the games. The incident was a passing cloud, scudding across the otherwise serene Korean sky.

The Bulgarians were mentioned in passing by Juan Antonio Samaranch. And like all positive tests, these were presented as evidence that the system was working: the cheats were being caught. On Sunday, Johnson's was one of around a hundred urine samples tested by Park and his team. The lab director must have known that, among them, were the four top men in the 100m. But nobody in the lab had any way of matching the code on the bottle with the name of the athlete.

In testing one urine sample, Park detected metabolites of the anabolic steroid Stanozolol. Though this was not a requirement, he immediately re-tested it – he wanted to be sure. He was sure. The amount was significant: 80 nanograms. Next, Park informed Robert Dugal, the Canadian official supervising the lab that day, and Prince

Alexandre de Mérode, the head of the IOC medical commission. And he gave de Mérode the code from the bottle. De Mérode was the only man with the codes; he kept them in a safe in his temporary office at the Shilla Hotel, where the IOC had its headquarters. We must assume that four years on, he was more careful with his safe.

When he received notification from Park, de Mérode checked the code on the bottle against his list, matching the sample with the athlete. And then he took a deep breath. De Mérode now sat down and dictated a letter, on behalf of the IOC medical commission, to the athletes' Olympic association, giving them the news that every association dreaded: one of their athletes had tested positive. The fate of the athlete now rested on the analysis of the B sample – or a credible explanation for the presence of a banned substance.

SUNDAY 25 SEPTEMBER, 11.30 P.M.

Don Catlin and Robert Dugal were having a late dinner in Seoul. They ate late every night, after their shifts supervising proceedings in the lab. Dugal was distracted; he had something on his mind. Eventually, he told Catlin what it was:

'Well, your guys got another medal today.'

Catlin looked baffled. Dugal said it again, 'America have got another medal today.'

'What do you mean?'

'You got the 100m.'

MONDAY 26 SEPTEMBER, 1.45 A.M.

De Mérode's letter, on behalf of the IOC medical commission, was hand-delivered to the Canadian Olympic team's headquarters in the athletes' village. It was opened by Carol Anne Letheren, the team's *chef de mission*. It stated that Ben Johnson's A sample had tested positive; it didn't name the substance detected in his urine.

Letheren stared blankly at the letter but kept the contents to herself. She decided not to inform Johnson or Charlie Francis – who had other athletes competing the next day – until the morning. Instead, she spent much of the night wandering the athletes' village. And as dawn broke over Seoul on Monday morning, she spoke to William Stanish, Canada's chief medical officer, and Dave Lyon, the athletics team manager.

At 7 a.m. Lyon was dispatched to Francis's apartment, in the same block, several floors above the team headquarters. When Francis answered the door, Lyon didn't beat around the bush. 'We've got to get over to the medical commission,' he told him. 'Ben's tested positive.'

When Francis entered the team headquarters he met Letheren and Stanish. They discussed what had happened; Francis was anxious, but most of all he was confused. He wasn't putting it on: he was genuinely baffled, which reassured his colleagues. They assumed his surprise came from his confidence in Johnson.

But Francis's mind was processing quite different information. He was thinking about Johnson's final steroid cycle, and concluding that he had stopped taking them in plenty of time before Seoul, that the drugs would have cleared his system; they always did. It made no sense.

The man at the centre of a slowly gathering storm was still in the Hilton Hotel, oblivious. Johnson lay in bed in suite 2718, with his mother and sister in adjacent rooms. Francis didn't want to tell him yet. Instead, at 10 a.m., he, Lyon and Stanish drove to the anti-doping laboratory, where they met Manfred Donike and Arnold Beckett, in their capacity as members of the medical commission, and Jong Sei Park.

First there were the formalities: Beckett confirmed that a banned substance had been detected in Johnson's urine. 'But before we tell you what the substance is,' he said to Francis, 'can you think of anything that might have caused it?'

Francis replied that he couldn't. The metabolites found in Johnson's urine, Beckett then told him, were Stanozolol: the substance for which Donike had developed a test with the help of his guinea pig, Don Catlin. This baffled Francis even more: his athletes had been on Estragol, not Stanozolol.

By now, Johnson was being driven to the laboratory. When he joined them, he was carrying a gym bag containing bottles of the vitamins he had been taking – all legal – and he had a handwritten note from Jamie Astaphan, confirming that he was not taking any banned substances. 'He was less upset than I might have expected,' Francis observed. 'A lot less upset than I was.'

Johnson was quizzed by Beckett for fifteen minutes. Though Don Catlin has said that athletes will sometimes admit to having taken something illegal when they visit the lab after a positive test, Johnson stuck to the mantra Francis had drilled into all his athletes, 'Deny, deny, deny.' But he did say that there had been a third party in the anti-doping room, someone besides the official observer, Arne Ljungqvist, and his physical therapist, Waldemar Matuszewski.

'I knew something was funny – that guy in the testing room must have messed me up,' said Johnson. Beckett asked if he knew who the mystery man was, and Johnson replied, 'It was a tall black guy.' (He apparently didn't remember the name André Jackson until years later.)

Beckett had also asked Francis about the 'mystery man'.

'It was a white guy,' said Francis.

'Come on,' said Beckett, 'get your story straight.'

This discrepancy, and his conversations with the lab staff, seemed sufficient for Beckett to dismiss the 'mystery man' explanation.

Johnson returned to the Hilton, while Francis and the Canadian officials travelled to the Shilla Hotel, where they met Dick Pound, not just IOC vice-president but, as he puts it now, 'the only Canadian lawyer in Seoul at that moment'.

Pound had only recently been made aware of the impending drama. First thing in the morning he and his wife, Julie, had been at the diving pool, watching Greg Louganis, before returning to the Shilla for a reception with the board of one of the IOC's commercial partners, Coca-Cola. The function was being held in the hotel's most opulent suite, occupied, of course, by the IOC president, Juan Antonio Samaranch.

When Pound arrived, he found Samaranch in a state of distress, but trying not to let the sponsors see it. 'Have you heard the news?' he asked quietly.

'Greg Louganis won…?' asked Pound.

'No!' said Samaranch. 'The *news*!'

'What is it – somebody died?'

'No it's worse!' said Samaranch. He led Pound into his bathroom and closed the door. 'Ben Johnson has tested positive.'

'Oh, shit,' said Pound.

He and Samaranch returned to the meeting with the Coca-Cola board. 'We had to sit with these guys,' says Pound, 'and they're saying, "We're so glad your nice Ben Johnson beat that dreadful Carl Lewis."' Through gritted teeth Pound replied: 'Thank you very much.'

'As soon as I could escape,' Pound recalls, 'I called Carol Anne Letheren, who said, "What are we gonna do?" I said, "I don't know." She asked if they could come to the Shilla Hotel, and I said, "Sure." I had an extra sitting room in my suite, because I was a vice-president. And down they came with Charlie. When they arrived we gathered in my room and I said, "So what's the deal?"

'They told me what was going on. And I told them that it was more likely they would fail to find something in a sample than have a false positive. The only option was to challenge the process.' Johnson had already signed the paper saying he was happy with the doping procedure, so that was a problem. 'I said, "What about the scientific results? Can we challenge the science?"

'Someone said it was Stanozolol and Charlie reacted oddly. He said, "But I don't want my guys on Stanozolol on race day! It tightens them up. I want them loose... "

'I thought,' says Pound, 'my God, the issue here might not be *whether* but *what*."

Then they said, 'Will you help him?' which put Pound in a difficult position. There was his role in the IOC to consider. He was on the executive board that, if the positive was confirmed, would have to disqualify Johnson. There was also Pound's unease with what Francis had just said. The Canadian delegation was insistent, though, telling him, 'We just want to make sure he gets a chance to say whatever he has to say... '

'Well if I'm going to defend him,' Pound replied, 'I've got to meet him.'

Pound's wife was sent to rendezvous with Johnson in the Shilla Hotel lobby. Since there were always journalists hanging around there, it was important for him not to attract attention. Not that a visit to the Shilla would automatically be deemed suspicious. After all, since his success Johnson had been in demand almost as much by officials as by fans. On the Sunday, twenty-four hours after his triumph, he spent much of the day in the royal box at the Olympic Stadium as Primo Nebiolo's guest.

Julie Pound met Johnson in the lobby and escorted him to the lift, standing in front of him to try and hide him. It wasn't that difficult: she was surprised how small he was. When they arrived in the suite, Pound took him into the bathroom and shut the door.

'Ben, are you on anything? I can't go and lie for you. I don't do that as a lawyer; I won't do it here. Tell me: are you on anything?'

'No, no.' (Deny, deny, deny.)

'Well, I'll do what I can, but I gotta tell you, this is going to be a pretty steep curve. Because they've found something in your system... '

Like Francis, Pound was struck by Johnson's calmness; he seemed utterly unperturbed. 'I don't know that he really understood the seriousness of the situation,' Pound suggests. 'My view now is that I guess he knew he was taking something he shouldn't, but he would've been putty in the hands of Charlie and everybody else.'

Johnson told Pound about the 'mystery man' in the dope control centre, who handed him cans of beer. Still, though, he could not recall the man's name. But when he heard this angle Pound's eyes lit up: it was a shaft of light. 'We should go and find him, maybe there's a story,' suggested Johnson. Pound thought about it, then decided, 'No, don't. Speaking as a lawyer, whoever he is, he'll have an explanation for having been there, and there goes your defence.'

There was another possible source of contamination, suggested Johnson: the drinking bottle with the honey and vinegar concoction he had been handed by Desai Williams before the final. Though he barely touched it, he told Pound he had taken a sip.

'If that was spiked, it's your problem,' Pound told him. 'You're responsible for what you put in your body.'

The only 'spiked drinks' defence that might work – and only in exceptional circumstances – would be if Johnson could prove that a drink had been spiked after the race. Only the mystery man could have done that; but this just seemed too implausible.

'As a legal exercise,' says Pound, 'it was pretty hopeless.'

MONDAY 26 SEPTEMBER, 10 P.M.

That afternoon Jong Sei Park, in the presence of two Canadian officials, as well as Francis and Johnson, had tested the B sample. Johnson opened the bottle himself, as is the custom, to guard against accusations of tampering. The B sample also tested positive. But even then, Park wanted to be doubly and triply sure. After Johnson and the others had left he tested the sample twice more. Only then did he inform Alexandre de Mérode that the tests had been conclusive.

As soon as he heard, de Mérode called a meeting of the IOC medical commission for 10 p.m. in the Shilla, to hear Johnson's case and decide his fate.

Despite the hopelessness of the situation, Dick Pound appeared on Johnson's behalf and mounted what one observer described as 'a passionate defence'. He opted not to identify a single cause or explanation. As Pound tells the story, 'I'm explaining about the lack of security and the informality in the doping control station, and the presence of this mystery person, and saying there was too much opportunity for something to go wrong. But I'm not making much contact with the audience.

'And then Donike, Manfred Donike, he hits me with it. "Mr Pound," he said, sounding like Colonel Klink, "Mr Pound, would you be interested in the scientific results of the tests?"

'And I tell you, if you're a lawyer, you know you're dead at this point,' Pound says. 'I said, "I'm not sure, but our chief medical officer might." And I look over at Stanish, our medical guy, who's about that colour.' Pound points to the while walls in his office.

Pound conferred with Stanish. 'What have we just heard?' he asked him.

'What we've just heard is that, not only did they find Stanozolol in the urine sample, but his entire renal cortex function is so depressed that it's clear this is not the first time he's used all this stuff.'

After almost three hours of deliberations, the medical commission found against Johnson, and told the Canadian contingent they would recommend his disqualification the next day.

Pound remained in the meeting; the other Canadians waited in his suite. By now Francis was nursing toothache – perhaps stress-induced, as in Rome the previous year. But he found comfort in the time the meeting was taking: the longer it went on, the more optimistic he became. 'The commission must be split,' he thought. Eventually, Pound phoned and gave Francis the news: official disqualification would come at 9 a.m. After the hearing, at 1 a.m., Francis met Pound in the hotel bar, where they were joined by John Holt among others.

Pound was pragmatic. But in defending Johnson he had taken a major gamble – one that could have compromised his position in the IOC. Did he feel compromised? He was disappointed Francis and Johnson had lied to him but he insists, 'As a lawyer, it's a professional thing. You've either got bullets to shoot or you've got no bullets to shoot. I had none.'

Defending Johnson in Seoul did not affect Pound's position – far from it. Twelve years later, he would be appointed founding chairman of the World Anti-Doping Agency and become recognised as the most influential and most outspoken figure in the anti-doping movement. But, as Don Catlin puts it, 'It was a strange moment in Dick's career.'

Catlin also baulked at the intervention of his friend Donike. The German chemist's use of additional scientific evidence during the medical commission hearing was unprecedented. But it was based on an analysis by Donike of Johnson's previous urine samples, including the one given in Zurich five weeks earlier, which was negative. This enabled Donike to establish Johnson's 'endocrine profile', and with this, he was able to determine his 'normal' levels of hormones such as testosterone. These levels, he discovered, were all over the place: a sign of steroid use.

Francis was furious when he heard about the endocrine profile – reasonably asking, 'If such an analysis were reliable, why wasn't it used for everyone?' Catlin was also surprised that Donike produced this evidence. 'It provided a nail, and helped seal the case. It shouldn't have, but it did.' As far as he was concerned, the analysis of Stano-zolol in his urine was enough in itself. He was not even convinced Donike's profiling was wholly reliable.

'But that next morning was... ' continues Catlin, leaving the sentence unfinished, but screwing up his face, shaking his head at the memory. 'It stopped the Olympics cold for one day. I found a room in the basement of the Shilla Hotel, a laundry room. And I found a desk and I just sat and read and worked there all day. I kept outta the way. Because the press were just... hammering.'

TUESDAY 27 SEPTEMBER, 2 A.M.

The phone rang at 2 a.m., waking Charlie Whelan, a journalist with Agence France-Presse, one of the world's biggest news agencies. He was in bed in one of the AFP apartments, which he shared with a colleague, Ron Wall, in a high-rise tower in Seoul's 'media village'.

On the phone was Patrick Minn, chief of AFP's Seoul bureau. 'Ron came into my room,' recalls Whelan. 'I remember him opening my door, and saying: "There's been a big drugs bust. We think it could be Ben Johnson."'

'You are joking,' replied Whelan.

He wasn't. They entered panic mode – but silently. They could not yet know whether it was true, untrue, an exclusive, or something their rivals were already on to. Whelan alerted the agency's desks including the sports editor of the French-language service, Michel Hénault. Five minutes later the AFP men crept outside, shutting doors as quietly as possible, speaking in whispers. Outside, they sneaked into a car and began to drive away. An AFP colleague, returning from a night out, spotted them leaving. He was suspicious, so he followed them in a taxi.

A ten-minute drive through deserted streets took them to the press centre. They found the vast building blacked out. They entered, turned on the lights and found their assigned desks. From Whelan's seat he could look out on a clear Seoul night, and make out the towers of the media village, in silhouette.

A course of action was quickly decided. 'Hénault made the decisive call,' says Whelan. 'We didn't know if it was Johnson: that was just a rumour. But we had good information that it was a massive bust, and that it was from the 100m.'

Hénault covered Olympic politics and knew who was who at the IOC. He phoned the one man who would know the identity of any athlete who had failed a drugs test: Prince Alexandre de Mérode. He woke him up. 'Did an athlete test positive after the men's 100m?' Hénault asked him. De Mérode's mumbled response – neither a confirmation nor a denial – satisfied Hénault that he was right. 'Is it Johnson?' asked Hénault. De Mérode went silent.

'If you don't hang up in ten seconds then it's Ben Johnson,' said Hénault. De Mérode stayed on the line for more than ten seconds. Then he hung up, and unplugged his phone. 'It meant,' says Whelan, 'that he confirmed it without saying it. He had "deniability": if he was asked whether he'd told a reporter that it was Johnson, he could say no.

'Now we felt we had confirmation that was strong enough to run the story,' Whelan continues. 'We weren't 100 per cent certain – there was certainly doubt in our minds. In fact, there was a possibility that we were wrong, and would all be fired. But we were prepared to be fired. It was such a huge story. And Hénault was the boss, he was a heavyweight, and he said, "Go with it."'

Whelan and his colleagues quickly filed what they called a bulletin, or flash report: a top priority news story. Meanwhile, they worked the phones, calling contacts everywhere. For them, it was almost as exhilarating as Johnson's run.

That first flash report had the impact of a bomb detonating. In Britain, Des Lynam, presenting the BBC's evening Olympics programme, was handed a printout of the AFP bulletin. A solemn and clearly shaken Lynam came out with the line that still reverberates: 'I've just been handed a piece of paper here that, if it's right, it'll be the most dramatic story out of these Olympics, or perhaps any others.

'It says Ben Johnson of Canada has been caught taking drugs and is expected to be stripped of his Olympic 100m gold medal, according to International Olympic Committee sources.'

Lynam understood the impact of his words; he also understood the risks. 'We didn't trust the French agency all the time,' he explained some years later, 'but we decided to go with it and apologise later if it was wrong.'

He kept reading, 'A report from the IOC medical commission, to be presented to the medical board later this morning, Seoul time, reveals that Ben Johnson took anabolic steroids before his historic victory over Carl Lewis on Saturday. The result of the dope test will be officially announced by the IOC at nine o'clock; that's twenty-three hours GMT. Eleven o'clock tonight.'

Lynam placed the sheet to one side. 'That would be absolutely sensational. It's unconfirmed as yet, we've got it from a news agency.

'We'll push on for the moment,' he added. 'The women's 400m hurdles... '

In Seoul, Charlie Whelan gazed out of the window, in the direction of the media village. A few minutes ago it had been shrouded in darkness. Now he watched as 'one light came on... then another light came on, and another, and another, and another. Within an hour it was blazing with light.'

Whelan manned the phones, taking calls from journalists around the world, all wanting to know the source of the scoop. Whelan didn't tell anyone, other than to say that the story had been 'confirmed' by a high-level IOC source. The truth was, he didn't know, at that point, the actual source: he had no idea who had told Patrick Minn.

It was not until 2005 when Whelan was back in Seoul, and working as AFP's bureau chief, that an elderly man approached him and outed himself as the person who'd broken 'the most dramatic story of these or any other Olympics'.

His name was Yong-suk Shin, and in 1988 he was the Olympics editor of the *Chosun Daily*, Korea's oldest and biggest newspaper. 'I had fifty reporters working for me,' Shin explains, in perfect English, when I track him down. 'And I had one reporter who smelled that something was going on with the IOC medical committee.' Shin will not say who the reporter was, only that she was a woman. 'She told me it was a really big story. So I went to the Shilla. I had to see what my reporter told me with my own eyes; it was too big a story, too important.

'At the Shilla I saw many IOC members whom I knew, members of the medical commission. And I saw the IOC spokeswoman, Michele Verdier. I asked her if Ben Johnson had a problem. She said she couldn't say, but she did not deny it. It confirmed to me that something was going on with Ben Johnson. I decided to send the news to the front page. But my publisher kept asking, "Are you sure, are you sure?"

'I confirmed through another source at the IOC, at the highest level. We knew Samaranch at the time. I'm not saying it was Samaranch. Our source didn't say yes, but they didn't deny it. So I said to my publisher, "You can believe me."'

Shin was not quite as confident as he allowed his publisher to believe, though, not confident enough for his paper to go out on a limb. 'I feel it's better to have some support,' he explains, 'so we needed some foreign media to run the story.' He spoke to the *Chosun*'s sister paper in Japan. And then he spoke to his friend Patrick Minn. He thought it was appropriate to go to a French agency, since a Frenchman had started the modern Olympics. I had heard a story that Shin had found Minn in the pub and told him there that Johnson had tested positive.

'In a pub?' Shin asks, incredulous. 'I had no time to go to a pub. I was the busiest man in Korea!'

TUESDAY 27 SEPTEMBER, 3 A.M.

With the *Chosun Daily* hitting the newsstands in the early hours of Tuesday morning, shortly after the detonation caused by AFP's bulletin, there was a stampede of journalists to the Shilla Hotel. Phones had been ringing off the hook in the media village, and in those days before ubiquitous mobiles, long queues formed outside phone boxes.

At the Shilla, journalists surrounded the usually composed IOC spokeswoman Michele Verdier. But in the early hours of Tuesday morning, as the greatest Olympic scandal began to unfold, Verdier was less attack-dog, more rabbit-trapped-in-headlights. Tensions were running high. Dressed in a green business suit, and with a bag over her shoulder, Verdier looked as though she was trying to leave – probably to go to bed. But a mob of journalists pressed in, pushing for answers.

'So there'll be no official IOC statement tonight?' asks one.

'No, no, at the press centre in the morning.'

'Who'll be at the press centre?'

'I'll be at the press centre.'

'And there'll be a statement?'

'Yes, if there is something to announce.' She shrugs, and turns away, adding, 'I don't know.'

'Ooooh, come on!' says another journalist.

Verdier turns sharply back, and snaps, 'Oh, come on what? Come on what? Why do you think I've been up until 3 a.m. Uh? It's my fault?'

In the Lewis house in the Seoul suburbs, the phone rang at 4 a.m. Reporters had been calling Joe Douglas's Santa Monica office and Lewis's Houston home, as well as associates, friends and family members. When he was finally tracked down to his rented house in Seoul, Joe Douglas answered the call. 'It was an American reporter,' says Douglas. 'He asks, "What do you think of Ben Johnson testing positive?"

'"Whoa! Whoa! What did you say?"'

'I let Carl sleep, I didn't tell him. I wasn't going to wake him at four. He was still competing. I told him in the morning. But we knew he was going to test positive. We knew he was on drugs. So I wasn't surprised. What surprised me was that they didn't cover it up.

'I guess I was happy. Happy that maybe this would stop the use of drugs: knowing they could get caught. Carl's reaction was similar to mine. We weren't exhilarated. But it was good; good for the sport.'

But Douglas's version of events contradicts the scene described in Lewis's book. When the phone rang, according to that version, the news travelled quickly around the house. 'Everyone in the house was up, and there was a lot of excitement. What justice, if Ben had indeed been caught. What a shock, too. All these years he had been getting away with using drugs. Finally, this might be the end of the line for him.'

TUESDAY 27 SEPTEMBER, 4 A.M.

Before the IOC's official announcement of Johnson's positive test, and his disqualification, Carol Anne Letheren had to retrieve his gold medal. Letheren had become fond of Johnson, even slightly protective of him. In the company of Francis and Stanish, she wandered through the labyrinthine corridors of the Hilton Hotel to room 2718, located, as she later put it, 'in the hinterlands of the hotel'.

Entering the suite, they found Johnson with his mother and sister Jean, both of whom were distraught and sobbing quietly. Ben had broken the news to his mother earlier. Gloria Johnson recalled the scene years later for a BBC documentary: 'He said to me, "Mom, guess what." He wasn't looking so happy. He said, "I test positive."

'I said, "Oh no – that can't be." And he lay down in the bed, his hands crossed behind his head, and he stretched out. I said, "Don't worry, everything is going to be OK." That's all I could say to him at that moment.'

Also in the room were the agent Larry Heidebrecht, already counting the lost millions (an anticipated $10 million in 1989, according to Heidebrecht, $25 million over the course of his career), and a stunned Jamie Astaphan. Francis quietly asked him whether Johnson could possibly have taken Stanozolol. Astaphan responded by shaking his head. Johnson, meanwhile, was impassive. He was 'the calmest person in the room,' according to Francis. 'He hugged his mother and said, "Come on, Mom, nobody's died."'

Letheren became emotional when it came to asking for the gold medal, which, on Saturday evening, Ben had presented to his mother. 'Ben, this is very hard for me to do,' said Letheren, 'but I have to take back the medal.'

'Here it is,' said Johnson. 'I can't lose something I never owned.'

'Ben was very cooperative,' said Letheren. 'He didn't really say anything. He gave the medal back. It was like a wake at a funeral: it had that sense of grieving, and pain, and disappointment, and probably some anger. And, I would suggest, some denial and disbelief at what had really happened.'

Johnson, Letheren reflected later, 'appeared to be in a complete state of shock, apparently not comprehending the situation and not comprehending the information. It was like he didn't quite know what was going on around him.'

Johnson says now that his main concern was for his mother. 'At the time, I just wanted to get my mom out of there safe. I didn't care if it was embarrassing. I just wanted to get my mom safely home. When everything was going crazy all over the world, I was nice and calm. I did nothing wrong, I didn't kill anybody. Nobody died in my family, so why should I worry?'

For Letheren, the handing over of the medal seemed almost unbearably poignant. But for Johnson, as she said, the emotional impact was hard to judge. Perhaps Letheren's diagnosis of denial was accurate – and remains so, even twenty-three years on, with Johnson still believing he can 'clear his name'. But he offers another explanation for the apparent absence of shock: he says it wasn't a surprise. 'Well, I was expecting something like that to happen in my career,' says Johnson with a shrug. 'I had fear that I was in jeopardy. I knew there were people who wanted to sabotage me. So I wasn't surprised.'

Yet still he didn't seem angry. 'Because I know what the real truth is,' he says. 'And once you know the real truth, then nobody can break you.'

As Letheren left with a gold medal that would now be presented to Carl Lewis, Francis and Heidebrecht set about planning Johnson's exit from Seoul. Francis wanted him to head somewhere he wouldn't be harassed – a return to St Kitts was mooted – but Johnson insisted on Toronto, where his dream house was being built. He had intended to move in soon after the Olympics. Toronto was home, he said.

What Johnson didn't know was that his new home was as doomed as the rest of his world. Within hours of the news getting out, the builders, fearing they wouldn't be paid, abandoned the site.

TUESDAY 27 SEPTEMBER, 8 A.M.

As Seoul woke up, and the athletes learned the news, the other 100m finalists were sought for comment. Carl Lewis initially said nothing; he had the 200m finals to concentrate on, and then the relay. He had already won the long jump on Sunday, the day after the 100m. But he had given a recorded interview just before the news broke. Now it was broadcast. He said he was surprised by Johnson's improvement from the opening round, 'Because he wasn't the same person Friday as he was Saturday. That race was shocking. I just don't know how he does it or whether he gets a hypnotist or something, but he does something to stimulate himself for the finals.'

Linford Christie, when he heard, was in tears. He and Johnson were friends. 'It's a sad day for Ben because he's been a very good ambassador to the sport,' said Christie, his head bowed and eyes down – the impression was of someone who was in mourning, though Christie would later point out that he had been reading a prepared statement.

Later, asked about Johnson's positive, Christie told reporters, 'I don't really know how I feel about that exactly. I suppose I don't care what the other athletes are doing as long as I'm a drug-free zone. It's not a nice way to win a medal; there's a certain sadness about that. It's a very sad day for athletics as a whole. Anybody who gets caught is at the end of the road. It's a real shame for the sport.'

Calvin Smith, the man who had finished out of the medals in fourth, struck a slightly different note. 'I've got mixed emotions. It's a strange feeling to be told you've won a bronze medal three days after the event. I'm not surprised or shocked about Ben, because I've always suspected he was taking something. This should clean up the sport and make it better for everyone.'

Now, he reflects, 'First of all, I was very disappointed to finish fourth in the first place. I wasn't happy about the people that beat me. When I heard about Ben, it wasn't a surprise that he was taking drugs; it was a surprise he was caught. Everybody knew certain people were on drugs. I even feel that if they could've covered it up, they would've done. I think there must have been a breach at the lab; that's the reason it must've come out.'

Smith proposed a new medal ceremony, in front of the crowds at the Olympic Stadium, but the idea was quickly rejected by the IAAF. 'There was no ceremony,' says Smith. 'Nothing.' Instead, Primo Nebiolo presented Lewis, Christie and Smith with their medals in an obscure office inside the Olympic Stadium a week after the final. 'They had us come over from the village,' recalls Smith. 'They didn't want any publicity.'

Smith's sense of frustration has only increased over the years as, one by one, his fellow 100m finalists from Seoul have either tested positive or found themselves implicated in a drugs case. Of the eight, only two, Smith and Robson da Silva, the Brazilian who finished sixth, have retained unblemished reputations. Lewis, of course, had tested positive for stimulants at the US trials, and – even before he had received his 100m silver to replace his bronze – Linford Christie tested positive for Pseudoephedrine after coming fourth in the 200m. The IOC accepted his defence of inadvertent use, because he had drunk ginseng tea, and cleared him by a vote of eleven to ten. 'He's very lucky,' said Arnold Beckett. But Christie was less lucky eleven years later when he tested positive for the steroid Nandrolone.

The other three fell over the following years and decades. Dennis Mitchell, who was fifth, served a two-year ban for using testosterone in 1998, and later testified that his coach had injected him with human growth hormone. Desai Williams, who was seventh, told the Dubin Inquiry that he had used anabolic steroids, though he escaped punishment. And Ray Stewart, who pulled up injured, was banned for life in 2010 for offences while coaching,

'I have my bronze medal here in my house,' Smith says, nodding towards the stairs. And with uncharacteristic conviction, he adds, 'I feel I should've been the gold medallist. That's what I feel.'

TUESDAY 27 SEPTEMBER, 9 A.M.

By the time Michele Verdier read the IOC statement confirming Johnson's positive test and disqualification, and Prince Alexandre de Mérode, sitting alongside her, had answered the media's myriad questions, Johnson was on his way out of Seoul.

Whatever he had done, it is impossible to watch the pictures of Johnson making his way through Kimpo airport and not feel a pang of sympathy. In many ways it mirrored his chaotic arrival. The atmosphere was febrile. Johnson was jostled and manhandled, surrounded by a mob of reporters and camera crews – and fifty security guards, struggling to keep order. In the middle of it all Johnson was again expressionless: and yet he didn't look like someone in the depths of an existential crisis. Here was a man who had fallen from the summit of Everest, and was still falling. But Johnson, in a black leather jacket, with his boarding pass in his mouth, might have passed for a holiday-maker beset by a minor difficulty: a lost bag or a delay through fog.

It wasn't the picture the press wanted: they wanted the despair of a man whose dream had been snatched away. Yet Johnson wouldn't, or couldn't, oblige.

Still, one reporting team went to extraordinary lengths to get the shot of Johnson alone, lost in his thoughts, coming to terms – or not – with the collapse of his world. John Iacano, a photographer with *Sports Illustrated*, bought a ticket for the same flight to New York, along with Shelley Smith, the magazine's reporter. Smith even managed to sit beside Johnson for forty-five minutes, obtaining a first, exclusive, interview, throughout which Johnson followed the mantra: deny, deny, deny. Smith and Iacano caught a flight back to Seoul the next day.

When the plane stood on the tarmac in New York the in-flight crew were more sympathetic than the reporters waiting outside. They invited the Johnsons to hide in the cockpit. But eventually the fugitives had to catch their onward flight to Toronto, and the scenes at Kennedy airport were similar to those in Seoul. The BBC's Martin Bell described the 'tumult and pandemonium' as, behind him, a mob of reporters and New York police officers formed a swarming mass around Johnson. Bell was an experienced war correspondent and here he was reporting from the latest front line.

Later, when Johnson landed in Toronto, he was booed. The mood in Canada was a mix of disappointment, anger, hurt and shame. The anger had been expressed that morning by Earl McRae, a column-ist with the *Ottawa Citizen*. McRae began by describing Canadians huddled around TV sets, enjoying a moment they would always remember, when Johnson 'made this small nation prouder than any nation in the world'.

Then came the bombshell, prompting McRae's open letter:

So, thanks Ben.

You bastard.

Thanks for the humiliation, the embarrassment, the international disgrace.

I won't remember, if I can help it, too much longer exactly where I was and what I was doing when you cheated and won; but I'll remember for a long time exactly where I was and what I was doing when I heard the news of your death.

I'll remember the time, 4:35 in the afternoon, and Beverley waking me up from a nap and saying, you won't believe this, it can't be true, it just can't be true but a Canadian track and field athlete has tested positive for drugs in Seoul and the rumour is it's Ben Johnson.

And then she cried, Ben; she cried because like all Canadians, we believed in you and respected you and maybe even worshipped you a bit and you said you'd do it and you did and you made the whole, wide world look at that Canadian flag you held; you made us a somebody in the eyes of the whole, wide world...

And so it went on, until McRae finished where he had started:

Thanks, Ben.

You bastard.

Johnson was vilified, and, in some reports, no longer referred to simply as a 'Canadian', but as a 'Jamaican-born Canadian'. He was dehumanised: 'a monster created by drugs', an 'outcast of the sporting world', a man for whom drugs had, according to one claim so absurd that it might have made Francis smile, 'turned an also-ran into an Olympic champion'.

Brian Mulroney, the prime minister who had telephoned his congratulations to Johnson after the final, spoke now of 'a moment of great sorrow for all Canadians, especially the younger generation'. His sports minister, Jean Charest, was decisive: he banned Johnson for life from all 'amateur' competition.

But such reactions said more about the depth of the hurt felt by Canadians. Johnson sought refuge in his house as the anger began to abate, even if the disappointment and shame remained. A crowd gathered outside his home. It included the media, of course, and a large proportion of teenage fans. Some seemed to be there out of voyeuristic curiosity, and many were supportive, one banner reading, 'We believe in you, Ben.'

For McRae's fury was not quite typical. The street scene was characterised by a peculiarly Canadian civility. Johnson emerged briefly to clean his Ferrari, and the crowd politely stepped back to allow him to polish the windows. His car also provided one way of escape, though one day Johnson was stopped for driving his Ferrari at 87mph as he tried to evade his media pursuers. After being booked by the police, he got into a scuffle with cameramen. A few days later a motorist complained that Johnson, this time driving his Porsche, had pointed a pistol at him. It was a starting pistol. In the media, a picture was starting to emerge: Johnson in meltdown.

But Canada was as ambivalent as its fallen hero. One anonymous Canadian coach described him as 'a victim of society'. And on the streets of Toronto in those early days, vox pop television interviews suggested widespread sympathy, as well as general cynicism about the pervasiveness of drugs in sport. 'I guess I feel most of the competitors probably use steroids at some point or other,' said one man. 'It's too bad he got caught.'

'I feel very sad for him but that's the price you gotta pay,' said another.

'I do feel sorry for him,' said one woman, 'and his mother especially.' And from her doorstep, Johnson's sister Clare mounted an impassioned defence, 'I can really tell anybody from the bottom of my heart that he is not guilty. He is not guilty.'

Back in Seoul, meanwhile, the Canadian team felt the sting of their highest profile athlete's disgrace. 'Our guys didn't want to wear their Canadian uniforms any more,' says Doug Clement, the athletics coach. 'Everyone just felt so ashamed.'

As for Lewis, he had the 100m gold: a replacement for the medal he had buried with his father. And he had become the first man in history to defend the title successfully. But the circumstances made it bittersweet. His last week in Seoul was all like that.

He won the long jump for his sixth gold medal. But he could only finish second in the 200m, behind his US and Santa Monica teammate Joe DeLoach, another man who, like Lewis, arguably should not have been in Seoul after his positive test for stimulants at the US trials.

But the order of the one-two proved awkward: DeLoach was his protégé – Lewis had persuaded him to go to Houston, and to join Santa Monica – and the result made them both uncomfortable. In their post-race interview, with DeLoach at pains to praise his mentor, Lewis's smile was stilted, his magnanimity forced, the tension unspoken but obvious. Not for the first time in Seoul, Lewis looked stunned, though at least the result vindicated one argument he had been having with Russ Rogers, which had centred on whether or not DeLoach should be in the relay team. 'Obviously Joe has proved he should be on it,' said Lewis.

But the nadir came in the relay, where Lewis failed to win his third gold medal. He did not even run. Rogers selected a makeshift quartet for the qualifying heat, omitting Lewis and DeLoach, who had turned up at the stadium in their tracksuits and warmed up, only to learn, ten minutes before the race, that they would be sitting it out.

From their seats, they could only watch in horror as the inexperienced Lee McNeill, running the anchor leg, turned to take the baton from Calvin Smith. He fumbled and seemed to panic. 'My hand was shaking so bad,' he said later. 'I gave Calvin a shaky target.' He tried to grab the baton with his left hand, then his right, and finally got a firm hold, but outside the passing zone. There was no red flag, but a protest by the Nigerian, French and Soviet teams was upheld and the US team was disqualified. 'To me it was probably a blessing in disguise,' Rogers told me. He explained that he was fed up with the feuding. But it seemed that his bitterness towards Lewis had, in the end, clouded his judgement.

Lewis was furious, calling the debacle 'an outrage'. It was hardly the only one of the Seoul Games. But it ended his second Olympics on a suitably discordant note.

15

THE MYSTERY MAN

'I was in too deep. I lied.'
BEN JOHNSON

Bob Armstrong watched the Seoul 100m final in a rural hotel north of Toronto. His law firm was on a weekend retreat in Georgian Bay, but the whole country was glued to the race, and three hundred lawyers were not going to miss it. At eleven o'clock at night, most of them crammed into the bar, craning to see the one television screen, then letting out an almighty roar as Ben Johnson ran the fastest race in history. 'Every Canadian knows where they were when Ben won the gold medal,' says Armstrong.

Afterwards, the drinks flowed.

Armstrong was a big sports fan, and he had a kindred spirit in his mentor, Charles Dubin, the chief justice of Ontario. They watched football, baseball and hockey games together. 'When we weren't talking law, we were talking sports.' But little did they know the extent to which the two would intersect and take over both their lives.

Less than a month after Johnson's return from Seoul, Brian Mulroney announced a government enquiry, to be headed by Dubin: the 'Commission of Inquiry into the Use of Drugs and Banned Practises Intended to Increase Athletic Performance'. Dubin immediately appointed Armstrong lead counsel. Armstrong describes it as 'a kind of marriage made in heaven, the two of us engaged in taking a detailed look at a very important part of the sporting world. We both went at it with great enthusiasm.'

Armstrong met Charlie Francis in the first week of October. He also began meeting athletes: members of Francis's group, and others. Although the inquiry was restricted to Canadian sport, he wanted to understand the wider context. He travelled the world, flying to the UK to meet Linford Christie, Frank Dick and Daley Thompson. He spent time in California, talking to, among others, Robert Kerr, the 'steroids guru' who had advised Angella Issajenko in 1983. It was, he says, eye-opening, and eye-watering.

Armstrong knew Francis's lawyer, Roy McMurtry, who told his client that he would only represent him if he told the commission the truth. Francis quickly agreed. 'Charlie broke the conspiracy, the brotherhood of the needle,' says Armstrong. He told him about the drug programmes his athletes had been on for more than seven years. But Johnson took a different tack. Right until the moment he appeared as the final witness at the Dubin Inquiry, he maintained his innocence. He even called a press conference in a Toronto hotel on 4 October, sitting alongside his parents, and his lawyer Ed Futerman, to insist that he had 'never knowingly taken any performance-enhancing drugs'.

This was too much for Issajenko. 'I came to the conclusion that BJ was going to lay the blame on Charlie and Jamie,' she said. 'I felt at the time that when someone has been very good to you, someone has done you a good turn... when someone is responsible for making you great, you shouldn't turn against them.' Like Francis, Issajenko decided to come clean. She also made her diaries available to Armstrong and his team, and supplied them with bottles of Estragol – the anabolic steroid supplied by Astaphan. Dubin commended her as an 'impressive witness... articulate, forthright, fair, and truthful'.

Just as in the months before Seoul, a divide opened between Johnson and his coach. He was represented by Futerman, and his agent, Larry

Heidebrecht, was still involved – or thought he was. In the days after Seoul, Heidebrecht, trying to make the most of a bad situation, sold an exclusive interview to the highest bidder, doing a deal with the West German magazine *Stern* for a reported $1 million, money that demanded a full confession.

When Heidebrecht turned up at Johnson's house, accompanied by a van-full of reporters and photographers from *Stern*, he found the door locked. 'Ben, let me in – open the door,' pleaded Heidebrecht. 'Ben, I've got to talk to you.' The door remained locked. Heidebrecht tried a side entrance. But eventually he had to admit defeat, retreating sheepishly past the throng of other journalists stationed outside.

The other team member who refused to cooperate was Astaphan. He had made a surprise appearance on television, turning up at the CBC studios only hours after landing in Toronto. He was interviewed by Barbara Frum, whose probing questions and tenacity turned Astaphan into a gibbering wreck. As he repeatedly denied ever giving Johnson Stanozolol – 'I have never made it available or accessible to him, and I don't know of any incident where Ben was exposed to this, even visually' – he squirmed and sweated, and his face was overcome by his tic. It was an interview that did very little to persuade anyone of Astaphan's – or Johnson's – innocence.

Astaphan then returned to St Kitts. He had no intention of attending the inquiry, he said, or not unless certain financial conditions were met. When he was threatened with a subpoena, he relented. Armstrong flew to St Kitts to meet him.

Armstrong did not meet Carl Lewis, or any of his team. The only other Seoul finalist called to the inquiry was the second Canadian, Desai Williams. Armstrong admits there was discussion about calling Lewis to testify, but explains, 'We decided we didn't want to turn the inquiry into a circus. We saw no point in turning this thing into a Johnson versus Lewis controversy. It would look like Canadian sour grapes, and there was no point to that.'

Nevertheless, Armstrong's travels left him in no doubt as to the extent of the doping problem. Though the focus was on Canadian athletes, 'I had to know what was going on elsewhere, and it became very clear to me that steroids were absolutely de rigueur in the United States. It was common in those days to say that the East Germans and the Russians were all on steroids. That probably was so, but make no mistake about it, the Americans were at the forefront.

'It was also absolutely clear that complicit in all this were the IAAF and the IOC, to the extent that they were aware of the problem and they did nothing about it. If they had wanted to do something about it, they would have done out-of-competition testing. Their in-competition testing was a complete waste of time.'

Few would disagree. But it raises an obvious question: why was the biggest fish of them all caught in Seoul?

The Dubin Inquiry began sitting in February 1989. It lasted eleven months and called 122 witnesses, culminating in a 600-page report, culled from 1,400 pages of testimony. In his report, many of Dubin's conclusions were damning of the culture of elite sport, which he came to regard as an ethical vacuum. He spoke of the 'moral crisis' afflicting sport. In many respects, he seemed to be broadly in agreement with his first witness, Charlie Francis, who spent eight days giving evidence. But they disagreed on one point.

While Francis had lamented having to 'confront our limitations', and sought to overcome them by cheating, Dubin believed that this was at the very root of the issue. Some athletes took drugs, he said, 'because of their inability to accept the limitations of their natural ability and because of a flawed system of values'. Moreover, he worried about how their loss of ethical standards would seep like poison into other areas of the competitor's life: 'We cannot allow sport, which we expect to build character, to become a means of destroying it.'

But he did not just blame Francis and the athletes. In his summing up, Dubin said, 'The failure of many sports governing bodies to treat the drug problem more seriously and to take more effective means to detect and deter the use of drugs like anabolic steroids has contributed in large measure to the extensive use of drugs by athletes. Added to the laxity of enforcement has been a laxity of investigation.

'When an athlete was detected using performance enhancing drugs, only the athlete was disciplined and the incident was treated as an aberration,' Dubin continued. 'No enquiries were made about the circumstances under which the athlete took drugs and whether responsibility should also attach to coaches, physicians, or indeed to the athletic organisations themselves. Thus, no investigation was made into the true extent of the use of drugs and what influenced the athlete to use them.'

Francis told the inquiry about his experiences as a young sprinter at Stanford and what he witnessed at the Munich Olympics, about becoming a coach, about his conversations about steroids with East German coaches, and his belief that, if his athletes were clean, they might as well set up their starting blocks a metre behind their rivals.

Many, if not all, of the athletes who testified were just as candid – in total, forty-six admitted to steroid use during the inquiry. It was the fact that Issajenko had kept bottles of the 'Estragol' given to her by Jamie Astaphan that meant the substance could be analysed, and shown to be Winstrol V, a veterinary product that – crucially – contained Stanozolol. The milky white product was intended for animals, to build up their lean muscle mass before slaughter.

It was the same for Johnson. He was built up. And then he was slaughtered.

Johnson appeared as the final witness on 12 June 1989. Having heard the testimonies of Francis and Issajenko, he had, as Bob Armstrong puts it, 'nowhere to hide'. And so he admitted, 'I lied.'

Despite all the past lies, both Armstrong and Dubin seemed to feel affection, and some sympathy, for Johnson. Dubin found him 'a very polite and well-mannered young man'. He also felt that 'within the field of his own expertise, he had no difficulty in expressing himself'.

This was important, because Johnson's defence had appeared to hinge on his lack of intelligence, with his legal team seeking to portray him as ignorant of what he was doing. Dubin rejected this. 'Although he placed great trust in his coach, his physician, and other members of his entourage, it is apparent that he has a mind of his own... From my own observations, I think it was unfair to Mr Johnson to describe him as unintelligent.'

Now, Johnson, who subsequently fell out with his lawyer, blames him for the fact that he initially lied. He says that Futerman 'tried to change the way I was thinking. I told him the truth from the beginning, I said, "This is what it is," and he said, "No, this is what we're going to say."'

Throughout the Dubin Inquiry, the atmosphere seemed less that of a judicial investigation, and more akin to a truth and reconciliation commission. The courtroom was brightly lit and modern; and Dubin created an unthreatening environment. When Johnson appeared, he seemed only slightly uncomfortable as he began to be quizzed by Armstrong.

On his relationship with Francis, he said, 'He's a nice person, he comes from a good family. His mother is very nice. Charlie has been very nice to me; we have a good relationship.' He wiped his face with his hand. 'If Charlie give me something to take, I take it.' It was on the second day that Johnson offered his apology: 'I was in too deep. I lied, and I, I was ashamed, for my family, my friends, other Canadian athletes. I was just in a mess.'

'If you're given the chance to run again, what country do you wish to run for?' asked Armstrong.

'I would like to represent my own country,' said Johnson. 'Canada.'

'And do you believe you can be the fastest man in the world without steroids?' Armstrong asked.

'I know I can be,' said Johnson. The end of his testimony was greeted with a round of applause.

Armstrong's careful, persistent probing, and his calm approach, was perhaps as important to the inquiry as Dubin. In a sense, Johnson and Francis emerged almost as victims – willing victims, but victims nonetheless. But Armstrong was less sympathetic towards Astaphan, still nervous-looking, who admitted to the inquiry that he had injected Johnson with steroids 'fifty or sixty times', though he insisted, 'I thought it was my responsibility to do this.'

'You,' said Armstrong, 'were playing Russian roulette with Ben's liver, with his Achilles tendon, and perhaps he indeed is very fortunate that he tested positive in Seoul, to ensure that at least people like you would be exposed.'

Following the inquiry, Astaphan was fined $5,000 by the Ontario College of Physicians and Surgeons and banned from practising medicine in the province for eighteen months. A remarkably light punishment, and of little consequence – as Astaphan, by then, was back in St Kitts.

Francis thought his honesty at the inquiry would serve two purposes. It would open the world's eyes to the reality – as he saw it – of sport at the highest level, and it would explain, and justify, his actions. Then, perhaps, he would be understood, if not ever fully rehabilitated. It could be said that he achieved the former, partially and briefly: his testimony sent shockwaves through the world of athletics and made global headlines.

And it was not just Francis's word. Others testified to the pervasiveness of drugs in elite sport, including Robert Kerr, who said that he had prescribed steroids to twenty US medallists at the 1984 Olympics. Revelations such as these, and the admissions of Manfred Donike, Robert Dugal and others about the ineffectiveness of an in-competition testing programme, garnered headlines for a day, and then the stories were forgotten. Many thought – or hoped – that the inquiry would provide a clarion call to action. But it was all too easily ignored.

Dick Pound, who also testified at the inquiry, thinks this was because Dubin, though he reached conclusions about sport in general, restricted the investigation to Canadian sport. 'Dubin confirmed a lot,' says Pound, 'but my feeling was, "Don't stop in Canada." This is an international problem. Dubin, for some reason or other, didn't want to make it international. We had problems in Canada, but it didn't end there.'

Yet part of the blame – as Dubin made clear – belonged to the IOC. The ambivalence of Samaranch, its president, was apparent in his words after Johnson's positive: 'I consider Ben Johnson a great champion. He's guilty because he's guilty. But maybe the most guilty people are the people surrounding Ben Johnson.'

Pound acknowledges that Samaranch 'would have been just as happy if the drugs problem had gone away. He was never willing to invest much of his personal political capital in going head-to-head with the international federations on it.' It could go a long way to explaining why, after Dubin, so little changed. Samaranch remained in office until 2001. Sport carried on as though Seoul had never happened.

For Dubin and others, the Ben Johnson affair revealed many unpalatable truths and supported the view that sport was suffering a 'moral crisis'. Robert Voy told me about a post-Seoul athletes' drugs helpline he helped establish on behalf of the US Olympic Committee. A large proportion of the callers, under the cover of anonymity, were preoccupied with one question, 'Where can I get what Ben Johnson was taking?'

Dubin believed that the only way for sport to confront the problem was to break the conspiracy of silence. But those who did were punished. Francis's reward for his candour was to be cast into the track and field wilderness – he was banned for life from coaching in Canada. Johnson and Angella Issajenko were also stripped of their world records – a decision Dubin criticised.

Francis did not detach himself from sport, however. It is doubtful whether he could: it was his own form of drug. He worked as a personal trainer to businessmen and sports people, some of them well known; and there were probably far more who never let on.

In 2003 he burst back into the sprinting limelight, when it was revealed that he was working with Marion Jones, the Olympic champion, and Tim Montgomery, whose 2002 world record finally surpassed the time Johnson ran in Seoul – by a hundredth of a second. Although both athletes were eventually found to have used drugs, and there was considerable suspicion around them already, Francis insisted that drugs formed no part of their programme. And it appears that, as far as his time with them was concerned, this may be true.

But Jones came under pressure from sponsors and officials to stay away from Francis, so the collaboration was short-lived. Charles Dubin, fifteen years after the inquiry, even re-emerged to say, 'Mr Francis has paid a high penalty with respect to his past mistakes. It is appropriate to allow him once again to work with elite track and field athletes.'

But, except for this ill-starred interlude, he never did.

He did, though, become the 'go-to' expert on drugs in sport for some in the media. He even became friends with Jim Ferstle, the American journalist whose main interest was uncovering drugs scandals. For Ferstle, the Dubin Inquiry changed his thinking, to an extent. 'I came into this whole thing being a black and white person, believing there is good and evil,' he says. 'Dubin got me to appreciate the grey areas. Charlie and I, in another context, would probably have hated each other, but we had common ground, we understood each other, and ultimately we became friends.'

And they spoke regularly. 'My son would pick up the phone and say, rolling his eyes, "Charlie is on the line." There were no short conversations with Charlie. But that was the fun part.'

According to Ferstle, Francis's 'main motivation at Dubin was to get the truth out. He thought that by doing that, not only would it expose what was going on, but it would help him. That didn't happen, though. And the hypocrisy of it all stuck in his craw.'

Dick Patrick was another journalist who developed a good rapport with Francis. He says, 'Even after Charlie was banned, a lot of coaches and athletes still came to him in an advisory capacity, to bounce ideas off, because he was a really smart guy, extremely knowledgeable. We spoke regularly.' But that created a problem; one of his editors at *USA Today* hated the idea of Patrick speaking to Francis, even when he was doing a series on drugs. 'I said, "I've gotta speak to Charlie for this." He said, "If I ever learn that you've talked to Charlie Francis, you're going to be fired."' Patrick's solution was to tell Francis to use a code-name. 'When he called, he said it was Harry Jerome.' Jerome was the top Canadian sprinter of the 1960s.

Patrick says that Francis remained bitter, 'because I think in his mind he really wasn't cheating. Instead of becoming famous as an innovator, he was considered a cheat. Although that was the view of the public – the people in the sport, they knew how effective a coach he was. But all the stuff that was still going on, it made Charlie's blood boil.'

With Francis and Johnson's admissions of drug-use, little time was spent on the suggestion that Johnson might have been sabotaged in Seoul. 'Other than talking to a number of people who knew about it, we did not investigate the mystery man theory,' says Bob Armstrong. 'We didn't have the time or the resources. And it wasn't within our jurisdiction to find out what went on in the dope-testing room in Seoul.'

Neither did he spend much time investigating Jack Scott's role in the build-up to Seoul. Armstrong interviewed Scott, not to find out if Scott had been spying on Johnson on behalf of Lewis, but to try to find out whether he had given Johnson drugs. He was convinced that he had not. Dubin, equally, declared himself 'satisfied that Mr Scott's relationship to Mr Lewis and his treatment of Mr Johnson with the myomatic machine, while appearing intriguing, were purely coincidental and irrelevant to the events which transpired'.

In as much as Justice Dubin did come to a conclusion as to why Johnson tested positive in Seoul, he suggested that, after his problems with injury and his defeat to Carl Lewis in Zurich in August, he returned to Toronto and began his final, mini-steroid programme too close to competition. 'There had been a dramatic deterioration in his performance, and I think they panicked,' said Dubin of the Johnson camp.

Today, however, Johnson dismisses this theory as vehemently as at any time in the years that have passed since Seoul. He doesn't protest his innocence, exactly – he can hardly do that. But he still insists he was set up. In some respects it is curious. It doesn't tally with Francis's description of Johnson as someone with vast reserves of inner strength, who didn't much care what others thought of him. As Jim Ferstle says of Johnson, 'He is a survivor. Most people faced with that kind of vitriol and disgust would just fold up the tent and go away, but there is a part of Ben that has ultimate self-belief or self-confidence. He is still standing and he is still out there.'

And what Johnson has continued to say, to the dwindling numbers who will listen, is that he was sabotaged. He has resurrected the 'mystery man' thesis, basing much of his 2010 autobiography, *Seoul to Soul*, on this theory. It is a strange book, half of it Johnson's story, the other half 'discernments' from his spiritual adviser, Bryan Farnum, who claims to have a direct line to people's souls, living or dead. He can also discern previous lives, telling Johnson he was the Egyptian pharaoh Cheops, builder of the Great Pyramid. Carl Lewis was, according to Farnum, part of the dynasty that fought Cheops for the leadership, 4,500 years ago. So they have been at loggerheads for quite some time.

'My gift allows me to connect to anyone's soul,' Farnum tells me, after greeting me with a bear hug. 'I can talk to Jamie Astaphan, to his soul – even right now.'

This allows Farnum to confirm that Astaphan, who died from a heart attack in 2006, was not responsible for Johnson's positive test in Seoul.

So who was?

'André Jackson was,' says Johnson. He explains that the mystery man, whose name Johnson couldn't quite remember that day in the anti-doping centre, suddenly resurfaced in 1995. 'André Jackson contacted me out of the blue, and said he wanted to speak to me, he had something very important to tell me. He was coming through Toronto airport, in transit. He'd be waiting for a few hours and he wanted to talk to me about what happened in Seoul: the true story.'

Johnson claims he went to Toronto airport in the company of a friend with a tape recorder in his chest pocket. But after a few minutes Jackson realised he was being recorded, said 'I got you, motherfucker', and left.

Nine years later, in 2004, Jackson made contact again. This time, says Johnson, 'he said, "This thing's been on my mind for so long, I have to tell you the truth".'

Jackson invited Johnson to come and see him in California. At the time, Johnson's mother was dying of cancer in hospital, and he was reluctant to leave her, but his curiosity compelled him to go. He flew into Los Angeles with a female friend and checked into a hotel, where Jackson visited him. 'He comes into my hotel room with a six-pack of Budweiser,' says Johnson. 'That was his joke.'

With the beer rekindling memories of their time together in the anti-doping room in Seoul, they made small talk, mainly about Jackson's diamond business. Eventually, Johnson asked him why he had wanted to meet. 'He told me he wanted to discuss the events surrounding the 1988 Seoul Olympics and my positive test results', according to Johnson's book. 'From then on, the conversation was, at times, much like a chess game, mentally tiring and frustrating. He spoke in riddles, telling me a piece of the story, and then pausing to ask a question about my own recollection of events.'

This is what Johnson says Jackson told him:

1. That the strange business in San Jose in 1986, when Johnson had no hotel room, was organised by the Lewis camp.
2. That the plan to sabotage the drugs test was formulated after their initial meeting at the 1986 Weltklasse. 'He brazenly admitted the intent was to set me up for a positive test, to place a steroid in my system.'
3. That he carried out this plan. While Johnson was being massaged, Jackson reached 'inside a Mizuno pouch he wore around his waist to retrieve the Stanozolol... And put one capsule into each beer.' Carl was not 'completely apprised of the plan', but others in the Lewis camp were.

Johnson says he taped Jackson's hotel room confession. 'Yes,' he says, 'we taped it; I have a tape. But I can't find it.'

Ah.

'Bryan Farnum took some shorthand when I got back. But we kept the hotel receipt, everything.'

What was his reaction to what Jackson told him? How did he feel?

'I said, "You almost killed me, man!" Because Arnold Beckett, he told me the amount of Stanozolol in my system was enough to kill me.* André said, "I had to put food on my table." I said, "Who put you up to it? Carl Lewis?" He said, "Carl Lewis was not involved in this."'

Has Johnson spoken to Jackson since that last meeting? 'He called me a couple of times and sent a few emails wishing me happy birthday, and to be careful what I'm saying, or whatever.'

Strangely, André Jackson had been outed as the mystery man long before this alleged meeting with Johnson. When Carl Lewis's first book, *Inside Track*, was published in 1990, it included blurry photographs of Jackson and Johnson sitting side-by-side in the dope control centre.

---

* A claim Don Catlin describes as nonsense.

'My friend André Jackson,' read the caption, 'with Ben Johnson in the drug-testing area at the 1988 Seoul Games. At the time, André had no idea he would be labelled "The Mystery Man".'

Lewis paid attention to the Dubin Inquiry, and was bemused when Francis 'included me in his conspiracy theory. The theory went like this: an "unidentified stranger" had sat with Ben in a waiting room before he was tested. The stranger and Ben talked, watched television, and drank beers together. One of the drinks could have been spiked by the stranger. He could have placed a steroid in it. He had no other reason to be in the waiting area. And – here is where the plot thickens – two witnesses told Francis that the stranger had spoken with me in another area of the waiting room. Conclusion: Carl is the bad guy, and we have to find the unidentified man.'

When Francis mentioned the theory during the Dubin Inquiry it prompted a brief flurry of media interest. What if it were true? A newspaper-driven manhunt was launched. A Canadian businessman offered $10,000 if the 'Mystery Man' came forward and testified. But Jackson didn't come forward, and, as Bob Armstrong has said, it wasn't considered too important. He wasn't called.

As far as Lewis was concerned, there was no mystery. His book is explicit, 'The mystery man is André Jackson, the friend who stayed with my family in Seoul... I've known André for about five years. He loves to travel, so he often shows up for track meets. He has become friends with a lot of people on the track circuit. Seoul was one of the few trips André actually planned ahead. Usually, he just shows up.

'I'm not sure how André got into the drug-testing area. Either he had one of my passes for admission to the area or he got one from an Olympic official. The passes were amazingly easy to get, considering how strict the overall security was. Anyway, I was surprised when I looked in the waiting area and saw André sitting with Ben. Once I had provided my urine sample, I left the drug-testing room and found André to ask him what was going on. André did not really have any reason to be in the drug-testing area. He was just going to wait for me, to see what goes on in drug testing, then leave.'

When I meet Joe Douglas I have to ask him about André Jackson. By now Johnson's book has come out, with his renewed claims that he was sabotaged – not to mention Jackson's alleged confession. The story had garnered a few column inches, but not as many as Johnson hoped. The world, it seems, has grown tired of his conspiracy theories. Still, though, Douglas must have been aware of what Johnson has alleged.

'What did I make of it?' Douglas asks, before suffering a coughing fit. When he recovers, he pauses. 'I hesitate to give you the truth,' he says. And he pauses again, staring at the table. 'OK, I'll tell you the story. We wanted to make sure that he didn't take, ah, any, ah, masking agents. That everything was done legal and fair. That he was gonna be tested, etc. I don't even remember how the heck… But anyway, André went there and he just sat down in the room. That's all he did.'

Jackson was planted by Douglas? 'I think he had a camera,' Douglas replies. 'He was to take a picture of Ben if he takes anything. In case he takes any masking agents, he's got the picture of him. We just wanted to make sure it was done legally and honestly. And that was our purpose. So Carl said, "You go in… " The purpose was to keep Ben from cheating. Because, I think there were some things went on in 1987, in Rome. Some things happened there.' That was where Francis was overheard threatening to say that Johnson had gonorrhoea if they found traces of probenecid.

So Douglas has confirmed it: he did plant André Jackson in the drug-testing centre. But to monitor Johnson, he says, not to sabotage him. It doesn't answer another question: how on earth did he get him in when Jackson was not a member of the US team? Douglas smiles, 'We made sure he got accredited.'

You must be well connected, I suggest. 'Yuh,' he nods, speaking softly. 'I played some games… '

*

All this leaves is the man himself: André 'Action' Jackson. The chairman of the Angola-based African Diamond Council – whose motto, 'insist on the truth', bodes well – is not very difficult to track down. He responds quickly to an email, and supplies a phone number.

The email reads: 'Hello Richard... I will allow you the opportunity to (at least) explain your project as well as your intentions.'

When I call Jackson, he tells me, 'I won't talk about this today. But what Joe says, or Jamie Astaphan, or Charlie Francis says, it really has no relevance. It boils down to Carl, Ben and myself. If these guys feel they can talk about this whole situation after such a long time, you know, I would be willing to participate. But I'm not going to be the lead guy to solve the mystery for everybody.'

Jackson suggests that I talk again to Johnson and Lewis and find out what they're willing to say. Johnson is clear: he wants Jackson to come forward and tell 'the truth' – which, according to Johnson, is that Jackson spiked his beer in Seoul. And Lewis? Lewis, it is clear, has other priorities.

With that, my conversation with Jackson ends. But two months later I call him again. I haven't got Lewis to tell me his side of what happened in Seoul, but I hope that Jackson will open up, anyway. 'Insist on the truth' is his organisation's motto, after all. When he answers, I cut to the chase: is Johnson telling the truth?

'Is that the only thing you're interested in right now?' Jackson replies.

'Yes.'

'Look, I've spoken to Ben three or four times since I spoke to you,' says Jackson. 'He called me, gave me his cell number. He's been in India and Kenya. I've spoken to him a few times. And I've spoken to Carl. I'll probably talk to him today.'

Jackson says he's reluctant to say anything more, but he keeps talking. He's soft-spoken and engaging. 'Whatever I say at this point, it won't change much.' He says he's been called by lots of journalists, all keen to ask him about his role as the 'mystery man'. 'I don't discuss this with Joe, I don't discuss this with Carl, I don't discuss this with Ben. The conversations I have with Carl today are conversations relevant to 2011.

'It's about Ben and Carl. I'm in the middle of this, both of these guys I speak to on a regular basis. At this point in my life, regardless of what has happened in the past, we've all grown older, we're more mature, we have reached a level of understanding, regardless of what I've done, or what has happened. I mean, we found a truce between the three of us.'

There doesn't seem to be much of a truce between Johnson and Lewis, I say.

'I mean my relationship with Carl and my relationship with Ben, not between them,' says Jackson. 'I don't try to push these guys together.'

It seems strange that Jackson can maintain good relations with a man accusing him of sabotage.

'There are consequences to that, of course, and he has to realise that. Even still, Ben is guilty of making mistakes in terms of what he says, the people he associates with, the power he gives to other people.

'And regarding Carl, he really doesn't want to open this subject. He's running for public office now and he's trying to do a lot of things outside of this.'

But why would Johnson continue to make his accusations?

'You have to put things in perspective. What are Ben's objectives? He has an underlying desire to clear his name, and he would do it at any cost. Of course, everyone is curious to know what my version is. I was very straightforward with Ben when we sat down to discuss this. In terms of him having a taped conversation, if he has a taped conversation, then let's play it. That's my response.

'If you saw someone put Stanozolol in your drink, show me where you actually see me doing that. Did I give him the beer? Of course I did. Was I in there? Of course I was. Was I accredited? Of course I wasn't. Did I violate any laws or regulations? No, I didn't.'

Johnson had said Jackson spoke in riddles. And he does. It's difficult to follow everything he says. But it's very simple, I say to him. He could end the speculation. He could set the record straight on whether or not he put Stanozolol in Johnson's beer in Seoul.

'Of course I can say I didn't,' says Jackson. 'But I can also say I did, too. What's the benefit?'

DIFFERENT ERA, DIFFERENT TIME ZONE, SAME THING

LONDON, NOVEMBER 2010

He moves a little stiffly, and his hair is flecked with white, but the boyish face is familiar, the small, dark eyes possess the same energy, the same intensity, and they sparkle like the tiny diamonds in his ears.

As Carl Lewis strolls on to a stage in the flagship Nike store in London he waves a hand at the small crowd, mainly comprising schoolchildren too young to know who he is, or what he did. 'I was going to read through all your medals, but we've got to get through this in half an hour,' says the MC as Lewis sits on a stool in the middle of the stage, a dazzling smile fixed to his face.

'Awright!' says Lewis, clapping his hands together. 'Yeah, yeah.'

When Lewis is interviewed he swivels, like a politician, from his inquisitor to his young audience. Other athletes wait in the wings, including Premiership footballers, and a tingling sense of anticipation is evident in the schoolchildren at the prospect of seeing the twenty-first century stars, Didier Drogba, Ashley Cole and Cesc Fabregas. In the meantime, other, lesser sports personalities are invited to the stage, and they orbit Lewis, sitting on stools arranged around the man in the middle. Lewis, dressed casually in dark jeans, with a pale grey Nike hoodie over a bright red T-shirt, interacts with each of them, chuckling and clapping, always making eye contact and exchanging a smile. Your eye is drawn briefly to the newcomer, then immediately back to Lewis. He radiates charisma.

When the footballers appear, the atmosphere changes, as though a switch has been flicked on. But Drogba, the Chelsea and Ivory Coast star, is bewitched by Lewis. He sits behind him, stares at him, reaches for his hand and appears not to want to let it go. When he is asked to name his sporting hero, he reaches towards Lewis again and says, 'This man. Carl Lewis. I used to watch him run in the Olympics. Amazing.'

'Awright!' says Lewis, turning to face Drogba and accepting his hand.

After the on-stage formalities, Lewis strolls across the shop floor to speak to the three journalists who have requested an interview.

'No!' he says emphatically, but smiling, as he sits down, after shaking each of us firmly by the hand, and making eye contact. 'That's always my answer to the first question. Hey, hey. But they always say, "Do you miss it?"'

'Do you miss it?'

'Ha ha, you see?'

Lewis tells us what he does now. He runs a marketing and branding company, he says. 'Believe it or not, I also import a tequila. And there's my relationship with Nike and McDonalds.' He was reconciled with Nike, after his acrimonious post-LA departure, following his final Olympics in 1996, and has been an ambassador ever since. But that's only part of his portfolio. 'I basically manage my own brand. That's what I do.' Just like when he was an athlete. 'Right, as an athlete, I was my own CEO.'

Yet, for an athlete named the Olympian of the Century by *Sports Illustrated*, and Sportsman of the Century by the IOC and by Unesco, Lewis keeps a fairly low profile. He seems to have drifted away from the sport. Some attribute that to the revelation of his failed drugs tests at the 1988 Olympic trials. When that story broke, Lewis was said by friends to have taken it badly. It cut to the heart of the image he had cultivated: of the cowboy in the white hat, fighting the evil Johnson.

A week after that news, he crashed his Maserati into a wall next to Interstate 110 in Los Angeles. The California Highway Patrol found him alone following the incident. A breath test revealed that he was intoxicated, though – a little like the drugs tests in 1988 – the level of alcohol put him only just over the threshold. He was sentenced to three years' probation and two hundred hours' community service and ordered to attend Alcoholics Anonymous.

In defending himself against the drug test revelations, Lewis sought to differentiate between his case, and that of his old foe, Johnson. In his case, it was just a herbal remedy, he said. In a BBC interview he told another former runner, Steve Cram, 'I think that people say, "Aha!" They wanted that smoking gun. The parts that were in my system at the time were so low they didn't even have a performance-enhancing quality at all. Ben was out taking steroids, and we know what the intention is with that.' He also told the *Guardian*, 'It's ridiculous. Who cares? I did eighteen years of track and field and I've been retired five years, and they're still talking about me, so I guess I still have it.'

Lewis has suffered from arthritis, first feeling the symptoms of the condition in 1993, a year after he won Olympic gold number eight in the Barcelona long jump, and three years before his fourth and final Olympics, in Atlanta, where he won the long jump yet again for number nine. 'I've always known that sporting people frequently suffer from joint problems,' he said. 'But somehow I never thought it would happen to me.' He blamed it on 'over-training and the amount of painkillers I took to help me get over injuries'.

After retiring he moved to LA, bought a large house in the wealthy Pacific Palisades hilltop suburb, and threw himself into acting with the same commitment and ambition he'd applied to sport. 'I don't want to play cameo parts walking on as Carl Lewis the athlete. I want to go on stage or screen and be taken seriously.'

Acting, he said then, was 'the next big challenge that could really fulfil me'. But after eight movies his career as a character actor seemed to stall. His most recent part was in 2007, a minor role in *Tournament of Dreams*, about an inner-city girls' high school basketball team. Otherwise, he has appeared in forty-three movies, TV programmes and documentaries as himself. It's hardly a ringing endorsement; and of course it is exactly what he did not want.

He moved back to New Jersey, and five months after we meet, in April 2011, he announced his intention to run as a Democratic candidate for the state Senate. Local Republicans protested that he was ineligible, having voted in California in 2009, and there followed a six-month battle through the courts, with a federal appeals panel eventually deciding against him. After that ruling, he appeared unfazed – and wearing a Nike polo shirt – at a press conference, laughing and winking, then shrugging when asked what he would do next. 'I let the spirit move me.'

Now, not for the first time, Lewis might appear slightly directionless and lost. He seemed a little like that after the LA Olympics, when the question was: how do you follow perfection? Yet LA, as his athletics career panned out, was only a microcosm. The question of what he does post-athletics has been even bigger. How does Carl Lewis the athlete become anything other than Carl Lewis the ex-athlete? It's a question that hovers over his every move, even as he affects indifference. He is outgoing and garrulous, unrecognisable as the shy teenager Joe Douglas described. But it seems to act as a shield, deflecting more probing enquiries about his goals and motivations. His private life, too, remains private. The method is effective: he talks so much that he leaves only the briefest of openings. When he does, you have to react with all of his old speed just to ask a question.

In London, he tells us that, although his interest in top-level athletics has waned, he now devotes much of his time to coaching youngsters. 'Honestly, right now, my relationship with the sport, I kind of cut off or limit it at eighteen and under. I volunteer at my high school two or three days a week. My foundation sponsors youth programmes. That's kind of where my relationship with track and field is.'

It is admirable. But it hardly seems a fitting role for the sportsman of the century – not when it is his only role in the sport. Of course, Lewis might also claim another coveted title: that of greatest sprinter of all time, not least because so many of his rivals – past and more recent – have been undone by drugs scandals. As Lewis talks about the latest sprinting phenomenon, Usain Bolt, I am reminded of his disdain towards Johnson when he emerged and started to beat him. He talks of Bolt as though he is a rival. But could it be that he is even more dangerous than Johnson, because Lewis is powerless to take him on – on the track, at least?

Off the track might be a different matter. Because when Lewis talks about Bolt, his speech slows down and he weighs his words carefully. 'It's… interesting. It's just… interesting.' The pauses, accompanied by a narrowing of the eyes and thin smile, are so heavily pregnant that they seem about to give birth; only for Lewis to laugh and lighten the tone, 'I don't follow it as much because track and field is really hard to follow in the States. You have to follow it on the internet, but I just watch the results like everyone else and wait… for time to tell. Ha!'

It is clear what Lewis is implying. When Bolt ran a world record 9.69 at the Beijing Olympics it was, many agreed, the most thrilling 100m final since 1988. But the post-race reaction was quite different. Though there was scepticism in Seoul, it was largely confined to journalists and the tiny number of those in the know. Twenty years later, the world knew not only about Johnson's secret, but also that three of his successors – Linford Christie, Maurice Greene and Justin Gatlin – had been subsequently discredited. Only Donovan Bailey, whose win in Atlanta in 1996 represented a glorious moment of redemption for Canada, had survived with his reputation intact. By the time Beijing came around, that was perhaps not enough for the 100m to retain its credibility. Lewis cites Greene as an example, 'When Maurice was running around saying, "I'm the greatest of all time," I said, "Well, time will tell."'

The similarities between Bolt's run in Beijing and Johnson's in Seoul were striking. Both represented a dramatic improvement on the previous record; both were heart-stopping. But whereas in Seoul even the sceptics in the press seats were thrilled by what they witnessed, in Beijing the questions and raised eyebrows followed as inevitably as the world record. For many, celebrations were checked for fear they might be premature. This was not Bolt's fault. It is the legacy of Seoul, a legacy of knowing that the race might not be decided by the finishing line, but in the laboratory.

This seems to be what Lewis is acknowledging when he tells us, 'History defines the greatest. Time always tells. We're old enough to know that. Wait around long enough and you'll get your answers.'

Still the questions are about Bolt. That must infuriate Lewis. What does he think Bolt would have to do to replace him as the best of all time? For once he is lost for words. 'I mean... You... I mean... I don't even think about that. Is that his goal?'

Perhaps if Bolt successfully defends his Olympic 100m title in London he will be acknowledged as the greatest ever. 'It's very rare to repeat success,' Lewis replies. 'To win two Olympic 100m titles, nobody has ever done it.'

'It's interesting that you say nobody's done it,' I say, 'because technically, you have... '

'I said "else"!' says Lewis sharply. 'Nobody else has done it.' He forces a laugh. 'I don't look at it that way, some people might. The reality is, if Ben hadn't cheated, I'd have won. I'm really proud of that race in Seoul. It goes up there with the top ones because everyone could've chosen to get on drugs to try to beat Ben, because we all knew he was on it. But we chose not to do it. So at the end of the day the right people got the medals and the right people won.'

As he says: wait around long enough and you'll get your answers.

So his memory of the race isn't sullied at all. 'Not really,' he shrugs. 'You know, my father died in 1987 and the last thing I told him was I'd win that medal back. And when I crossed that line and originally Ben was in front, I remember this clearly: I went over to shake his hand and he kinda looked away and he was boastful and everything. And I knew he was dirty. So therefore I made him shake my hand.

'When you do the right thing, right comes by you. That's a real simple thing we always say, but I try to live by that. And it all worked out.'

His rivalry with Johnson did contain a pantomime aspect, he suggests. It was cultivated, it was deliberately stirred up, but that served him and Johnson, and the sport. 'What the sport needs is rivalries,' says Lewis. 'I enjoyed all of that. I understood the importance of that. I worked it!

'I mean,' Lewis adds, 'the Ben thing, everyone's like, "You must hate him." I say, "What, are you kidding me? That guy made me so much money it's ridiculous!"'

TORONTO, FEBRUARY 2011

After we enter the Metro indoor track and field centre, Johnson and I head in separate directions, he to the track, me upstairs to the bench seats. I sit down and watch as he paces across the arena, towards the 60m straight, and his athletes, who have been waiting, gather around him. The session starts, but several times Johnson glances up at the seats and waves. It's a friendly gesture, but also a self-conscious one, as though he's not fully comfortable.

Johnson, still in his smart black shoes, his big overcoat and woolly hat, supervises a group of 15 to 23-year-olds, boys and girls. The atmosphere seems relaxed – very different, I would imagine, from the days when Charlie Francis was in charge in this same venue. There is an easy rapport between Johnson and the kids; the girls laugh and flirt with their coach. The image is in stark contrast to the one I have of Francis, which has Johnson's old coach standing off to the side, a stopwatch in his hand, exuding intensity, alternately putting an arm around an athlete, or barking out instructions at Johnson, Issajenko, Williams, McKoy and the others.

It will seem odd that Johnson, Canada's most famous disgraced sportsman, now coaches young athletes. He has argued so vehemently that drugs are a necessity for any athlete who wants to reach the highest level, yet he had insisted to me, 'I never speak to any of my athletes about performance enhancing drugs.'

Never? 'They can reach the top without drugs. But, well, let me say this: over the last twenty-three years doctors and scientists are improving the natural vitamins, so they have the same effect as performance enhancing drugs. But this way is much cleaner, it's safe, there's no harm to the body. It's legal. Most athletes I know now are using these vitamins and running pretty good. Things have changed.'

Yet Johnson contradicts himself later when he says that, at the highest level, the sport is still tainted. 'It's still tainted. No doubt about that. That's the way it is. The more money you put on the table... '

But surely, I suggest, it's a different era, people are being caught for doping now, where previously they mostly weren't. 'Different era, different time zone, same thing,' he says dismissively. 'Same 100m. Everybody wants to be the fastest man.'

But Johnson has been entrusted with young athletes, with people's children. Is this what he tells them: that they are going to have to make the same choices as him? 'I say to them, be the best you can be. If you become a 100m finalist in the Olympic Games or world championships, or make the top three, that's good enough. These kids are smart.'

It isn't clear if Johnson finds coaching fulfilling. It doesn't appear to be his *raison d'être*, as it was for Charlie Francis. 'I don't want to do this for more than a couple of years,' he had said in the car. 'I just want to help these athletes to get from point A to point B, then whoever coaches them can move them on and develop them.'

After he served his two-year ban, following Seoul, Johnson made a comeback, competing at the Barcelona Olympics, but failing to make the final when he stumbled out of the blocks. In January 1993 he went close to the 60m indoor world record but tested positive again, this time for testosterone. He was banned for life by the IAAF, but he appealed and, six years later, a Canadian adjudicator said that procedural errors meant he could compete again – though only in Canada. Nobody would race against him, however, and at one meeting in Ontario he ran alone, recording 11.0 seconds for the 100m. Then he tested positive for a third time, this time for a diuretic. 'I was nailed,' says Johnson. Three times? 'They catch who they want to target,' he shrugs.

Using 'Charlie's training methods' he coached Diego Maradona – 'a very nice person if you get to know him, but don't cross him' – and also an aspiring footballer, Al-Saadi Gaddafi – the third son of the late Libyan dictator, Colonel Gaddafi. That arrangement was reportedly worth $50,000 to Johnson for a ninety-day spell in Tripoli. His spiritual adviser Bryan Farnum was anxious to point out that Johnson never even met the colonel.

'Tripoli was very nice,' says Johnson. 'My mom always said I'd live near the water.' Two years later, Gaddafi junior's football career was halted in its tracks, after one match for Perugia, when he tested positive for Nandrolone. Stopping off in Rome on his way home from Tripoli, Johnson was mugged by a gang of children. Some of his earnings from Tripoli – more than $5,000 – had been in his wallet, and it was all gone. Johnson gave chase, only to be outsprinted by all but one of the young gang members. It made a brief, amusing story in the international media, and confirmed Johnson in the fall guy role he has played since Seoul. Still, as he had been since joining Francis's training group, an easy target, the butt of most jokes.

At various times Johnson has been persuaded to cash in on his notoriety. He advertised 'Cheetah' energy drinks. But he claims he needed the money; when he returned from Seoul, he says, there should have been $4 million in his trust fund. 'That was the money I needed to live on, to do the things I wanted to do in life,' he says. 'But all that money was gone.'

In August 2008 he filed a $37 million lawsuit against the estate of the lawyer, Ed Futerman, who had encouraged him, in the aftermath of Seoul, to deny 'knowingly' using drugs. Apart from his financial problems, he suffered with the death of his mother, whom he still lived with, in 2004. 'I can't cook,' he explained when she died, 'and my mother used to take care of me.' He moved briefly into his sister's house, but 'thought things over and accepted it'. He lives on his own now, though he has a daughter and a granddaughter. His eyes light up when he speaks about his granddaughter; he sees a lot of her. But he says he's careful about relationships. Where once he was fearless, even reckless, now he claims to be more wary of women.

He says he watches replays of his races – including Seoul; especially Seoul – on YouTube. 'Sometimes, yeah.' He laughs. 'My granddaughter watches it and says she can beat me now; she can run faster. She's five years old. She told me she wants to go to the track with me. There are signs she's going to be a runner.'

He says he gets fits of depression but doesn't just stay in bed. He treats what Farnum calls the 'heaviness in his head' by working out. 'I still go and coach and train myself, but in the back of my mind, there's this sadness. That my mother's gone. Or at a certain time of the year, like Christmas time, when everybody's on holiday with their families and other stuff, it really hits you, you know?'

Ever since he forged such a close relationship with Charlie Francis it has seemed that Johnson has craved a father figure. I wonder if Farnum is the replacement. Farnum, a former merchant banker, is a towering, big-bellied, dark-featured man with an unsettlingly steady gaze. He is not that much older than Johnson, but their relationship seems more like father–son. When he leaves his house to head to the track, Farnum pulls him close and, with feeling, tells him, 'You drive carefully, Ben.'

But when I put that theory to him, Johnson shakes his head, 'No, no, I don't need a father figure. But people trying to take from me, those days are over.'

'You know,' Farnum interjects, 'these last twenty-two, twenty-three years Ben has gone through a psychological rollercoaster that most people, by now, would have a very serious disease, or be dead. They'd commit suicide based on what Ben's gone through the last twenty-two years with the media. But he's strong. He's very strong, very determined.'

'I either trust people or I don't,' says Ben. 'There's no in-between.'

And there is no in-between when, within weeks of our meeting, Farnum tells me he and Johnson have parted company. 'I no longer represent Ben Johnson,' reads the email. 'Ben is on his own and we wish him well.' Apparently, he lost trust in Farnum.

If he could say anything to Carl Lewis now, I ask Johnson, what would it be? 'I would say to him, "We were all running for the same title. I beat you fair and square. And you only beat me in the doping room."'

But it is plain that, even if he really believes this, it offers no comfort. The pain of his defeat remains etched on his face, his anger unconcealed as he spits the words out. Only one thing, to which he clings stubbornly, wilfully ignoring that his name has been wiped from the record books, offers consolation to Johnson. Or two things: his run in Rome and his run in Seoul. Abruptly, he sits forward and, with the faux aggression of a boxer at a pre-fight weigh-in, asks, 'Hey, you tell me: who was the first guy to beat 9.9?'

'It was you, Ben.'

'And who was the first guy to beat 9.8?'

'You.'

'OK.' he laughs, settling back into the large leather chair in Farnum's office. The chair is so big and so dark that it seems to consume him. He disappears into it. He looks tiny.

And then he springs forward, repeating his boast for the umpteenth time, 'Fifty years! I was fifty years ahead of my time. Make sure you print that.'

WHERE ARE THEY NOW?

THE FINALISTS: SEOUL OLYMPICS, 100M

Raymond Stewart

Stewart finished injured and last of the eight finalists in Seoul. He now lives in Texas and works in finance. In 2008, when Stewart was coaching several top athletes, he was implicated in a drugs scandal and charged by USA Track and Field, now the American governing body, for the alleged trafficking and administration of a prohibited substance. It followed claims that he had purchased human growth hormone. Stewart said the drugs were for his own use, to treat football-related health issues. He continues to protest his innocence. 'They make it look like I killed somebody,' says Stewart. 'People are entitled to make some mistakes – come on! It's not a big money sport, but they ban me for life.'

Desai Williams

Williams, who finished seventh, 0.32 of a second behind Johnson, still lives in Toronto and, like Johnson, coaches athletes at the Metro centre, as well as working as the speed coach to a Canadian football team, the Toronto Argonauts. During the Dubin Inquiry Jamie Astaphan testified that he had supplied Williams with steroids. It was also claimed that in 1985 Williams told a Canadian team manager about Johnson's use of steroids. Though Williams was training with Francis and Johnson again in 1988, and they celebrated together when

Johnson won gold in Seoul, Johnson says that relations between them are now frosty. 'There's a rift between us now. He wants to take my athletes over to his camp, so he can build a name for himself.'

Robson da Silva

Da Silva, sixth in Seoul, a microsecond ahead of Williams, competed in four consecutive Olympic Games (1984–96) and won two bronze medals, in the 200m at Seoul and the 4x100m relay in Atlanta. He now lives in Brazil, where it is understood he runs a discotheque. 'He sent me his number on Facebook,' said Ben Johnson of Da Silva. 'He wants me to go and visit him in Brazil. A nice guy.' Da Silva is one of the two Seoul finalists never tainted by drug allegations.

Dennis Mitchell

Mitchell, fifth in Seoul, won a gold medal in the 4x100m relay and bronze in the 100m at the 1992 Olympics. In 1998 he tested positive for testosterone, for which he blamed 'five bottles of beer and sex with his wife at least four times', explaining that, 'it was her birthday, the lady deserved a treat'. USA Track and Field accepted his explanation. But the IAAF did not, and banned Mitchell for two years. Mitchell also testified at the trial of his former coach, Trevor Graham, that Graham had injected him with human growth hormone. Today, Mitchell coaches at the National Training Centre in Clermont, Florida, and at his own club, Star Athletics.

Calvin Smith

Smith, having finished fourth in Seoul, was promoted to the bronze medal. He lives outside Tampa, Florida, where he is a social worker. His son, also called Calvin, is a 400m runner who competed for the USA at the 2008 Beijing Olympics. Like Robson da Silva, Smith has never been implicated in any case of doping. He has said he feels like the moral winner of the 1988 Olympic gold medal.

Linford Christie

Christie, who finished third in Seoul, was promoted to the silver medal. Four years later, he won the gold when a sickly Lewis failed to qualify for the event at the US trials. Christie reached the final again in 1996 when he was thirty-six and already a grandfather, but was disqualified for two false starts. Having avoiding punishment following his positive test in Seoul, he tested positive in 1999 for the anabolic steroid Nandrolone and was banned for two years, though he has always denied any wrongdoing. 'He's funny,' said Johnson of Christie. 'I called him last year; he said he was riding his bicycle. I said, "Man, get off the bicycle – you'll break it. You're too big."'

OTHER MEMBERS OF THE CAST

Charlie Francis

Francis died on 12 May 2010, in Sunnybrook Hospital in Toronto, aged sixty-one. He had been diagnosed with non-Hodgkin's lymphoma five years earlier. His funeral was attended by all his former star athletes, including Ben Johnson, who acted as pall-bearer. He is survived by his wife Angé Coon, a former hurdler, and his son James.

Jamie Astaphan

In 2004, a British sports journalist, on holiday in St Kitts, sat in a beachside bar and got chatting to a deeply tanned, dark-haired man. He was cheerful, friendly and talkative and said he was a doctor. It was only later that the sports journalist recognised the name: Astaphan. But that is perhaps an indication of how far Jamie Astaphan drifted from the world of sport. He didn't stay away from trouble, though. In 1994 he was arrested in New York and charged with acquiring and distributing steroids and cocaine. After two years in a Florida jail he was released with 'time served' on the steroid charges;

the cocaine charges were dropped. He returned once more to St Kitts, where he continued to practise medicine until he died of a heart attack in 2006. He was sixty. At his funeral, his brother Dwyer, then the island's national security minister, said, 'Jamie was not a good loser. He was tenacious, stubborn, questioning and strong-willed.' Dwyer added, 'His time in international sports medicine was made a hell for him and those whom he loved, faced as he was, with all of his ability, by a powerful establishment built on greed, arrogance and hypocrisy. Back home after his international ordeals, and given a chance to start over, he got down to work, healing our people, caring for them, and saving lives.'

Tom Tellez

Tellez continued to coach Carl Lewis throughout his senior career. In 1998 he retired as head coach at the University of Houston – to be replaced by another of his former athletes, Leroy Burrell – though he stayed on as a volunteer, and coaches to this day. These days, Houston's athletes train and compete on the Tom Tellez Track, which forms part of the Carl Lewis International Complex.

Manfred Donike

The German anti-doping scientist died of a heart attack while on a flight from Frankfurt to Johannesburg in August 1995. He was en route to Zimbabwe, to set up the laboratory for the following month's All-Africa Games. He was sixty-one.

Prince Alexandre de Mérode

'The Prince' continued as head of the IOC medical commission until Juan Antonio Samaranch stepped down as IOC president following the 2000 Olympics. He was disappointed not to be appointed chair-man of the new World Anti-Doping Agency when it was founded in 1999, losing out to Dick Pound. It is thought he was overlooked because another Belgian, Jacques Rogge, was on the verge of replacing Samaranch. De Mérode was such a heavy smoker that he was nicknamed 'Marlboro Man' by American sportswriters. He died of lung cancer in November 2002, aged sixty-eight.

Primo Nebiolo

Nebiolo served as president of the IAAF until his death, from a heart attack, in November 1999. He was seventy-six. Samaranch described him as 'one of the leading men in sport of this century'; the *Guardian* said in its obituary, 'What Nebiolo did not appreciate was that even leading athletic officials believed that he was, if not part of, then close to, the Mafia.' The athletics stadium in Messina, Sicily, was named the Stadio Primo Nebiolo in his honour.

Dick Pound

Pound was founding chairman of the World Anti-Doping Agency from 1999 to 2007, and he is widely credited with some of the advances made in testing and anti-doping. When he met Carl Lewis at the Athens Olympics in 2004, according to Pound, Lewis approached him and said, 'We should get together – I have some great ideas on anti-doping. I'll call you.' 'That'd be great,' Pound told him. But he didn't call.

Don Catlin

Catlin founded Anti-Doping Research, a not-for-profit organisation, with his son, Oliver, in 2005. Its mission is 'to help rid sport of performance-enhancing drugs by uncovering new drugs being used illegally and developing the tests to detect them'. Catlin describes the Seoul 100m as 'an incredible landmark' in the fight against drugs in sport, but is not confident the fight is being won. 'There are schemers out there. The rewards are so enormous that, for every one of me, there are probably fifty people on the other side.'

David Jenkins

In December 1988 Jenkins was sentenced to seven years in prison for conspiring to produce, smuggle and distribute steroids. 'You had it all,' the judge told him. 'You have brains, you're bilingual. In addition, you have great health and a fantastic, God-given athletic ability. Then enters greed and the whole thing seems to go down the toilet bowl.' Jenkins apologised to the court, saying the enterprise 'had got out of hand'. He was released after nine months in Mojave Desert Prison. In 1993 he set up a sports supplement company, Next Nutrition. He still lives near San Diego, having established and sold various (legal) nutrition companies and appears to be prosperous again.

Andy Norman

The former policeman who, in his role as British Athletics Federation's promotions manager and athletes' agent, became one of the most powerful men in the sport, was sacked in 1994. This followed an inquest into the suicide of the athletics journalist Cliff Temple, who had written an article highly critical of Norman's methods in the *Sunday Times* in August 1993. Temple's suicide, said the coroner, was partly due to Norman's intimidation of him. Norman, who was married to the javelin thrower Fatima Whitbread, died in 2007.

Jack Scott

The man who appeared to straddle the Johnson and Lewis camps in the build-up to Seoul was just fifty-seven when he died of throat cancer in February 2000. The obituary writers struggled to describe him succinctly.

STATISTICS

1. BEN JOHNSON V. CARL LEWIS
HEAD-TO-HEAD RESULTS
(OVER 100M, UP TO 1988*)

29/8/80: Sudbury, Canada (Pan-Am Junior Games) – 1. Lewis, 10.43: 6. Johnson, 10.88

20/8/82: West Berlin – 1. Lewis, 10.08: 8. Johnson, 10.61

22/8/82: Cologne (heat) – 1. Lewis, 10.47: 4. Johnson, 10.55

04/08/84: Los Angeles Olympics (semi-final) – 1. Lewis, 10.14: 2. Johnson, 10.42

04/08/84: LA Olympics (final) – 1. Lewis, 9.99: 3. Johnson, 10.22

20/8/84: Budapest – 1. Lewis, 10.05: 4. Johnson, 10.33

22/8/84: Zurich – 1. Lewis, 9.99: 3. Johnson, 10.12

11/5/85: Modesto – 1. Lewis, 9.98: 4. Johnson 10.16

21/8/85: Zurich – 1. Johnson, 10.18: 4. Lewis, 10.31

25/8/85: Cologne – 2. Lewis, 10.27: 3. Johnson 10.29

31/5/86: San Jose – 1. Johnson, 10.01: 2. Lewis, 10.18

9/7/86: Moscow (Goodwill Games final) – 1. Johnson, 9.95: 3. Lewis, 10.06

13/8/86: Zurich – 1. Johnson, 10.03: 3. Lewis, 10.25

28/5/87: Seville – 1. Johnson, 10.06: 2. Lewis, 10.07

---

* On 8 July 1991, Johnson and Lewis had a much-publicised re-match in Lille, northern France. Johnson finished seventh in 10.46; Lewis ran 10.20 to finish second to Dennis Mitchell.

30/08/87: Rome (World Championships final) – 1. Johnson, 9.83*:
  2. Lewis, 9.93
17/08/88: Zurich – 1. Lewis, 9.93: 3. Johnson, 10.00
24/09/88: Seoul Olympics (final) – 1. Johnson, 9.79*: 2. Lewis, 9.92

2. 100M WORLD RECORD PROGRESSION

Hand-timed: | 10.2: Jesse Owens, 20 June 1936
| 10.1: Willie Williams, 3 August 1956
| 10.00: Armin Hary, 21 June 1960
| 9.99: Jim Hines, 20 June 1968

Electronic timing: | 9.95: Jim Hines, 14 October 1968
| 9.93: Calvin Smith, 3 July 1983
| 9.83**: Ben Johnson, 30 August 1987
| 9.79**: Ben Johnson, 24 September 1988
| 9.92: Carl Lewis, 24 September 1988
| 9.90: Leroy Burrell, 14 June 1991
| 9.86: Carl Lewis, 25 August 1991
| 9.85: Leroy Burrell, 6 July 1994
| 9.84: Donovan Bailey, 27 July 1996
| 9.79: Maurice Greene, 16 June 1999
| 9.78**: Tim Montgomery, 14 September 2002
| 9.77: Asafa Powell, 14 June 2005
| 9.74: Asafa Powell, 9 September 2007
| 9.72: Usain Bolt, 31 May 2008
| 9.69: Usain Bolt, 16 August 2008
| 9.58: Usain Bolt, 16 August 2009

---

* Johnson was stripped of the 1987 world title following his doping confession at the Dubin Inquiry, and of his 1988 Olympic title after testing positive in Seoul. The score, before Johnson was disqualified from these races, read: Johnson: 7, Lewis: 10.
** Stripped of world record for doping.

INTERVIEWS

(If no location is named then the interview took place over the phone, apart from two that were conducted by email, as noted below.)

Alex Baumann, 8 April 2011
Allan Wells, 11 April, University of Surrey, Guildford
André Jackson, 25 June 2011 and 27 August 2011
Andreas Brügger, 7 May 2011
Arne Ljungqvist, 5 August 2011
Ben Johnson, 24 February 2011, Toronto
Bob Armstrong, 9 November 2011
Calvin Smith, 28 February 2011, Tampa, Florida
Carl Lewis, 8 November 2010, London
Charlie Whelan, 29 May 2011
David Jenkins, 17 May 2011, Carlsbad, California
Dick Patrick, 20 March 2011
Dick Pound, 25 February 2011, Montreal
Don Catlin, 11 May 2011, Los Angeles
Doug Clement, 5 August 2011
Don Coleman, 20 June 2011
Doug Gillon, 16 April 2011, London
Frank Dick, 6 April 2011, London
Gary Smith, 13 July 2011
Jan Hedenstad, 10 November 2011, email
Jayanti Tamm, 13 November 2011, email

Jim Ferstle, 13 April 2011
Joe Douglas, 12 May 2011, Santa Monica
John Goodbody, 8 April 2011, London
John Holt, 20 April, Lochgilphead, Argyll
Morris Chrobotek, 13 April 2011
Neil Wilson, 31 March 2011, London
Randy Starkman, 13 April 2011
Ray Stewart, 9 June 2011
Robert Voy, 11 April 2011
Russ Rogers, 9 June 2011
Sherri Howard, 21 November 2011
Simon Barnes, 11 April 2011
Tom Tellez, 21 November 2011
Wayne Williams, 10 April 2011
Yong-suk Shin, 3 June 2011

BIBLIOGRAPHY
AND FURTHER READING

A 2008 episode of the BBC Radio 4 series *Archive Hour*, about the 100m final in Seoul, and called 'The Dirtiest Race in History', provided a useful source of material, as well as a catchy title. In fact, that 'Dirtiest Race in History' claim was not original to the BBC, either. In 2003 the *Guardian* claimed it in a headline for a story prompted by the revelation that Carl Lewis failed a drugs test at the 1988 US Olympic Trials.

The Seoul final has featured in numerous films, radio programmes and books. There was a good TV documentary, which focused on Ben Johnson in particular, directed by David Belton and broadcast in 2001 as part of the BBC's *Reputations* series. Chris Bell's more recent film, *Bigger, Stronger, Faster: Is it still cheating if everyone's doing it?* (Magnolia Pictures, 2008), is a fascinating look at drug use in sport, with contributions from Johnson and Lewis. As well as the numerous newspaper archives in which I delved (thanks to their online archives, and also with special thanks to the British Library at Colindale), the *Sports Illustrated* online 'vault' proved a treasure trove of contemporary reports and feature articles.

The books that proved most useful, in vague order of importance:

Speed Trap: Inside the Biggest Scandal in Olympic History, by Charlie Francis with Jeff Coplon (Lester & Orpen Dennys, 1990)
Inside Track: My Professional Life in Amateur Track and Field, by Carl Lewis with Jeffrey Marx (Fireside, 1992)

313

Seoul to Soul, by Ben Johnson with Bryan Farnum (Ben Johnson Enterprises, 2010)

Running Risks, by Angella Issajenko with Martin O'Malley and Karen O'Reilly (Macmillan of Canada, 1990)

Linford Christie: An Autobiography, by Linford Christie with Tony Ward (Arrow, 1990)

Inside the Olympics, by Dick Pound (Wiley, 2004)

Drugs, Sport and Politics: The Inside Story about Drug Use in Sport and its Political Cover-up, with a Prescription for Reform, by Robert Voy, MD, with Kirk D. Deeter (Leisure Press, 1991)

Drug Games: The International Olympic Committee and the Politics of Doping, 1960–2008, by Thomas M. Hunt (University of Texas Press, 2011)

Running Scared: How Athletics Lost its Innocence, by Steven Downes and Duncan Mackay (Mainstream, 1996)

Dishonored Games: Corruption, Money & Greed at the Olympics, by Vyv Simson and Andrew Jennings (S.P.I. Books, 1992)

Doping's Nemesis, by Arne Ljungqvist with Göran Lager (Sports Books, 2011)

A History of Drug Use in Sport 1876–1976: Beyond Good and Evil, by Paul Dimeo (Routledge, 2007)

Death in the Locker Room: Drugs & Sports, by Dr Bob Goldman and Dr Ronald Klatz (Elite Sports Medicine Publications Inc., 1992)

ACKNOWLEDGEMENTS

Of the main protagonists in the 1988 drama in Seoul, I would like to thank Ben Johnson and Joe Douglas for agreeing to be interviewed, and for giving their time generously. Charlie Francis's widow, Angé Coon, initially agreed to be interviewed, then changed her mind, but kindly wished me well. She looks after her late husband's legacy through charliefrancis.com, an online tribute to 'the greatest speed coach the world has ever known'.

It was a pleasure to meet Don Catlin and Dick Pound, both of whom continued to be helpful in subsequent correspondence. The modest Calvin Smith and Allan Wells are two relatively unsung heroes. David Jenkins was quirky, charismatic and disarming, and his dry humour continued in emails following our interview. In one, he explained the presence of a child-sized Buddha sitting in the back seat of his car: 'He allows me to drive in the car-pool lane.'

From the sports world, I'd like to thank Alex Baumann, Andreas Brügger, Arne Ljungqvist, Don Coleman, Doug Clement, Frank Dick, John Holt, Morris Chrobotek, Ray Stewart, Robert Voy, Rob Woodhouse, Russ Rogers, Sherri Howard, Tom Tellez, Wayne Williams and Carl Lewis. And, of course, I'd like to thank the 'mystery man', André Jackson, for his cooperation. Colleagues in the media who provided expert help and shared vivid memories include Charlie Whelan, Dick Patrick, Jim Ferstle, John Goodbody, Neil Wilson, Randy Starkman, Gary Smith, Peter Nichols, Jan Hedenstad, Simon Barnes, Yong-suk Shin and Doug Gillon. Anders Christiansen of Norwegian newspaper *VG* was also extremely helpful, as was Jayanti Tamm. And I am grateful to the Honourable Justice Robert Armstrong for his fascinating reminiscences about the Dubin Inquiry.

Charlotte Atyeo of Bloomsbury responded with enthusiasm when I first mentioned my idea for this book, and I'm grateful for her encouragement and for helping to persuade Matthew Engel, editor of the Wisden Sports Writing imprint, to take it on. Matthew came with a reputation and lived up to that by subjecting every line and word to rigorous examination. Thank you, Matthew.

Thanks to Dan Gordon, with whom I compared copious notes as he sought to tell the same story on film; to my agent, Mark Stanton; to Becky Arnold and Dave Hunter for their editorial assistance; to Janet Kim for her help on the West Coast of the United States, my brother Robin and his wife Iciar for theirs on the East Coast; to Tim Noviello for his Willingboro connections; and thanks to Karen Olianti for allowing me to use her beautiful apartment in Chamonix as a writer's retreat, on the condition that I looked after her cat, Daisy. It is a sign of how focused I was on the writing that Daisy was perhaps a little neglected and, at the conclusion to our month together, suffering from depression. I am pleased to report that she has made a full recovery and hope she can find it in her heart to forgive me. Thanks also, and as ever, to my dad, Brian, and brothers, Peter and Robin. And finally, to Virginie for her love and support.

INDEX